Reliable Financial Reporting and Internal Control

A Global Implementation Guide

Reliable Financial Reporting and Internal Control

A Global Implementation Guide

Dr. Dimitris N. Chorafas

JOHN WILEY & SONS, INC.

New York • Chichester • Weinheim • Brisbane • Singapore • Toronto

ISBN 0 471 38261 2

Printed in the United States of America.

10 9 8 7 6 5 4 3 2 1

Foreword

One of the great challenges facing the financial system is the risk inherent in increasingly complex financial instruments and strategies undertaken by increasingly complex financial organizations. Under normal circumstances, the sophistication of these instruments and strategies permits precise definition and pricing of risk, creating a wider ranger of financial products and spreading risk across a broader range of market participants to the benefit of all concerned. However, experience shows that even broad and deep international capital markets are susceptible to shocks and crises, to which even sophisticated financial intermediaries can fall victim.

In a crisis situation, the precise measurement and careful parsing of risks on which sophisticated financial strategies are premised can become irrelevant. Financial distress in an individual country or at a single financial intermediary can trigger losses that balloon and spread through the system. If the mechanisms by which this occurs are sometimes obscure, the implications for markets and market intermediaries in developed and emerging markets alike are clear enough. The 1987 stock market crash, the failure of Barings, the Asian crisis, the collapse of speculative investment in Russia, and the near collapse of LTCM suggest the variety of ways in which trouble may arise in international capital markets.

If shocks are inevitable, then it is essential that internationally active financial institutions and especially the large, sophisticated institutions that are the pillars of the international system are fortified against them. This has been a primary focus of concern for the Group of Thirty in the last 15 years, resulting in a series of recommendations for reducing clearance and settlement risks, strengthening risk management of derivatives, and promoting stronger management, greater transparency, and comprehensive supervision of the risks facing global firms. Since the Mexican crisis of 1994–1995, these issues have also become a central focus of international financial supervisors and a standard feature of G-7 Summit communiques.

The starting point for sound management of financial risks is the subject of this book: an effective system of internal controls established by the board of directors and management to provide feedback on the way the financial institution functions at all levels. As the author argues, this is not simply a matter of financial results but of command and control mechanisms, personnel management, and other performance characteristics of the firm. To be fully effective, controls must involve a range of techniques, supported by real-time monitoring, sophisticated computer systems and modeling techniques. Because all systems can malfunction and decay with time, internal controls must be regularly audited.

Professor Chorafas offers a comprehensive review of the issues involved in an effective control regime, including grand themes, key concepts, and detailed requirements, presenting them all in a very practical way. He has surveyed actual practice through extensive interviews and is not afraid to offer his best judgement about what makes sense. A particularly appealing feature of this analysis is that its basic approach is operational. Major institutions have been decomposing the risks they face and addressing them one by one, while supervisors have similarly taken a building block approach to risk-based capital requirements. Market and credit risks have been most thoroughly analyzed, while attention is only now focusing on operational and legal risks. This book argues that all risks should be evaluated in the context of performance failure.

The other appealing feature of the analysis is its broad, interdisciplinary approach. The analysis examines assessment techniques and measurement rules embodied in COSO, FASB, and the international accounting rules exercise. It examines how human and system errors are measured in other industries and contexts and suggests how they might be applied to financial services. In an industry with as many repetitive transactions as banking and as much data gathering on financial performance, it is interesting that quality control approaches and methodologies that have become commonplace in other industries have not been applied in this sector. Professor Chorafas may not have answers to all the questions that he raises, but he very usefully gets many of the questions on the table. In doing so, he provides an important public service.

JOHN WALSH
Director, Group of Thirty

Preface

Financial reporting is, fundamentally, a process of knowledge exchange. This process is, too often, simplistically equated with codifying information, feeding it into computers, shifting it around, and handling it through supposedly sophisticated models. In contrast, true knowledge integration is the outgrowth of financial, technical, and social processes—and, of course, of *internal controls* that assure the right thing happens at the right time. This is what underpins reliable financial reporting.

One of the main difficulties in global management of credit risk and market risk is that knowledge is often taken out of context. Something that is understood about counterparty exposure in one business environment may change meaning in another. Or, alternatively, the message may be wrongly interpreted, fail to arise management's sensitivity, or lead to absurd decisions.

Addressed to investment bankers, commercial bankers, institutional investors, treasurers, chief financial officers, company accountants, as well as certified public accountants, auditors, and financial analysts, this book brings under the same cover three crucial issues to the modern institution and the financial function at large: Internal control and international accounting standards; reliable financial reporting as defined by the Committee of Sponsoring Organizations (COSO) of the Treadway Commission; and the New Capital Adequacy Framework by the Basle Committee on Banking Supervision.

Part One is dedicated to internal control concepts and processes, as well as to the controversy between International Accounting Standard (IAS) and the Generally Accepted Accounting Principles (GAAP). Accounting is the language companies speak among themselves and with regulators. A common accounting language is just as important as the establishment of a timely and accurate internal control system.

The subject of Chapter 1 is the board's accountability for internal control. After a brief review of the effects of globalization and consolidation on inventoried exposure, the text defines internal control, shows its synergy to risk management, examines formal and informal solutions to internal control challenges, and demonstrates the impact of transparency on management's ability to be in charge.

Chapters 2 and 3 address the issue of international accounting standards. They compare IAS to GAAP and, based on the results of my research, elaborate on the likelihood GAAP and IAS will merge into a global accounting system. This would be a great boost to global financial accounting reporting standards—assuring better understanding in capital markets and money markets, as well as in connection with derivative financial instruments. But its likelihood is not that high.

It is both legally and operationally necessary that financial conditions are correctly reported, but that is not enough. The reports must be done efficiently and effectively—two themes dominating this book. Peter Drucker defines *efficiency* as doing things the right way; and *effectiveness* as doing the right things. Efficient and effective operations are the second major requirement of COSO.

Part Two addresses efficient and effective operations. It reviews the work of the Treadway Commission and COSO, emphasizes behavioral controls, demonstrates the contribution quality control—and most particularly statistical quality control—brings to efficiency and effectiveness, and documents that many COSO guidelines have already filtered into Statements of Financial Accounting Standards by FASB.

Chapter 4 elaborates on the work that has been done by the Treadway Commission and the objectives that it targeted. This presentation starts with control environments, involves issues associated to fraudulent financial reports, emphasizes the critical role played by internal controls, and explains the benefits from implementation of COSO, whose first practical application took place at the Federal Reserve Banks of New York, Boston, and Chicago, in 1998.

Fraudulent financial reporting and its avoidance are the theme of Chapter 5. The Treadway Commission's guidelines for audit of financial reports are examined, focusing on the command and control system necessary to master an entity's financial operations. Chapter 6 emphasizes the importance of behavioral controls, drawing on the guidelines by COSO, COCO, and IOSCO as well as capitalizing on interdisciplinary cross-fertilization in behavioral studies.

Chapter 7 explains why a crucial subject in the assurance of reliable financial reporting is measuring and managing the quality of financial services. It covers the work of the Quality Control Inquiry Committee (QCIC) and the role of statistical investigation in quality assurance. Chapter 8 completes this presentation through practical examples on the use of statistical quality control (SQC) in banking. It discusses sampling plans and presents quality control charts by attributes, variables, and percent defective.

Analytical solutions work best when they are tuned to the observance of rules and regulations. For this reason, Chapter 9 concentrates on statements by the Financial Accounting Standards Board and associated reporting practices, including the assessment of hedge effectiveness. Chapter 10 addresses specifically SFAS 133, compares its clauses to SFAS 119 (which it replaces), and brings attention to the aftermath of the new regulation.

Part Three takes a close look into the issues which many experts consider to be the counterparties of reliable financial reporting—therefore, of COSO. These are capital adequacy and capital at risk. Quite often, creative accounting practices come into the picture because capital reserves are inadequate and/or more capital is put at risk than what the institution can afford under normal conditions.

The theme of Chapter 11 is the New Capital Adequacy Framework by the Basle Committee on Banking Supervision. This Framework is one of the best examples on the application of COSO's principles. In 1988, the Group of Ten central bankers, who form the Basle Committee, established the Capital Accord that addressed credit risk. In 1996, capital requirements were enriched with the Market Risk Amendment. In 1999, a new capital accord was drafted in a much more sophisticated way than the 1988 original.

Preface

Published in June 1999, the New Capital Adequacy Framework is still a discussion paper and there are many issues that will be debated before it becomes the new standard. Chapter 12 contributes to these issues by explaining the key factors that enter the redefinition of a bank's capital—specifically the role and use of internal ratings-based (IRB) models.

Following this process through, it leads us to capital at risk and earnings at risk, the issues of Chapter 13. The reader is first presented with the notions underlying a sophisticated application of capital at risk metrics and measurements. Then the discussion focuses on commitments whose impact is felt on current exposure, prudential limits, the volatility on capital at risk, and the need for literacy in high technology.

After having outlined the supervisory rules for greater transparency in financial reporting, including clauses still in the making, the text turns to those issues that present financial institutions with a somewhat greater freedom of choice. Market value accounting (Chapter 14) is an example, including issues such as fair value, present value, replacement value, and net replacement value.

Reliable financial reporting as well as efficiency and effectiveness in operations are not only regulatory issues. They are also the best way for financial institutions to look into the future, helping top management to identify what practices must stop. They also assist in projecting into the future some of the things senior management should be considering. The present is conditioned by the future, not by the past.

Never before has it been possible to look as far into the future as it is today, and with as much confidence about events to come. "Political ability," Winston Churchill once suggested, "is to foretell what is going to happen tomorrow, next week, next month, and next year. And to have the ability afterward to explain why it didn't happen."

DR. DIMITRIS N. CHORAFAS

Acknowledgments

Let me first take this opportunity to express my thanks to everybody who contributed to this book: my colleagues for their advice and the insight they provided; the people who took part in my seminars for the puzzling and most interesting questions; the senior executives who contributed thoughts and ideas during my research; Timothy Burgard for his care and interest in publishing this book; the staff at Publications Development Company for book editing and production; and Eva-Maria Binder for compiling the research results, typing the text, and preparing the artwork and index.

The following organizations, through their senior executives and system specialists, participated in the recent research projects that led to the contents of this book and its documentation (countries are listed in alphabetical order):

AUSTRIA

National Bank of Austria
Dr. Martin Ohms
Finance Market Analysis Department
3, Otto Wagner Platz
Postfach 61
A-1011 Vienna

Association of Austrian Banks and Bankers
Dr. Fritz Diwok
Secretary General
11, Boersengasse
1013 Vienna

Bank Austria
Dr. Peter Fischer
Senior General Manager, Treasury Division
Peter Gabriel
Deputy General Manager, Trading
2, Am Hof
1010 Vienna

Creditanstalt
Dr. Wolfgang Lichtl
Market Risk Management
Julius Tandler Platz 3
A-1090 Vienna

Wiener Betriebs- and Baugesellschaft mbH
Dr. Josef Fritz
General Manager
1, Anschützstrasse
1153 Vienna

GERMANY

Deutsche Bundesbank
Hans-Dietrich Peters
Director
Hans Werner Voth
Director
Wilhelm-Epstein Strasse 14
60431 Frankfurt am Main

Federal Banking Supervisory Office
Hans-Joachim Dohr
Director Dept. I
Jochen Kayser
Risk Model Examination
Ludger Hanenberg
Internal Controls
71–101 Gardeschützenweg
12203 Berlin

ACKNOWLEDGMENTS

European Central Bank
Mauro Grande
Director
29 Kaiserstrasse
29th Floor
60216 Frankfurt am Main

Deutsches Aktieninstitut
Dr. Rüdiger Von Rosen
President
Biebergasse 6 bis 10
60313 Frankfurt-am-Main

Commerzbank
Peter Bürger
Senior Vice President, Strategy and Controlling
Markus Rumpel
Senior Vice President, Credit Risk Management
Kaiserplatz
60261 Frankfurt am Main

Deutsche Bank
Professor Manfred Timmermann
Head of Controlling
Hans Voit
Head of Process Management, Controlling
    Department
12, Taunusanlage
60325 Frankfurt

Dresdner Bank
Dr. Marita Balks
Investment Bank, Risk Control
Dr. Hermann Haaf
Mathematical Models for Risk Control
Claas Carsten Kohl
Financial Engineer
1, Jürgen Ponto Platz
60301 Frankfurt

GMD First—Research Institute for Computer Architecture, Software Technology and Graphics
Prof. Dr. Ing. Wolfgang K. Giloi
General Manager
5, Rudower Chaussee
D-1199 Berlin

FRANCE

Banque de France
Pierre Jaillet
Director, Monetary Studies and Statistics
Yvan Oronnal
Manager, Monetary Analyses and Statistics
G. Tournemire, Analyst, Monetary Studies
39, rue Croix des Petits Champs
75001 Paris

Secretariat Général de la Commission Bancaire— Banque de France
Didier Peny
Head of Big Banks and International Banks
    Department
F. Visnowsky
Manager, International Affairs
Supervisory Policy and Research Division
Benjamin Sahel
Market Risk Control
73, rue de Richelieu
75002 Paris

Ministry of Finance and the Economy, Conseil National de la Comptabilité
Alain Le Bars
Director International Relations and Cooperation
6, rue Louise Weiss
75703 Paris Cedex 13

HUNGARY

Hungarian Banking and Capital Market Supervision
Dr. Janos Kun
Head, Department of Regulation and Analyses
Dr. Erika Vörös
Senior Economist, Department of Regulation and
    Analyses
Dr. Géza Nyiry
Head, Section of Information Audit
Csalogany u. 9–11
H-1027 Budapest

Hungarian Academy of Sciences
Prof.Dr. Tibor Vamos
Chairman, Computer and Automation Research
    Institute
Nador U. 7
1051 Budapest

ITALY

Banca d'Italia
Eugene Gaiotti
Research Department, Monetary and Financial
    Division
Ing. Dario Focarelli
Research Department
91, via Nazionale
00184 Rome

Istituto Bancario San Paolo di Torino
Dr. Paolo Chiulenti
Director of Budgeting
Roberto Costa
Director of Private Banking
Pino Ravelli
Director Bergamo Region
27, via G. Camozzi
24121 Bergamo

Acknowledgments

LUXEMBOURG

Banque Générale de Luxembourg
Prof.Dr. Yves Wagner
Director of Asset and Risk Management
Hans Jörg Paris, International Risk Manager
27, avenue Monterey
L-2951 Luxembourg

POLAND

Securities and Exchange Commission
Beata Stelmach
Secretary of the Commission
1, Pl Powstancow Warszawy
00–950 Warsaw

SWEDEN

Skandinaviska Enskilda Banken
Bernt Gyllenswärd
Head of Group Audit
Box 16067
10322 Stockholm

Irdem AB
Gian Medri
Former Director of Research at Nordbanken
19, Flintlasvagen
S-19154 Sollentuna

SWITZERLAND

Swiss National Bank
Dr. Werner Hermann
Head of International Monetary Relations
Dr. Christian Walter
Representative to the Basle Committee
Robert Fluri
Assistant Director, Statistics Section
15 Börsenstrasse
Zurich

Federal Banking Commission
Dr. Susanne Brandenberger
Risk Management
Renate Lischer
Representative to Risk Management Subgroup, Basle
Committee
Marktgasse 37
3001 Bern

Bank for International Settlements
Mr. Claude Sivy
Head of Internal Audit
Herbie Poenisch
Senior Economist, Monetary and Economic
Department
2, Centralplatz
4002 Basle

Bank Leu AG
Dr. Urs Morgenthaler
Member of Management
Director of Risk Control
32, Bahnhofstrasse
Zurich

Bank J. Vontobel and Vontobel Holding
Heinz Frauchiger
Chief, Internal Audit Department
Tödistrasse 23
CH-8022 Zurich

Union Bank of Switzerland
Dr. Heinrich Steinmann
Member of the Executive Board (Retired)
Claridenstrasse
8021 Zurich

UNITED KINGDOM

**Bank of England, and Financial Services
Authority**
Richard Britton
Director, Complex Groups Division, CGD Policy
Department
Threadneedle Street
London EC2R 8AH

British Bankers Association
Paul Chisnall
Assistant Director
Pinners Hall
105–108 Old Broad Street
London EC2N 1EX

Accounting Standards Board
A.V.C. Cook
Technical Director
Sandra Thompson
Project Director
Holborn Hall
100 Gray's Inn Road
London WC1X 8AL

Barclays Bank Plc
Brandon Davies
Treasurer, Global Corporate Banking
Alan Brown
Director, Group Risk
54 Lombard Street
London EC3P 3AH

ABN-AMRO Investment Bank N.V.
David Woods
Chief Operations Officer, Global Equity Directorate
199 Bishopsgate
London EC2M 3TY

Acknowledgments

Bankgesellschaft Berlin
Stephen F. Myers
Head of Market Risk
1 Crown Court
Cheapside, London

Standard & Poors
David T. Beers
Managing Director, Sovereign Ratings
Garden House
18, Finsbury Circus
London EC2M 7BP

Moody's Investor Services
Samuel S. Theodore
Managing Director, European Banks
David Frohriep
Communications Manager, Europe
2, Minster Court
Mincing Lange
London EC3R 7XB

Fitch IBCA
Charles Prescott
Group Managing Director, Banks
David Nadrews
Managing Director, Financial Institutions
Travor Pitman
Managing Director, Corporations
Richard Fox
Director, International Public Finance
Andrew Philbott
Transition Matrices
Eldon House
2, Eldon Street
London EC2M 7UA

Merrill Lynch International
Erik Banks
Managing Director of Risk Management
Ropemaker Place
London EC2Y 9LY

The Auditing Practices Board
Jonathan E.C. Grant
Technical Director
Steve Leonard
Internal Controls Project Manager
P.O.Box 433
Moorgate Place
London EC2P 2BJ

International Accounting Standards Committee
Ms. Liesel Knorr
Technical Director
166 Fleet Street
London EC4A 2DY

City University Business School
Professor Elias Dinenis
Head, Department of Investment
Risk Management & Insurance
Prof.Dr. John Hagnioannides
Department of Finance
Frobisher Crescent
Barbican Centre
London EC2Y 8BH

UNITED STATES

Federal Reserve System, Board of Governors
David L. Robinson
Deputy Director, Chief Federal Reserve Examiner
Alan H. Osterholm, CIA, CISA
Manager, Financial Examinations Section
Paul W. Bettge
Assistant Director, Division of Reserve Bank
    Operations
Gregory E. Eller
Supervisory Financial Analyst, Banking
Gregory L. Evans
Manager, Financial Accounting
Martha Stallard
Financial Accounting, Reserve Bank Operations
20th and Constitution, NW
Washington, DC 20551

Federal Reserve Bank of Boston
William McDonough
Executive Vice President
James T. Nolan
Assistant Vice President
P.O. Box 2076
600 Atlantic Avenue
Boston, MA

Federal Reserve Bank of San Francisco
Nigel R. Ogilvie, CFA
Supervising Financial Analyst
Emerging Issues
101 Market Street
San Francisco, CA

**Seattle Branch, Federal Reserve Bank of
    San Francisco**
Jimmy F. Kamada
Assistant Vice President
Gale P. Ansell
Assistant Vice President, Business Development
1015, 2nd Avenue
Seattle, WA 98122-3567

Acknowledgments

Office of the Comptroller of the Currency (OCC)
Bill Morris
National Bank Examiner/Policy Analyst,
Core Policy Development Division
Gene Green
Deputy Chief Accountant
Office of the Chief Accountant
250 E Street, SW
7th Floor
Washington, D.C.

Federal Deposit Insurance Corporation (FDIC)
Curtis Wong
Capital Markets, Examination Support
Tanya Smith
Examination Specialist, International Branch
Doris L. Marsh
Examination Specialist, Policy Branch
550 17th Street, N.W.
Washington, D.C.

Office of Thrift Supervision (OTS)
Timothy J. Stier
Chief Accountant
1700 G Street Northwest
Washington, DC, 20552

Securities and Exchange Commission, Washington DC
Robert Uhl
Professional Accounting Fellow
Pascal Desroches
Professional Accounting Fellow
John W. Albert
Associate Chief Accountant
Scott Bayless
Associate Chief Accountant
Office of the Chief Accountant
Securities and Exchange Commission
450 Fifth Street, NW
Washington, DC, 20549

Securities and Exchange Commission, New York
Robert A. Sollazzo
Associate Regional Director
7 World Trade Center
12th Floor
New York, NY 10048

Securities and Exchange Commission, Boston
Edward A. Ryan, Jr.
Assistant District Administrator (Regulations)
Boston District Office
73 Tremont Street, 6th Floor
Boston, MA 02108-3912

International Monetary Fund
Alain Coune
Assistant Director, Office of Internal Audit and
   Inspection
700 19th Street NW
Washington DC, 20431

Financial Accounting Standards Board
Halsey G. Bullen
Project Manager
Jeannot Blanchet
Project Manager
Teri L. List
Practice Fellow
401 Merritt
Norwalk, CN 06856

Citibank
Daniel Schutzer
Vice President, Director of Advanced Technology
909 Third Avenue
New York, NY 10022

Prudential-Bache Securities
Bella Loykhter
Senior Vice President, Information Technology
Kenneth Musco
First Vice President and Director,
Management Internal Control
Neil S. Lerner
Vice President, Management Internal Control
1 New York Plaza
New York, NY

Merrill Lynch
John J. Fosina
Director, Planning and Analysis
Corporate and Institutional Client Group
World Financial Center, North Tower
New York, NY 10281-1316

International Swaps and Derivatives Association (ISDA)
Susan Hinko
Director of Policy
600 Fifth Avenue, 27th Floor
Rockefeller Center
New York, NY 10020-2302

Standard & Poors
Clifford Griep
Managing Director
25 Broadway
New York, NY 10004-1064

Moody's Investor Services
Lea Carty
Director, Corporates
99 Church Street
New York, NY 10022

ACKNOWLEDGMENTS

State Street Bank and Trust
James J. Barr
Executive Vice President, U.S. Financial Assets
    Services
225 Franklin Street
Boston, MA 02105-1992

MBIA Insurance Corporation
John B. Caouette
Vice Chairman
113 King Street
Armonk, NY 10504

Global Association of Risk Professionals (GARP)
Lev Borodovski
Executive Director, GARP, and
Director of Risk Management, Credit Suisse First
    Boston (CSFB), New York
Yong LI
Director of Education, GARP, and
Vice President, Lehman Brothers,
    New York
Dr. Frank Leiber
Research Director, and
Assistant Director of Computational Finance, Cornell
University, Theory Center, New York
Roy Nawal
Director of Risk Forums, GARP
980 Broadway, Suite 242
Thornwood, NY

Group of Thirty
John Walsh
Director
1990 M Street, NW
Suite 450
Washington, DC, 20036

Edward Jones
Ann Ficken (Mrs)
Director, Internal Audit
201 Progress Parkway
Maryland Heights, MO 63043-3042

**Teachers Insurance and Annuity
    Association/College Retirement Equities Fund
    (TIAA/CREF)**
Charles S. Dvorkin
Vice President and Chief Technology Officer
Harry D. Perrin
Assistant Vice President, Information Technology
730 Third Avenue
New York, NY 10017-3206

Massachusetts Institute of Technology
Ms. Peggy Carney
Administrator, Graduate Office
Michael Coen, PhD Candidate,
ARPA Intelligent Environment Project
Department of Electrical Engineering
and Computer Science
Building 38, Room 444
50 Vassar Street
Cambridge, MA, 02139

**School of Engineering and Applied Science,
    University of California, Los Angeles**
Dean A.R. Frank Wazzan
School of Engineering and Applied Science
Prof. Richard Muntz
Chair, Computer Science Department
Prof. Dr. Leonard Kleinrock
Telecommunications and Networks
Westwood Village
Los Angeles, CA 90024

University of Maryland
Prof. Howard Frank
Dean, The Robert H. Smith School of Business
Prof. Lemma W. Senbert
Chair, Finance Department
Prof. Haluk Unal
Associate Professor of Finance
Van Munching Hall
College Park, Maryland 20742-1815

Contents

Contents

PART ONE

Internal Control and Global Accounting Standards

CHAPTER 1

The Board's Accountability for Internal Control

The investing public, the firm's clients and suppliers, regulators, tax authorities, and people who are in charge of the economy are most interested in the way a company's management carries out its duties, including its financial reporting responsibilities. A reliable implementation of management control must be able to assure that the board and senior executives are fully accountable for their decisions and actions. This is a pragmatic consideration. Internal control is doable if there is a firm policy and the will to be in charge.

Internal control is the responsibility of the board and top management. Since the late 1980s, the Treadway Commission (see Chapter 4) recommended that all annual reports to stockholders be required, by rules by the Securities and Exchange Commission (SEC), to include a management report signed by the company's chief executive officer, chief financial officer, and chief accounting officer who may be the controller. As the mirror of the company's financial health, this report should:

- Acknowledge management's responsibilities for financial statements and their content.
- Discuss how these responsibilities have been fulfilled and confirm that they are fulfilled.
- Provide management's assessment of the effectiveness of the company's internal control.

The thread linking these issues is *accounting,* which also underpins reliable financial reporting. Therefore, Chapters 2 and 3 focus on international accounting norms, including GAAP and IAS. *If* internal control is the mind of the enterprise, then accounting is the body of evidence on which this mind rests.

Promoted by the Committee of Sponsoring Organizations (COSO) of the Treadway Commission as of 1998, in the United States the concepts outlined in the three bullets above became the law of the land with first implementers being the Federal Reserve Banks of New York, Boston, and Chicago. Part Two is dedicated to COSO, most specifically to efficiency and effectiveness—one of the pillars on which rest COSO principles.

3

Behavioral analysis, statistical quality control, and Statements of Financial Accounting Standards Board (FASB) are covered.

Reliable financial reporting and capital adequacy correlate. In June 1999, a year after the first practical implementation of COSO, the Basle Committee on Banking Supervision published "A New Capital Adequacy Framework." Still a discussion paper, in a couple of years it should become the law regulating capital adequacy in countries of the Group of Ten (G-10). This document, inspired by COSO, places great emphasis on internal control. Part Three examines the New Capital Adequacy Framework as a counterpart of COSO, and with it discusses the concepts of capital at risk, market value, and the control of exposure.

GLOBALIZATION AND CONSOLIDATION INVOLVE RISKS, NOT ONLY OPPORTUNITIES

Internal control and management responsibility correlate. In my research on management accountability and internal control, the majority of senior executives commented that traditional approaches to risk management are not working. Though many companies have implemented some type of internal control for monitoring their exposure, classical solutions still tend to focus on:

- Realized financial profits and losses.
- After-the-fact accounting methods.
- Certain formal checks of authority (i.e., signatory power, approval procedures, database access controls, and similar guidelines).

These actions are necessary but not enough. Investigations into recent serious financial scandals suggest that the culture of internal control accompanied by a structure that is dynamic in nature can be far more significant in:

- Unearthing breaches in exposure limits.
- Identifying causes for unexpected losses.
- Bringing problem areas to senior management's attention.

Another significant finding of my research has been that when organizations are gratified by huge profits, inefficiencies embedded into their operations are hidden. The same is true of risks. "Competition brings out the best in products and the worst in men," David Sarnoff once commented—particularly, the more lucrative types of competition.

Fat profits bring the best in short-term stockholder value and the worst in medium- to long-term exposure. This should induce the board and senior management to be doubly careful in the implementation of an efficient and effective internal control system. Using Peter Drucker's definition:

4

- *Efficiency* is doing things the right way.
- *Effectiveness* is doing the right things.

Both are important in an age where globalization and consolidation bring forward new opportunities, but also many unknowns and many risks. The cutting edge of competition sees to it that this is not a time for featherbedding executive suites or a technology suffering from diminished geriatric returns.

Since the early 1980s, globalization has joined deregulation, high technology, and innovation as a keyword in banking and in practically any other industry. Exhibit 1.1 suggests that at the core of these four concepts is a growing business opportunity that has pushed market capitalization at an unprecedented level, albeit more so in the United States than in any other country—but it also brought along the prognostication of a $1 quadrillion ($1.000 trillion) exposure in derivatives. Many chief financial officers consider this quadrillion to be ominous.

According to some estimates, having passed the $170 trillion in notional principal amounts in 1999, the global derivatives market is headed for the astronomical $1 quadrillion mark. How are the experts reacting to this forecast? Nobel prize winner Dr. Merton Miller suggests that derivatives have made the world a safer place (though he does not explain how and why). But George Soros warns, quite to the contrary, that derivative financial instruments will destroy society.

One of the Soros concepts which is worth noting is that there are so many derivatives of esoteric characteristics that they present a problem to investors. The risks being involved

Exhibit 1.1   The Main Forces Propelling Rapid Growth of Business Opportunity in Finance and Other Industrial Sectors

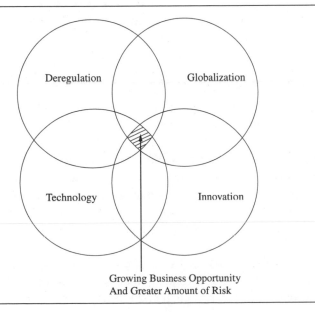

Deregulation

Globalization

Technology

Innovation

Growing Business Opportunity
And Greater Amount of Risk

are not properly understood, while some derivative instruments masquerade as being "low risk." This makes it feasible for institutional investors to make gambles that are not permitted by statutes of their organization. Greed induces financial institutions and other companies (even supposedly conservative investors) to take an inordinate amount of exposure.

- *Risks* have to be monitored and managed.

The greatest amount of exposure comes from the fact that very few people are able to see through to the limits of growth, and identify the *nonlinear* nature of exposure being assumed. Even these people have no hint how far the damage would go if the market crashes.

- The challenge in managing risks is *uncertainty.*

Uncertainty has become a cornerstone notion of the globalized service economy. In classical economies, prices are typically established on the basis of one's own cost of production and distribution. Today, this process has been inverted and pricing increasingly resembles the nonlinear process employed in insurance: Risk is connected to the uncertainty of an outcome.

- The number of risky instruments continues to grow.

The challenge of risk management does not relate only to derivatives. It concerns all products handled by financial institutions—whether exchange-traded or over the counter (OTC). Extended over a number of years, laxity in internal control as well as plain incompetence saw to it that by October 1998, the shares of Japan's big banks have been at a fifth of their value at the start of the decade of the 1990s. Other institutions of the G-10 countries did not fare so much better.

The search for "greater shareholder value" can hold many surprises. Following heavy losses in derivatives exposure and in imprudent loans, many banks quoted at the New York Stock Exchange, as well as in London, Zurich, Frankfurt, and Paris lost half their capitalization. Exhibit 1.2 dramatizes the drop in price of Bankers Trust stock compared to the S&P 500 Composite Index. Bankers Trust was subsequently bought by Deutsche Bank.

The risks taken by large financial institutions must be seen in conjunction with the quality of their internal control system. This is influenced by the consolidation that is taking place. The result is that as big banks have become bigger, they also became more exposed, because they assume the total of risk by the merging institutions. In the United States, the 10 largest credit institutions now have 66 percent of banking assets, compared with about 50 percent in the 1970s.

It is not the scope of this book to discuss the merits and demerits of mergers and acquisitions. The fact is that consolidation requires *more internal control,* not less. Yet, this is not the typical outcome. Musical chairs and other reasons see to it that megamergers

Exhibit 1.2 Equity Price Performance of Bankers Trust Contrasted to the S&P 500 Composite Index

are very difficult to consume, and the integration of internal controls is not a foregone conclusion.

The North Carolina National Bank became NationsBank which, after dozens of acquisitions, took over BankAmerica. The new BankAmerica, currently the largest deposit-taker in the United States with 7 percent of insured deposits, is active in 23 of 50 states. Next on the list of deposit-taking, with 3 percent apiece, are Bank One and First Union.

•   The hypothesis is that as banks have expanded across the country they have become less susceptible to shocks in specific geographical areas, product lines, or counterparties.

But while the days when banks could be hit by a slump in oil prices or by a collapse in property prices are thought to be over, the risk of losses remains. The same is true of exposure taken with emerging countries. Size may have advantages but it also involves risks—and therefore imposes prerequisites.

- At a time where *leveraging* is king and credit risk escalates, balancing risk and reward requires the greatest *transparency* ever. (This is a program to be initiated by policy makers at the top.)

The aftershock of high gearing can be devastating to the institution. The mismanagement of assets coupled with inability to control risk saw to it that in September 1998, at Wall Street, Long-Term Capital Management nearly collapsed after having taken about $200 billion in loans with only $4 billion in capital—a 50-to-1 leverage. At the same time, BankAmerica provided $1.4 billion against losses in the third quarter of 1998—with $400 million against an unsecured loan to D.E. Shaw.

Inordinate risks and negative effects on shareholder value correlate. No matter what is said and written about expected benefits from, and positive effects of, consolidation and globalization, the serious financial officer and the wise investor would examine both sides of the equation. They will also challenge the obvious. If we look at statistics, we will appreciate that there exists an asymmetry between economic power in terms of global gross domestic product (GDP) and capitalization in the world's stock markets:

- In 1999, in terms of Global GDP the United States represented 27 percent, European Union 31 percent, Japan 17 percent, Asia-Pacific 11 percent, Latin America 6 percent, Russia 1 to 2 percent, and the rest of the world about 6.5 percent.
- But also in 1999, in terms of capitalization the $11 trillion U.S. stock market represented 53 percent of global value of all stock markets. A decade earlier, in 1989, this was equal to only 24 percent—a 221 percent increase.

At one side, a shrinking world presents enormous opportunities for a company that can think beyond its own borders, both physically and psychologically. To benefit, it must pursue this strategy with a relentless brand of energy in every market—and be able to constantly communicate to its clients' high product quality at the most competitive cost. Executives who are not able to deliver on sales and profit goals they help set will not stay in the job.

THE SYNERGY BETWEEN INTERNAL CONTROL AND RISK MANAGEMENT

In the opinion of talented people in the financial industry working for central banks, commercial banks, investment banks, brokers/dealers, and treasury departments, internal control responsibilities start at board level. These responsibilities affect the way managers and professionals think and operate in every corner of the institution. But what's exactly meant by *internal control?*

I have posed this question to central bankers, the members of professional associations, and cognizant executives of commercial and investment banks. In reply, they brought to my attention different definitions of the term by reputable organizations. See the Appendix for five definitions, by:

1. The Committee of Sponsoring Organizations of the Treadway Commission (COSO).
2. The Institute of Certified Public Accountants (AICPA).
3. The Institute of Internal Auditors (IIA).
4. The Basle Committee of Banking Supervision.
5. The European Monetary Institute (EMI), now European Central Bank (ECB).

Indirectly, each of these definitions looks fine. The problem is that they contradict one another. Therefore, I combined them together and tested versions of this integrative definition of internal control until the opinions of knowledgeable people converged. The result is presented at the end of the Appendix.* Here is a condensed version of it:

- The chairman of the board, the directors, and senior management are responsible and accountable for internal control.
- Internal control is a dynamic system covering all types of risk, addressing fraud, and assuring transparency.
- Beyond risks, internal control goals are preservation of assets, account reconciliation, and compliance with laws and regulations.
- The able management of internal control requires policies, organization, technology, open communications, access to all transactions, real-time quality control, and corrective action.
- Internal control must be regularly audited by internal and external auditors to ensure its rank and condition.

"This is consistent with the COSO model of efficiency and effectiveness," said David L. Robinson of the Federal Reserve Board in Washington, DC (for the COSO criteria, rules, and methodology see Part Two). Other regulators pressed the point that well-tuned internal control helps to assure that the information senior management receives is timely and accurate. Opinions converged on two facts:

1. Internal controls are valid only as far as the people working for the organization observe them.
2. Controls should be designed not only to prevent cases like Barings and Orange County, but also to underline everyone's accountability.

The Basle Committee on Banking Supervision states that a credit institution's board of directors should be responsible for understanding the risks run by the institution, setting acceptable levels for each type of exposure, and assuring that senior management takes the necessary steps to identify, monitor, and control the entity's exposure. The Committee's thesis upholds the principle that the board of directors must provide senior management with:

---

* This definition is reflected in all subsequent chapters since it constitutes a consensus.

- Governance.
- Guidance.
- Oversight.

"It is the responsibility of senior management to define the internal control structure," said Claude Sivy of the Bank for International Settlements. "The definition of internal control should not be limited to banks," observed Robert A. Sollazzo of the Securities and Exchange Commission in New York. "If internal control is going to work, management must be committed to it," added Edward A. Ryan, Jr. of the Securities and Exchange Commission, in Boston.

Hans-Dietrich Peters and Hans Werner Voth, of the Deutsche Bundesbank, stated that the first level responsible for internal control is the board. They added that all levels of management must be acutely aware of the need for internal control, and they must be accountable for exercising it in an effective manner.

"Internal control is a process effected by the board and senior management to ensure adequacy and accuracy," suggested Bill Morris and Gene Green, of the Office of the Comptroller of the Currency (OCC). John B. Caouette, of MBIA Insurance Corp., concurred with this statement, "Internal controls are only successful if embedded in a strict risk management culture." "Internal control is a concept which reaches all levels of management and the activities pertinent to that level," said Jonathan E.C. Grant, of the Auditing Practices Board, in the United Kingdom.

These expert opinions confirm what is known from organizational theory and practice. The board is responsible for setting the broad strategies and major policies of a company, including ways and means to face the challenges posed by globalization and consolidation. Not only is it part of the board's responsibility to ensure that an adequate system of internal controls is established and maintained, but a matter of personal accountability of each member of the board. Other questions linger:

- Is internal control part of risk management?
- Is it the other way around?
- Or, are these two activities independent from one another?

Curtis Wong, of the Federal Deposit Insurance Corporation (FDIC) posed this provocative query, "What's the difference between internal control and risk management?" To FDIC's opinion, there is no difference, because "risk management is the internal control of the institution." As shown in Exhibit 1.3, FDIC considers internal control as a subset of risk management.

The Securities and Exchange Commission disagrees with this viewpoint. It sees risk management as being part of internal control—rather than vice-versa. This thesis is visualized in Exhibit 1.4. Said Robert A. Sollazzo, "I don't see internal control as a separate box, but as one composed of two important functions: Risk management, and compliance and accounting reconciliation."

Other cognizant regulators expressed the opinion that the relationship between internal control and risk management is complex because the two concepts overlap—and this is also true of the ways banks put them in practice. According to Dr. Martin Ohms, of the

Exhibit 1.3   The FDIC Viewpoint on the Relation between Internal Control and Risk Management

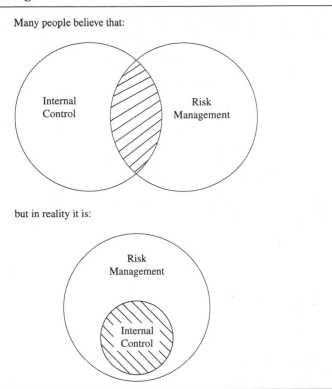

Austrian National Bank, "risk management (is) generally a part of internal control." Article 39 of the Austrian Banking Act specifies that "internal control has to be seen as a concept."

The Bank for International Settlements supported the principle that internal control is every department's responsibility. "Therefore," said Clause Sivy, "there should not be a single department or function dedicated to internal control—but all departments should be controlled by internal audit on whether they observe and follow internal control concepts and practices."

The Basle Committee bets on this process, as it seeks to assure that a credit institution's capital position is consistent with its overall risk profile and management strategy—an approach intended to encourage early supervisory intervention (see Part Three). Compliance is the keyword in this connection. Supervisors should have the ability to require banks to hold capital in excess of minimum regulatory capital ratios, if the situation warrants doing so. Concomitant to this is the drive to convince senior management about the need for:

• Developing a rigorous internal control and capital assessment process.

• Setting targets for capital commensurate with the bank's particular risk profile and internal environment.

Exhibit 1.4   The Viewpoint of SEC and of the Austrian National Bank

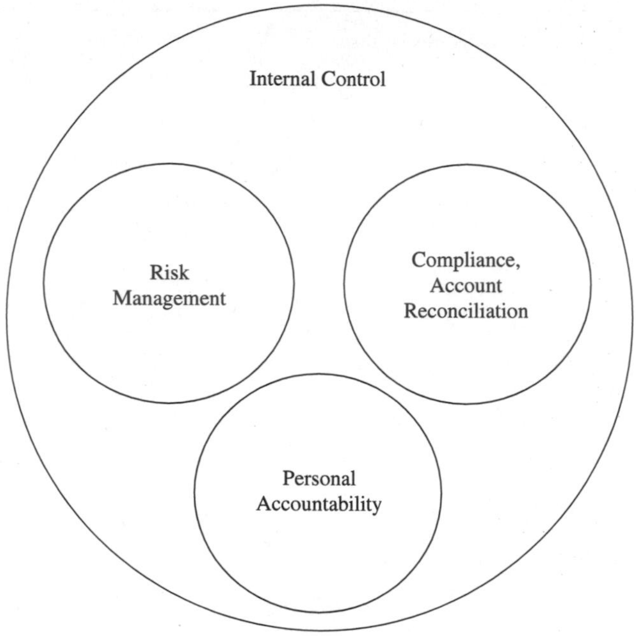

The expectation is that this internal control process would be subject to supervisory review and intervention, where and when such action proves to be appropriate. In a way emulating COSO guidelines, the Basle supervisors want to see that a bank should publicly disclose qualitative and quantitative information about its risk exposures:

- The risk profile inherent in on-balance sheet and off-balance sheet activities should be transparent.
- Transparency makes it possible to judge the stability of an institution's financial position.

Transparency is an integral part of *market discipline*—the third pillar on which rests the New Capital Adequacy Framework by the Basle Committee on Banking Supervision (see Part Three). Market discipline should characterize policies at the top before real improvements can be made by the people operating below top management. As Frederic Visnovski of the Commission Bancaire, Banque de France, stated during our meeting, "Market discipline is synonymous to reliable public information."

FORMAL AND INFORMAL SOLUTIONS TO INTERNAL CONTROL CHALLENGES

Internal control can be *formal* or *informal*. At the current state of the art, the most prominent examples of informal internal control are: management integrity, management competence, self-risk analysis, effective communications, training, merits and demerits, appropriate remuneration, and reward systems. These should supplement formal controls characterized by a clearly defined organizational structure subject to:

- Fully transparent transactions and positions.
- Analytical risk management procedures.
- Support through high technology.
- Rigorous internal and external auditing.

The last bullet raises the question: Is internal control part of auditing? If not, whose job is it? As the previous section indirectly suggested, there exists no simple answer to this question, neither is there a unique solution. A great deal depends on an institution's history, culture, and iron hand of management. My research has documented that:

- Some institutions see internal control as part of auditing.
- Others think it is part of accounting in a sense of extended responsibilities.
- Still others, among the more technologically advanced, see it as part of risk management.

I subscribe to none of these alternatives. Instead, internal control should convey a sense of responsibility. It should have an independent status, designed to be of service to the board, the chief executive, and all levels of management. As Exhibit 1.5 shows, internal

Exhibit 1.5   The Areas Covered by Accounting, Auditing, Risk Management, and Internal Control Overlap, but Each Also Has Its Own Sphere of Interest

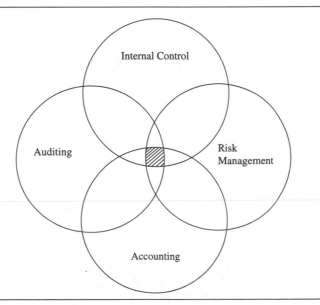

control, risk management, auditing, and accounting have a common ground—these subjects closely correlate. The functions of accounting and of internal control should not be confused:

- *Accounting* keeps the General Ledger, manages the financial records, and looks after the reconciliation of profit and loss.
- *Auditing* checks the correctness of all operations through a system able to flush out what has malfunctioned.
- *Internal control* underlines the accountability of every member of supervision, and most evidently of accounting and auditing.

While three of the four spheres of interest in Exhibit 1.5 are structured organizational units, one could consider internal control not as another department but rather as a system of limits, checks and balances—over and above its conceptual qualities, and the responsibilities it confers to the board and senior management:

- This system of internal control must be supported by every existing organizational unit.
- It should be served in real-time by intelligent networks, sophisticated software, agents,[1] and database mining.

Technology should help to create an integrative knowledge-enriched internal control with communications as the focal point, and computation seamless to the end user. The infrastructure must be reliable and user interaction with the systems through voice, signs, and forms should be ones that people are naturally comfortable with in their daily business. This is the financial environment of the early twenty-first century—with globalized internal control one of its basic requirements.

The use of advanced technology is part of a formal solution to internal control. It is rewarding, but also demands skill and vision. Under no condition should the information technology needs of internal control, and of banking at large, be underestimated. "One of the pillars of internal control," said the Deutsche Bundesbank, "is a complete and correct information system for management." Many regulators emphasized that effective management control depends on:

- Reliable information.
- Open communications channels.

Mauro Grande, of the European Central Bank, suggested that: "Both the executives responsible for internal control and the Audit Committee should see to it that the communications channels are open throughout the financial institution." Open communications channels are a basic requirement for transparency, and technology can be instrumental in keeping the information flowing in a dependable way.

The formal internal control solution we adopt must primarily serve senior management's "need to know" about every transaction, every position, every counterparty, and every commitment—anywhere in the world, for any product, at any time. At the same time, while there are many functions the internal control system should accomplish, it must not (and cannot) do management's own job.

Decisions connected to risk taking and risk control are management's own. Management must be brave both in planning and in control. As Shakespeare's Julius Cesar said: "Cowards die many times before their deaths. The valiant never taste of death but once." Immediate corrective action is an act of bravery. Hiding the bad news under the carpet until the whole edifice comes crashing down, is the financial equivalent of cowardice.

When risk estimates are underestimates, the board and senior management are kidding themselves—lying to their investors, business partners, and supervisors. Neither is liquidation of those directly responsible for huge exposure a way of improving things all by itself. Changing the personnel is a waste of time, when:

- Defective internal control policies remain the same.
- The board shies away from its responsibilities.
- Tough decisions are pushed further out into the future.

Because of deregulation, globalization, consolidation, technology, and innovation, survival requires a rigorous management able to fend off unplanned exposure. The board must know itself deeply, its institution, its competitors, and the environment in which it operates. "If you know yourself and know your opponents, you do not need to worry about the outcome of 100 battles."[2]

Next to concept, principles, structure, technology, and analytical approaches, a formal approach to internal control depends a great deal on behavioral science (see Chapter 6). Decades of research in behavioral science and artificial intelligence allow organizations to simulate and institutionalize the patterns and processes of self-directed human activity, including learning. This potentially makes powerful decision support media available at all levels of operations.

Furthermore, as Chapters 7 and 8 explain through practical examples, formal internal control can benefit from an array of tools. Statistical quality control (SQC) charts are one of the most formidable tools. SQC has been effectively applied in the manufacturing industry for 55 years with great success. Banking has been slow in using SQC concepts and principles. The first significant reference is Risk Adjusted Return on Capital (RAROC) by Bankers Trust, which dates back to the middle-1980s.[3]

Both behavioral controls and SQC concepts and charts help in closing the gap that often exists in finance between the ideal and the real promises and products. Tracking behavior, including trader behavior, can be instrumental in controlling the disparity often characterizing expected and obtained results.

One of the ways to discover weaknesses in internal control is to establish whether no matter how significant this year's profits are, senior management always wants more. Usually, more is attained by taking on an increased amount of exposure, with some risks being ill-studied and some transactions being full of unknowns.

The aftermath is that the institution finds itself at the edge of its knowledge and experience—unable to neutralize a growing exposure by some bold action. A bad situation becomes worse through organizational ills such as overlaps in responsibilities or levels of management. When this happens, the chain of command is not functioning correctly. Senior members of management are no more fully aware of risks and/or fail to show initiative in:

- Evaluating exposure.
- Uncovering fraud.
- Taking corrective action.

This puts in question the prevailing concepts of internal control, its functions and distinguishing characteristics. An independent audit should establish whether these overlaps are between accounting, auditing, and risk management; if internal control can still hold the upper ground in deciding on organizational responsibilities; and how much responsibility for a twisted structure falls on the board.

Is the chairman directly responsible for organizational ills? The chief executive? The chief operations officer? The chief financial officer? Conditions vary from one institution to another. There is no unique answer to these questions because a unique definition of organization and structure best suited for internal control, and of the way in which it should be implemented does not exist. This is true even among supervisory authorities and standards-setting organizations.

FINANCIAL STAYING POWER REQUIRES A RIGOROUS INTERNAL CONTROL CULTURE

It is becoming increasingly clear that the wave of change in the global financial market expected to take place over the next 10 years will dwarf what has occurred in the last 30 years, or in any similar period in the past, in terms of risk and return in business. This is with the understanding that the world's largest markets undergo a series of transformations that increase both opportunity and exposure—hence the reasons for rigorous internal control.

The barriers that have traditionally separated national markets for goods and services are breaking down, creating larger and more dynamic regional markets which in turn add up to the global market. In a sense, whether internal control or risk management keeps exposure under a watchful eye and at any given moment provides the necessary damage control is immaterial. What is important is that the job is done in an able and timely manner.

What has damaged many financial institutions, some of them beyond repair, is that the board, the chief executive, and senior managers are afraid of taking bold control actions. Their behavior is reminiscent of General George McClellan, the commander of the Army of the Potomac during the American Civil War. According to historians, McClellan lacked the mental and moral courage required of great generals. He did not have the will to act, to confront the terrible moment of truth on the battlefield.

McClellan is a perfect example of why chief executives should be neither timid in their decisions nor possess one-track minds. Chief executives should appreciate that while a perfect organization is welcome, it is no substitute to action. The commander of the Army of the Potomac excelled at preparation, but it was never quite complete. The Army was perpetually *almost* ready to move. Prior to finally firing McClellan, Lincoln said to him:

"You remember my speaking to you of what I called your over-cautiousness?

"Are you not over-cautious when you assume that you cannot do what the enemy is constantly doing?

"We should not so operate as to merely drive him [Lee] away.

"If we never try, we shall never succeed.

"Will you pardon me for asking what the horses of your army have done since the battle of Antietam?"

All members of the board, chief executive officers, chief financial officers, risk managers, and internal auditors have a very clear job in keeping the institution healthy and solvent. If they don't, they should not be surprised if they, like McClellan, are asked to step aside and let someone else lead the battle. Or, as Lincoln put it, "If a man can't skin, he must hold a leg while somebody else does."

The executive in charge of risk management must be able at all times not only to give an objective factual account of events, but also make them meaningful, dramatic, and resonant to those who listen. Part of his job is to present the CEO with a sound plan of action:

- Fiction has no business in internal control and no place in risk management.
- The financial staying power of the institution depends on reliable reporting of both good news and bad news.

Concentration of exposure is an important criterion of looming trouble. Many bank failures have been caused by too much exposure to too few areas of business or clients, over too long a time, in an imperfectly controlled environment. Therefore, a vital test of financial health is the internal quality of objective financial reporting. Many banks do not provide themselves with real-time facts and figures that help provide accuracy in their decisions. There are many excuses for this failure, including:

- The current information technology supports no corporate memory facility.
- Disclosure on background decisions would submerge essential data into irrelevance.
- The risk of infringing customer confidentiality is unwarranted.
- Disclosures on decisions could affect the bank's competitive position and its safety.

Usually, however, the real reason is that there have been *too many* poor management decisions. If it were not for these, some of the largest global institutions would not have exposed to derivatives risk 1400 percent, 1600 percent, or 1800 percent of their equity— or about 100 percent of their assets. Observations on this level of superexposure are not often volunteered, but here are the facts.

The statistics in Exhibit 1.6 talk volumes about an unprecedented level of exposure that reduces financial staying power to a minimum. The figures about 14.5, 16.1, and 18.2 times equity are not connected to notional principal amounts (NPA) of derivatives contracts but to demodulated notional principal by a divisor of 30.[4] This demodulation gives the credit equivalent amount with the resulting exposure as a very conservative estimate. Had I used a divisor of 20, as some banks do, the ratio of equity of derivatives risk would have been, correspondingly, $\times 21.7$, $\times 24.1$, and $\times 27.3$.

Such numbers suggest that after doing away with all their equity 20 times over or more, some banks have put all their assets on the block and they are left with the liabilities. These assets don't belong to the credit institutions but to their clients, who entrusted them with management of their fortune. Many other major institutions from the Group of Ten countries are in the same position. The only reason I use examples from big U.S. banks is that Congress has passed laws making their exposure figures transparent.

Financial staying power is *weakened* by leverage. In the short term, provided the market moves the way management bets, leverage helps to improve the profit figures. The factor " $\times 18.2$ equity" basically means the bank has leveraged more than 18 times its equity. With some exceptions, even hedge funds don't gear themselves up to that amount. Of course, LTCM was geared 50 times up, but when the crash came its partners lost 90 percent of their equity. If the New York Fed had not brokered a refinancing solution, LTCM would have been bankrupt.

One of the fundamental characteristics of an internal control culture must be that such an amount of gearing is not doable because reason has the upper hand over greed. Time and again, high leverage turns into agony when top management participates in the gamble and the genie is out of the bottle. Short of a twelveth-hour salvage by regulators, a bank is left to its own devices to bring the situation under control.

Geared policies can be very costly when the market turns against the investor, or the instruments we deal with are not well understood. "Many businessmen are always establishing new headaches. They never ask: Is there a beach to the beachhead?" says Peter

Exhibit 1.6 Demodulated Derivatives Exposure Compared to Equity and Assets of Major Credit Institutions as of March 31, 1999 (in U.S.$ Billions)

	Equity	Assets	NPA in Derivatives	Demodulated Derivatives Exposure*	Ratio to Equity	Ratio to Assets
JP Morgan	11.3	261	8.861	295.4	× 16.1	1.132
Bankers Trust	4.7	133	2.563	85.4	× 18.2	0.642
Chase Manhattan	23.8	366	10.353	345.1	× 14.5	0.943
Citigroup	42.7	669	7.987	266.2	× 6.2	0.398
BankAmerica	45.9	618	4.438	147.9	× 3.2	0.239
Banc One	20.6	262	1.472	49.1	× 2.4	0.187

*By a factor of 30.

Drucker. A basic reason why internal control today plays a more vital function than ever is that the products offered by banks are becoming steadily more complex and more exotic.

Because the supervisory authorities tacitly or explicitly approve dealing in new financial instruments, it is part of the board's duty to assure that the internal control that is in place has the sophistication necessary to report exposure to new and old financial instruments in a timely and accurate manner and to determine whether the identified exposure is followed by corrective action.

Every executive and every professional working for the institution cannot be expected to keep tags on *every* trade. Internal control must produce *real-time patterns* to permit evaluation of individual and cumulative exposure, as well as ways and means to bend the curve. It must also make it possible for every manager to focus on detail to evaluate outstanding risk.

Finally, a great deal of attention should be paid to the synergy between internal and external controls—the latter being exercised by certified public accountants and supervisors—and to the standards being used. Quoting once more Peter Drucker: "We must stop talking of profit as a reward. It is a cost. There are no rewards, only costs of yesterday and tomorrow." The costs of yesterday are those we usually consider as expenses; those of tomorrow arc thc risks which we take.

TRANSPARENCY IS VITAL TO THE SUSTENANCE OF PERSONAL ACCOUNTABILITY

Many knowledgeable executives who participated in my research commented that while transparency today is greater than ever because of the expanding globalized market, it is still not enough. The concept of transparency is not evenly applied. In many emerging markets, crony capitalism sees to it that this notion has not taken root. It has not penetrated business ethics and regulatory reporting because management accountability is weak. And accountability is weak because business ethics are lacking (see Exhibit 1.7) and internal control is non-existent.

Only the best managed institutions appreciate that a thoroughly studied and clearly established internal control system is the best guarantee for commercial and investment banks, if they wish to achieve long-term profitability, keep risks under lock and key, and maintain a reliable reporting system. Timely and accurate controls help to assure that the organization will comply with laws and regulations, and management will be in charge even in time of turbulence.

The surge in interest that the issue of internal control experienced in the 1990s is a direct result of very important losses incurred by several banks during this decade. Much of this torrent of red ink could have been avoided if the institutions had established and maintained policies on transparency, effective risk management systems, and systems enabling early detection of problems. Such solutions would have limited the damage.

Just writing about plans for internal control is not enough. Many banks can produce volumes on what they intend to do through internal control. But who reads them? Is the chairman taking care of the negatives? Is the board looking after the necessary change in

Exhibit 1.7   Eight Top Reasons behind Emerging Market Risk According to a Recent Study

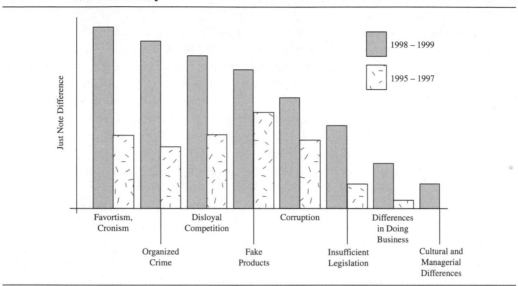

culture? The keywords in the board's policy regarding control of exposure should be those qualifying eligible external credit assessment:

- Transparency.
- Objectivity.
- Credibility.
- Staying power.

Setting and sustaining efficient internal control and risk management systems is a pressing issue. Lack of such systems can lead to loss of business confidence and eventually to bankruptcy. In many countries, the law and the regulators require the board of directors and top management to create a coherent internal control and reporting structure—and make the board members directly responsible for it. This is necessary to manage the many aspects of risk, and to safeguard the bank's business assets.

To avoid overlaps, internal control should differentiate among the responsibilities of the chief risk management officer (CRMO), auditors, and accountants. The responsibility of the auditors is to assure that the annual financial statements are free of material misstatement; that of the accountants is to provide a timely and accurate financial picture; while risk management should be proactive in exposure control.

From a risk management perspective, the key contribution of internal control is both as a filter and as a means for focusing attention.

Board members and senior managers who fail in their duty to identify and track exposure are turning the tables on themselves. Internal control should be steadily flashing the risks involved in the bank's transactions and its portfolio. In loans, for instance, this would include:

- Repayment history of counterparties.
- Analysis of loan losses according to strategic and tactical criteria.
- Poor loan mix and/or overconcentration.
- Profits from loans by customer class/loans type.
- Compliance to internal policies for granting loans.
- Compliance to regulatory directives and legal issues.

Stockholder activism has also pushed banks to institute and sustain a rigorous internal control. In July 1998, twenty BankBoston employees were either fired or reprimanded for negligence tied to a $73 million loan scandal. Ricardo Carrasco, an executive in the bank's New York office, was accused of embezzling money. The man and the money have been missing since February of that same year.[5]

The aftermath of leveraged trading losses, particularly those motivated by inordinate commissions, is no different than that of embezzlement. For this reason, stockholders have put the blame at the top of the organizational pyramid. In 1998, after the heavy losses in D.E. Shaw and other derivatives business, David Coulter the new BankAmerica president, was blamed for unexpected provisions against bad loans and had to resign. Also in 1998, at the United Bank of Switzerland, Mathis Cabiallavetta, the chairman, and three other senior executives had to resign after the LTCM scandal.[6]

At Dutch-based ING Barings, Marinus Minderhoud, its chairman, resigned over mediocre results in corporate and investment banking. At Kvaerner, the Anglo-Norwegian engineering and ship-building group, Erik Toenseth was ousted as chief executive officer. As shown in Exhibit 1.8, the company's shares lost 80 percent of their value over a 22-month period. This turned shareholder value upside down.

The BankAmerica/D.E. Shaw, UBS/LTCM, ING Barings and Kvaerner blow ups are not fuses that exploded because of a random spark. The company's degradation builds up over time, but is not visible because of lack of transparency. The moment of truth comes when things can no longer be hidden. Under conditions of secrecy, it is the last straw which breaks the camel's back and magnifies the chief executive's personal accountability.

A basic characteristic of well-run organizations is that the board and senior management fully appreciate the risks involved in any strategy which they establish. For example, huge investments in spite of the rather limited size of emerging market economies as well as the amount of unknowns and associated risks. One of the worst enemies of investors in emerging markets is *crony capitalism,* which is constantly rent-seeking at the expense of the local economy and foreign investors.

Typically, after the crash, IMF comes to the rescue with its classic tax hike/devaluation policy, which many experts believe is counterproductive. Others bash IMF policies that they believe contribute to moral hazard—and, most importantly, leave unaltered the general lack of transparency and accountability.

Exhibit 1.8 Kvaerner, 'A' Share Price Heads South

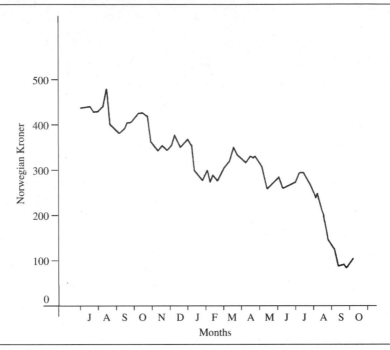

Many institutional and other investors disregard these negatives, yet ridding the system of crony capitalism is no simple matter. Part of the problem, though only part, is that with few exceptions these so-called emerging markets are not really emerging. Paul Volcker, the former chairman of the Federal Reserve, points out that the entire banking system of many an emerging country is no bigger than a typical regional bank in the United States or Europe—that is the size now considered too small for global financial markets, while it is full of traps and unknowns.

The ugly face of globalization is that for many emerging economies, small financial markets mean that exchange-rate volatility will be a structural problem, not a temporary one, and it will haunt them for years to come. If a hedge fund decides to play in its stock exchange or buy and sell its assets, or if a couple of mutual funds decide to make a serious investment, the country's exchange rate could rocket. Lavish foreign investments may start an unsustainable boom in real estate and banking, causing havoc for exporters, and currency collapse will take place the moment the financial invaders go home—as shown in Thailand, Indonesia, South Korea, Russia, and Brazil.

Lack of appreciation of nonconventional dangers in emerging markets leads to inordinate risks. This is true of credit institutions and of all other companies. In 1998, the cost of nonconventional risks reached $25 billion according to a study by Merchant International Group, a British firm. This study involved 7,500 companies with international operations.

Sixty percent of firms responding to the Merchant International Group study said that they suffered losses in these markets because they had not taken account of local morals and business habits. What is more, the pattern of corruption and disloyalty has significantly changed for the worse in 1998–1999 as contrasted to 1995–1997, while internal control is far less.

Let me conclude this chapter with a lesson I have learned from 40 years of experience in banking. While many bankers and other experts in finance pay at least lip service to the principle that key to internal control is good transparency, few institutions are willing and able to see to it that transparency carries the day. Yet, any management worth its salt should appreciate that it can catch a sophisticated crook only when it obliges him to be transparent.

Many financial institutions which "are not so transparent"—are, in fact, not transparent at all. This greatly diminishes management's supervision and it practically wipes out the contribution of a risk measurement system, particularly so when a trader or other professional has been for years a star performer. Because of good profits in the past, nobody seems to think that he or she can destroy the bank in the future. Barings thought that way, and complacency at the top let Nick Leeson lead that venerable bank to bankruptcy.

There is another lesson to be learned from Leeson's policies and Barings' debacle. It has to do with the practice of double books. In some cases, double books are a legend. When Dr. Enrico Cuccia, former chief executive and honorary chairman of Mediobanca (Italy's medium- to long-term lending institution) was asked by the judge if he knew that Gemina (a financial holding) kept double books, he responded: "In my long years, I never saw a company which did not have double books."

Double books are the best prescription for fraud, yet sometimes it is the law which makes them a necessity. This is particularly relevant with globalization, because down-to-earth accounting standards are so different from one country to another. Not only the way financial records are kept but also their interpretation changes tremendously with the jurisdiction. This is dramatized in Chapters 2 and 3 through real-life examples, which identify where some of the loopholes may be hiding.

NOTES

1. D.N. Chorafas, *Agent Technology Handbook* (New York: McGraw-Hill, 1998).
2. Sun Tzu, *L'Art de la Guerre* (Paris: Flammarion, 1972).
3. D.N. Chorafas, *Credit Derivatives and the Management of Risk* (New York: New York Institute of Finance, 2000).
4. D.N. Chorafas, "Managing Credit Risk," *The Lessons of VAR Failures and Imprudent Exposure,* vol. 2 (London: Euromoney, 2000).
5. *USA Today* (July 6, 1998).
6. D.N. Chorafas, "Managing Credit Risk," *The Lessons of VAR Failures and Imprudent Exposure,* vol. 2 (London: Euromoney, 2000).

CHAPTER 2

International Accounting Standards and the Global Accounting System

The markets for financial instruments are global, but risks are also global and rising. Therefore, to make profits, bankers, brokers, treasurers, and investors have to know with accuracy and in a timely manner their assets, liabilities, and exposure, the more so as counterparties become more sophisticated and new financial instruments are introduced practically every day—many with still unknown risks. An example is derivatives, which are popular because they are flexible and they are leveraged. Usually, they carry no initial cost; "merely" an agreement binding the two parties. However, whether this agreement is short-term or long-term, it may have embedded into it considerable future exposure. Therefore, accounting procedures must be adequate for pricing, inventorying, and controlling embedded risk.

Because institutions and other companies operate transborder, accounting rules and methods must also be global and homogeneous if they are to treat equal things in an equal manner. Fairly significant changes are now being considered in accounting standards and associated internal control policies and practices. The goal is to reflect the growing importance of new, sophisticated financial instruments, as well as to manage exposure in an able manner.

Current and forthcoming accounting changes are part and parcel of the ongoing switch between classical accounting methods and the more recent ones which have been evolving since the mid- to late-1980s. What should characterize emerging accounting standards?

While COSO is the metalanguage, accounting is the language companies speak among themselves and with the regulators. This language must be comprehensive and comprehensible by everybody, without loopholes and ways for twisting financial statements. It should reflect embedded value in a pragmatic way.

In addition, compliance to the rules put forward by the New Capital Adequacy Framework will be shown through financial statements that use rigorous accounting standards.

But which standards? With classical accounting procedures, everything is written at historical cost (accruals); with the new accounting procedures, the trading portfolio is marked to market or to model. Underpinning this new accounting strategy is the concept of *fair value* as contrasted to the method of accruals (see Chapter 14).

While fair value accounting has now been established for the trading book, the direction shown by the Framework suggests that eventually also the banking book will be marked to market or to model in an effort to reflect as close as possible its fair value. The challenge is to tune the new accounting rules in a way that fair value cannot be manipulated, but it has to be reported in a dependable and homogeneous manner throughout the global economy. This brings us back to the key question: Which standards should be used to reach this goal?

THE CHOICE OF ACCOUNTING STANDARDS ON A GLOBAL BASIS

The choice of accounting standards that fit modern business practices but also protect the investors is complex because of a number of reasons, with tradition and conflict of interest the most important. It is always difficult to abandon old accounting practices that have been handed down dating back to Luca Paciolo who, in 1494, published the "Summa di Arithmetica, Geometria, Proportioni et Proportionalita." But this is only part of the problem.

More fundamental is the fact that there are different conflicting interests that the new accounting standards, rules, and procedures should address and try to resolve. This can hardly be done through the time-honored method of compromises. To be valid, gain general acceptance, and pass the test of time, a new global accounting system must be characterized by:

- A top-down grand design addressing the general principles for reliable financial reporting (an example being the line drawn by COSO).
- A bottom-up modular building approach that makes system sense but also assures precision and makes it possible to handle detail.

A link between grand design, precision, and detail is *materiality* of which we spoke in Chapter 1. Materiality is a relative notion. A $150 million loss means something quite different to General Motors versus a small company. Any entity that loses $150 million on derivatives has to report it to regulators and investors. But the way the materiality principle works, a large corporation may not need to explain the details to investors because it can hide them between the other P&Ls.

A loss of that size is not so *material* to GE's, GM's, IBM's, or Microsoft's earnings (see also Chapter 13). But a small to medium-size company would be devastated by such a loss. Even if management tries to hide it, it would not remain hidden for long from public view. Should the materiality principle be flexible? If it is, the gates may open to "creative accounting." If not, it would be difficult to adapt the system to changing conditions.

Everyone agrees on the principle that good accounting practices can help to prevent swindling as well as assist in mitigating the effects of business catastrophe. The board and senior management must have in place a system capable of warning them of issues that are out of control before they become too serious. The challenge is how in practice to implement this principle.

Because of the importance of new accounting rules and regulations and the interests embedded in developing them, many efforts are currently underway. These parallel efforts are not necessarily compatible with one another. While each of the Group of Ten countries has its own accounting standards body, on an international level the three most prominent working groups are sponsored by:

- The International Accounting Standards Committee (IASC).
- The Basle Committee on Banking Supervision, through its Internal Control project.
- The European Union's Accounting Standards endeavor.

There is a collaboration between the International Organization of Securities Commissions (IOSCO) and IASC. IOSCO is the club of stock market regulators, like the Basle Committee is the club of the Group of Ten central bankers. This collaboration between IOSCO and IASC has aimed at establishing a uniform set of international accounting standards. One of their goals is to allow international firms to obtain listings on the world's major stock exchanges—which is in itself a vast project.

International accounting standards and requirements for listing in the world's stock exchanges correlate, but they are not necessarily the same thing. This is the message conveyed by Exhibit 2.1, which underlines the distinction between two different sets of players and the objectives they set out to meet. The parties whose interests must be protected through a suitable common ground are those in both sides of Exhibit 2.1.

The problems associated with developing a homogeneous set of accounting standards which can be applied worldwide are complex not only because of the differences in form and opinion prevailing today, but also because supervisory authorities have added value to local standards by implying precise regulatory requirements. In each country, the supervisory authorities for banks, securities, and exchanges have their own rules and

Exhibit 2.1   Accounting Standards and Supervisory Requirement Correlate, but They Also Cover Different Functional Areas

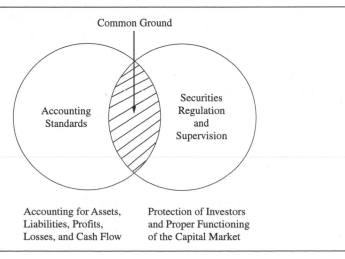

regulations for capital markets. Such rules evolve over time and are reflected into the prevailing reporting practices. This gives the local accounting procedures a better structure, but also makes it more difficult to untie the knots.

It is relatively easy to agree on the principles that should characterize the common accounting ground. The problem is to work out the details, keeping in perspective the prevailing regulatory requirements in the major exchanges of the world. For example, focusing on the International Accounting Standards (IAS), the basic principles are:

- Substance over form.
- Materiality.
- Value.

Under IAS, substance over form can be invoked so that accounting statements present a true and fair view of business transactions and other economic events. The underlying principle essentially states that financial statements and accounting for individual transactions and economic events should reflect financial reality. This representation of financial reality must be done in line with the principles and provisions of accounting laws.

Theoretically, there are no reasons to believe that any accounting standards body and its accounting rules would challenge this statement. A whole series of international accounting standards shown in Exhibit 2.2 abide by this principle. But in terms of practical implementation, there are challenges along the way. The problem starts precisely at this point which is the entry into the domain of accounting detail. The underlying economic reality of a transaction has no direct correspondence to the contractual terms and/or the legal form.

Exhibit 2.2 Accounting Standard Set in Collaboration between IOSCO and IASC

Subject	Standard	Effective Date
Income taxes	IAS 12 revised	January 1, 1998
Earnings per share	IAS 33	January 1, 1998
Segment reporting	IAS 14 revised	July 1, 1998
Presentation of financial statements	IAS 1 revised	July 1, 1998
Employee benefits	IAS 19 revised	January 1, 1999
Leases	IAS 17 revised	January 1, 1999
Interim financial reporting	IAS 34	January 1, 1999
Discontinuing operations	IAS 35	January 1, 1999
Impairment of assets	IAS 36	July 1, 1999
Provisions, contingent liabilities	IAS 37	July 1, 1999
Intangible assets	IAS 38	July 1, 1999
Financial instruments	IAS 39	January 1, 2001

While no one doubts the need for an internationally acceptable set of accounting standards, the question is one of different business realities, customs, opportunities, past experience, taxation, and prevailing laws of good conduct.

Still, the need for universal accounting standards acts as a counterforce to the differentiation which is prevailing today. With a growing number of companies becoming global in one way or another, there is an urgent requirement for a uniform accounting code which can effectively address five goals:

1. Investor information.
2. Management accounting.
3. General accounting.
4. Supervisory activities.
5. Taxation.

Let's take a closer look at investor information. Earnings per share (EPS) is one of the time-honored criteria. Both FASB and IASC recently issued new standards for computing EPS. These primarily deal with the denominator of the calculation of EPS since the numerator is always net income.

Under the Statement of Financial Accounting Standards (SFAS) 128, the U.S. computation becomes simpler and comparable to the international EPS. This is a welcome convergence, but SFAS 128 requires two EPS statistics and many experts think the spread between the two figures will in all likelihood widen. SFAS 128 substitutes basic earnings per share (BEPS) for primary earnings per share (PEPS).

BEPS is net income available to common shareholders divided by the weighted average number of common shares outstanding. Then comes another metric, the fully diluted earnings per share (FDEPS) which, generally, will be the same or higher than the ratio currently calculated and referred to as diluted earnings per share (DEPS). DEPS will be higher than FDEPS when stock prices rise at the end of a period.

DEPS will continue to be calculated using the *if converted* method for convertible securities, and the treasury stock method for options and warrants. But the specifics of the calculation diverge between FASB and IASC. The impact of this divergence will be financial figures reflecting the same facts but varying by company.

The example presented in Exhibit 2.3 helps to emphasize the difference between basic earnings per share and diluted. BEPS tend to be higher. In 1996, the difference was 7 percent; in 1997, 6.6 percent. Analysts use multiples of EPS to form a judgment and make a projection.

INTERNATIONAL ACCOUNTING STANDARDS AND GENERALLY ACCEPTED ACCOUNTING PRINCIPLES

While new departures are necessary in recording and reporting practices as well as new accounting rules, it is not easy to establish uniform global accounting standards and forms, let alone the fact that—in a universal accounting system—standards and rules are

Exhibit 2.3   Xerox Corporation Earnings per Share in 1996 and 1997

	1997			1996		
	Income	Shares	Per Share Amount	Income	Shares	Per Share Amount
Basic EPS			$4.31			$3.55
Income from continuing operations	$1,408*			$1,162		
Amount of shares		326,686			327,194	
Diluted EPS			$4.04			$3.32
Stock options and other incentives		3,964			5,321	
ESOP adjustment,† convertible debt	$ 47	29,986		$ 43	30,525	
Total income from operations	$1,455			$1,205		
Adjusted amount of shares		360,636			363,140	

*Minus accrued dividends on preferred stock.
†ESOP adjustment includes preferred stock dividends, ESOP expense adjustment and related tax benefit.

only the tip of the iceberg. What cannot be seen are the different regulations prevailing in each country regarding:

• The fine print of regulatory reporting.
• Disclosures connected to capital markets.
• Gains and losses beyond the yearly income statement.
• Different rules and practices for trading in stock exchanges.
• Reporting profits and losses for reasons of taxation.

These concepts are most critical at a time when the largest companies (even some mid-sized) seek overseas listings to widen their shareholder base and their source of capital. The equity markets would never have reached their current levels of *liquidity* and *efficiency* if it had not been for well-regulated financial disclosure. Under no condition should the tougher accounting standards and reporting rules in the United States be diluted.

This brings under perspective the other side of an accounting standards argument: Big firms in Europe and Japan would have liked to continue living in their protective national environment, but because of the quest for an increased capital base, they have been forced to get global—and no global company can afford to ignore the United States which is the biggest securities market in the world:

• In June 1999, the $11 trillion U.S. stock market has been equal to 53 percent of the total value of all global markets.

- Ten years earlier, in 1989, the U.S. stock market's share of global equity value was only 24 percent—a 221 percent increase in a decade.

The ability to tap the capital markets on a global basis through universal transparency in accounting rules has led IASC to consider as a first option the adoption of Financial Accounting Standards Board Statements and accounting rules. Such a move made sense, but it was not accepted by most of the other member countries. IASC's original proposal was based on:

- Universal fair value.
- A broader income statement.

The first key provision to which other IASC member countries objected is *transparency*. The second is that FASB standards link *hedging* to *management intent*. This did not please those IASC members whose legislation and regulations do not presently have rigorous clauses on management accountability. Lack of explicit rules helps to bypass the responsibility of senior management associated to hedging and therefore to derivatives.

The idea of adopting the Generally Accepted Accounting Principles (GAAP) as common international accounting language was neither irrational nor far-fetched. Rather than trying to reinvent the wheel, the IASC membership would have been well advised to take GAAP as a basis and improve it, as well as making it homogeneous. This is necessary because, as we will see in the following section, the GAAP used in Canada and the United Kingdom differs in certain respects from that in the United States. This is not surprising since each country uses a system of accounting rules that is home-grown and usually conflicts with IAS, but there are also different versions of IAS since it is being adapted to local conditions.

Is there a way of closing the gap created by these differences in accounting and in supervision and still end with a rigorous set of rules? Some experts point out that the rules embedded in the International Accounting Standards are a compromise, therefore they cannot be rigorous. Other experts answer that this sort of compromise does not necessarily imply the lack of iron-clad disclosures regarding transactions and economic events. Still others say that compromises in accounting are, in principle, a bad deal.

The problem faced by the different standards committees is that many of their members want to keep accounting, reporting, and regulation the way they are with only minor modifications. There is also strong opposition to IAS in the United States. We will examine some of the many significant differences in disclosure between the Generally Accepted Accounting Principles of the United States and the concepts underpinning the International Accounting Standards.[1]

Prior to presenting an IASC-U.S. comparison, let me use a couple of examples to show how far this issue goes. In October 1993, Daimler-Benz was the first German company to achieve a listing on the New York Stock Exchange. When its accounts were converted from German accounting rules to GAAP, a DM 168 million profit for the first semester of 1996 became a DM 949 million loss—nearly a DM 1 billion in red ink. Exhibit 2.4 shows a similar comparison for 5 years: 1990 to 1995.

Exhibit 2.4   Daimler-Benz's Net Profit and Loss over a 5-Year Period in DM Billion

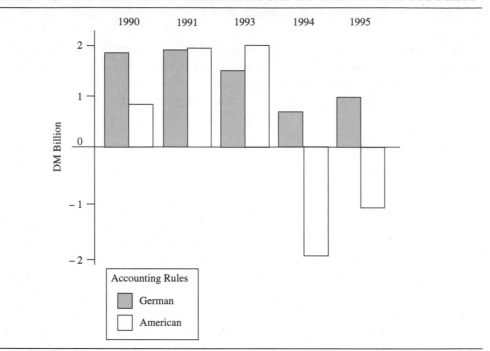

Hoechst, one of the three big German chemical firms, adopted IAS in 1994 when it listed in New York. In the process of reconciling its accounts with GAAP in the United States, an IAS profit of DM 1.7 billion turned into a GAAP loss of DM 57 million. Here, the gap in P&L between the two *standard* accounting methods has been bigger than in the case of Daimler-Benz.

This does not mean that GAAP is "better" than IAS, though it is more rigorous. Accounting standards have this in common with the military: Their value comes from their ability to continue to deliver, and GAAP delivers in the largest stock market in the world, in which so many continental European companies now want to be listed:

- In the last few years the number of foreign entrants filing with the SEC keeps increasing, now being past 750 firms.
- These firms come from 45 different countries, and they can be listed only if they satisfy GAAP requirements.

Behind fairly large accounting differences between GAAP, IAS, and other accounting standards are major cultural and supervisory considerations that cannot be ironed out just by making another draft and a few new compromises. Two most critical questions are:

1. For whom are accounts produced?
2. For what purpose are they established?

They are produced for investor information, management accounting, general accounting, supervisory authorities, and the income tax service. The next question concerns under whose jurisdiction a company's accounts should be made. For international standards the answer is under all jurisdictions. "All jurisdictions" follow neither GAAP nor IAS, though in the last couple of years IAS is gaining ground.

One of the challenges with both GAAP and IAS lies in the fact that internationalized accounting standards are not intended to override domestic accounting regulations. Their acceptance is on a voluntary basis. Recently, the IASC objective seems to be a change in this policy toward accounting standards that will be satisfactory for enforcement by securities regulators around the world.

At the same time, the shift in focus by IASC has led to pressure on the SEC to accept financial statements prepared in conformity with the new IAS which is currently under development. I doubt this pressure will succeed because the SEC will not give in while many non-U.S. companies have an aversion to transparency, being accustomed to a different regime on disclosures for over 50 years.

Recently, Credit Suisse wanted to switch to GAAP to register at the New York Stock Exchange, but it had problems with hedge accounting. Many other non-U.S. money center banks are faced with the same challenge. Transparency makes a great difference in corporate culture and management intent.

Arthur Levitt, chairman of the SEC, has warned that acceptance of the new IAS is not a foregone conclusion. The SEC, and by extension the New York Stock Exchange, NASDAQ, and other U.S. exchanges, has not budged from its position that any company seeking a listing in the United States must comply with GAAP.

In an effort to bridge the differences but also to strengthen its defenses, in May 1998, SEC appointed the vice president of an American high technology company as its new chief accountant. The SEC has an effective veto on IOSCO and its view is expected to signal whether the financial accounting passport in-the-making can be used on all exchanges.

In all likelihood, the interim solution regarding IAS will be near the GAAP standard, but it will not be identical. In London, other experts commented that unless national differences in common accounting language are ironed out, transparency will suffer, but they also added that a common solution is not for tomorrow.

The basic differences in management culture, measurements, recognition, display of ownership, and other issues continue. The IASC-U.S. Comparison Project identified 255 variations between IAS and the U.S. GAAP. Some of them have been resolved, but others remain. Major differences relate to impairment of assets, contingencies, income earned, profit and loss, cash flow, development costs, direct costs, government grants, goodwill, equity, derivative transactions, pension plans, and other issues of exposure.

DIFFERENCES BETWEEN VERSIONS OF GENERALLY ACCEPTED ACCOUNTING PRINCIPLES AND PRACTICES

One of the basic principles in business is that a company's accounting policies and procedures are influenced not only by the law of the land but also by the organization's size, culture, nature of its operations, and the industry in which it is active. Chapters 4 and 5 provide evidence that the quality of accounting policies and procedures has a significant impact on reliable financial reporting. Examples of issues that can aggravate quality of reporting are:

- Transactions with contentious, difficult, or evolving accounting issues.
- Decisions involving special valuation problems or uncertainties.
- Quality of the company's accounting records and whether these are kept in a conscientious fashion.

Even if there is only one accounting standard the company is using, for instance, GAAP, there may be an exceptionally aggressive, controversial, unusual, or liberal interpretation of GAAP. This might happen with regard to revenue recognition or any other issue leading to disputes between the company and its independent public accountants concerning the company's application of rules and its compliance to regulations.

Another situation where even the existence of only one set of accounting rules might lead to unreliable financial reporting is the way management uses these reports in controlling operations. The existence of financial statement elements that depend heavily on the exercise of subjective judgment or unusually difficult or complex calculations is also a source of unreliability in financial reports. Over and above that come external conditions, circumstances, and influences that affect operations beyond management's direct control. These may originate from:

- Crony capitalism.
- The business environment.
- The company's industry.
- Regulatory and legal sources.

With so many opportunities and inducements for unreliable financial reporting, it is not surprising that regulators have a tough job tracing fraud. This job becomes even more difficult if there are crevasses between standards or even versions of the same standard. As we have seen, differences exist among GAAP, IAS, and other national accounting systems. The surprise is that these exist *within* GAAP as well because of different versions: American, Canadian, and British.

Let's take the 1997 annual statement of Echo Bay Mining as an example. In accordance with Canadian GAAP, certain long-term foreign exchange contracts are considered to be hedges of the cost of goods to be purchased in foreign currencies in future periods. Gains and losses related to changes in market values of such contracts are recognized as a component of the cost of goods when the related hedged purchases occur. But under U.S. GAAP, changes in market value should be included in current earnings.

With Canadian GAAP, the present value of the principal amount of the capital securities issued, an event which at Echo Bay Mining took place in March 1997, is classified as debt within gold and other financing while the present value of the future interest payments is classified as a separate component of shareholders' equity, and related costs are allocated proportionally to defined financing charges. Under U.S. GAAP:

- The face value of the securities would be classified entirely as debt within gold and other financings.
- The related issuance costs would be classified as deferred financing charges within long-term investments and other assets and would be amortized to interest expense over the life of the securities, and
- The interest on the capital securities would be classified entirely as interest expense.

Also, in accordance with Canadian GAAP, in 1997 the company's portfolio of share investments was reclassified from long-term investments to short-term investments in light of the company's intent to dispose of these assets. Under U.S. GAAP, the company would have deemed the decline in fair values of its investments as other than temporary and the investments would have been marked to market with the unrealized losses included in earnings.

Let's look at the differences existing between American and British versions of GAAP:

- *Titles:* In the United States, GAAP stands for Generally Accepted Accounting Principles. In the United Kingdom, it is Generally Accepted Accounting Practice.
- *Writing and maintaining these standards:* In the United States, the Financial Accounting Standards Board, while in the United Kingdom, the Accounting Standards Board.
- *Content of financial statements:* U.S. GAAP requires three years' balance sheets, income, comprehensive income, cash flow, changes in equity, accounting policies, and notes. U.K. GAAP calls for the same statements but requires only two years—like IAS.
- *Correction of basic errors:* Both U.S. and U.K. GAAP call for restating comparatives. This contrasts to IAS which also permits effecting corrections in the current year. But there is a major U.S.-U.K. difference in definition of a subsidiary. The criterion with U.S. GAAP is controlling interest through majority voting shares. With U.K. GAAP and IAS, the evidence is based on voting control or actual dominant influence.
- *Definition of associate:* U.S. GAAP and IAS use the criterion of dominant influence—presumed if there is 20 percent of participation in the entity's affairs. The comparable clause at U.K. GAAP is based on actual exercise of significant influence. But the aforementioned pairs change when it comes to disclosure about significant associates.
- *Fair value on acquisition:* U.S. GAAP, U.K. GAAP, and IAS are rather comparable—with one exception. U.S. GAAP wants the entity to allocate value to all intangibles. U.K. GAAP takes no account of acquirer's intentions in determining asset values or provisions. Depending on the amount of money involved, this can make a significant difference.

- *Foreign entities within consolidated financial statements:* IAS and U.S. GAAP use closing currency exchange rate for the balance sheet, but average rate for income statements. U.K. GAAP permits use of either average or closing rate for income statements and it requires taking exchange rate differences to the Statement of Total Recognized Gains and Losses (STRGL).[2]

- *Contingent assets and liabilities:* U.S. GAAP and IAS are similar. They require that these are estimated at acquisition, then subsequently corrected against goodwill. With U.S. GAAP, contingent considerations are not recognized until the contingency is resolved or the amount being involved is determinable. IAS and U.S. GAAP capitalize and amortize goodwill (see also Chapter 3). IAS does so in the first 5 years with maximum 20 years. With U.S. GAAP, the maximum is 40 years while U.K. GAAP has a 20-year limit but exceptionally the time may be longer or even indefinite life.

- *Hyperinflation:* The IAS requires that prior to translation local statements of foreign entities are adjusted to current price levels. The relevant clause in U.S. GAAP says that prior to translation local currency statements must be remeasured using a temporal method. U.K. GAAP accepts either the U.S. GAAP or IAS approach.

- *Impairment of assets:* U.S. GAAP has established clear and elaborate procedures. Impairment review is based on undiscounted cash flows, but if these are less than carrying amount, then discounted cash flows should be used in measuring impairment loss. With IAS, current impairment rules are minimal and U.K. GAAP leans toward the IAS approach.

  A controversy between FASB and IAS is whether there should be a single fair value test—or assets should be measured against an internal assessment of value in use or net selling price, whichever is higher. There is as well a difference of opinion on whether an asset which has been written down because of impairment can subsequently be written up again if the impairment no longer exists.

Both U.S. GAAP and U.K. GAAP treat convertible debt as a liability. IAS accounts for convertible debt on split basis allocating proceeds between equity and debt. In regard to investments, the U.S. GAAP clause bifurcates on the classification of investment: If held to maturity, they carry at amortized cost; otherwise, they are written at fair value. U.K. GAAP wants to see the fixed asset investment carried at cost, market value, or other acceptable basis. The IAS rule is to carry long-term investments at cost or revalued amounts. But current asset investments should be carried at lower of cost and market value, or at market value.

CAPITAL MARKETS, NYSE, AND GLOBAL ACCOUNTING STANDARDS

Having explained the many differences that currently exist, it is clear that it will take years to iron these out. What a truly global, homogeneous accounting standard can do is to open up the international capital market, most particularly that of the United States.

That's the *Realpolitik* in finance. The SEC understands that, therefore it answers: "If you want our capital, you do it our own way."

There are still significant differences by country and region in terms of how financial statements should be made. Even if IASC reaches an agreement on a new IAS, it is up to IOSCO to decide whether to recommend it to its membership for adoption—and whether such adoption should be done without amendments.

Even this is an intermediate step, because it will be up to each jurisdiction to decide if the global accounting standard is acceptable to the capital markets that it regulates.

One of the stumbling blocks is that a global accounting standard would mean for practically every country and every company a change so radical that it may create a minor earthquake.

Yet, companies are not adverse to a conversion. During my research, the reasons I was given for converting to either IAS or GAAP are that the firm would like to improve its image as an international entity and, in the case of GAAP, it would make it possible to register at New York Stock Exchange (NYSE). Other fundamental reasons include:

- Benefits expected from a change in regulation.
- The need to do the conversion because of merger or other transaction.
- The ability to obtain lower interest rates from bankers or other financing sources.
- An anticipated favorable accounting impact.

It is proper to consider differences in taxation. GAAP requires goodwill to be amortized, written off over a period no longer than 40 years. This amount is not deductible for tax purposes, so it reduces both the pretax and after tax earnings by the amortized amount. Under GAAP:

- Provisions for losses may only be recorded once the loss is probable and the amount can be reasonably estimated.
- For revenue recognition, there are specific conditions that must be met GAAP before revenue and profits can be recognized.

Furthermore, U.S. regulations are very stringent on special payments, generally prohibiting them, particularly in cases of bribing public officials. They also require that pension plans are evaluated to determine their classification and accounting under GAAP.

For tax reasons, GAAP requires the recognition of both deferred tax assets and liabilities. As was briefly pointed out, there is also the interesting case of minority interest. These are generally presented separately in the company's balance sheet and income statement. GAAP also requires that certain related party transactions be disclosed because they tend not to be at arm's length.

Other issues are beneficial. By adopting GAAP, and therefore being able to list in the New York Stock Exchange, Daimler-Benz achieved higher volume production and won a slice of the American market. This was part of its strategy as Daimler moved into the volume market for smaller cars in Europe, with Mercedes' A-class and Smart models. Another component of Daimler's GAAP strategy was to buy components at huge discounts from a broad range of suppliers. But the coronation came with Chrysler:

- GAAP was a milestone in attaching Chrysler's annual 3 million production on to its own 1.2 million vehicles, making Daimler-Chrysler a big global competitor.
- Compared to this strategy, the other European car makers who stayed with their parochial accounting systems were left behind, and Renault's deal with Nissan pales compared to Daimler-Chrysler.

"The listing of large German firms at the New York Stock Exchange," said Dr. Rüdiger von Rosen, a former member of the Board of the Frankfurt Stock Exchange, "has helped them a great deal. The adoption of GAAP by Daimler-Benz for its listing was instrumental to its 1988 merger with Chrysler because major mergers need comparability of accounts, transparency, and public awareness."

Dr. von Rosen also pointed out that listing at NYSE changed the Daimler awareness toward being a public company. It adopted road shows and one-to-one meetings which before were not in its culture. It also led to a cooperation between German and American law firms working for Daimler-Benz, which had an evident impact on the merger talks. These are among the intangibles of a NYSE listing.

The management of all large global industrial and financial organizations would like to see their company quoted in the New York Stock Exchange. This makes the company more global and stimulates the investment of U.S. pension funds in its equity; but it also has evident implication on the adoption of GAAP accounting standards, while stockholder activism pushes in the direction of greater transparency and the delivery of shareholder value.

Changes in accounting standards may tip the balances toward the stockholders. Currently, the accounting system in Europe is more friendly to creditors than shareholders. On the other hand, stockholder activism tends to make companies more leveraged financially, and this is negative from the creditor's perspective.

The regulators themselves are at crossroads regarding national accounting standards, IAS, and GAAP. The Swiss Federal Banking Commission provides an example. Swiss banks currently report in the Accounting Reporting Recommendations (ARR) system. But international banks are allowed to choose GAAP or IAS as their system, provided they disclose the differences with ARR in the footnotes:

- Whatever the background reason may be, provided the regulation opens the possibility of choice, entities need to determine their overall objectives of the conversion in accounting standards.
- Any decision must take into account the difference in approach between the two main accounting standards, and clear reasons must be established prior to converting.

IAS tends to provide broader answers about how to account for a variety of transactions, events, or circumstances, while GAAP focuses on detailed accounting requirements. All material differences need to be identified for the entire operating history of a company, and such differences may have a major impact on the GAAP balance sheet. They also affect final financial statements because these involve disclosures and reconciliation of statutory balances to GAAP.

Finally, because of differences between statutory financial statements existing in their country and GAAP, many companies find it necessary to maintain two sets of financial records. Additionally, reliable financial controls must be in place to allow management to assess, on a steady basis, the impact of transactions on both the GAAP basis and that of the home country where the company operates. This needs sophisticated management.

THE BASLE COMMITTEE AND INTERNATIONAL ACCOUNTING HARMONIZATION

Within the perspective of ongoing international efforts aimed at harmonizing accounting principles and practices, in October 1998 the Basle Committee published the consultation paper "Sound Practices for Loan Accounting, Credit Risk Disclosure and Related Matters." This contains recommendations for supervisory authorities, accounting bodies, and financial institutions on:

- Valuation and reporting of loans.
- Setting up value adjustments.
- Disclosure of credit risk, and associated issues.

The paper presents the views of banking supervisory authorities regarding the appropriate method of loan accounting and disclosure for commercial banks. It is further intended to serve as a guide for prudential assessment of information quality, business principles, and reporting methods by credit institutions.

The ideas for evolving accounting principles and disclosure practices for lending, which have been submitted for consultation, are in line with the demands for greater transparency of the risks inherent in lending business made by finance ministers of the Group of Seven countries, central bank governors of the Group of Ten, and international organizations like IMF and World Bank.

In September 1998, the Basle Committee and the Technical Committee of the International Organization of Securities Commissions issued a paper, "Framework for Supervisory Information about Derivatives and Trading Activities." This revised the basic concept for improving the transparency of derivatives business, which was current practice since May 1995, and brought it into line with prevailing risk management practice in derivatives trades especially with regard to market risk.

This paper contains proposals for an internationally harmonized minimum standard of information on derivatives business known as the *Common Minimum Framework*. The Basle Committee and IOSCO committees are detailing what kind of accounting and other information should be made available to supervisory authorities.

In September 1998, the Basle Committee also published "Enhancing Bank Transparency," a recommendation for improving the disclosure requirements of credit institutions. The goal is strengthening market discipline by means of adequate transparency in the disclosure of information on key issues such as liquidity, incurred credit exposure, risk control practices, and internal risk monitoring systems.

These steps are necessary and cover not only accounting as a language for financial reporting but also metalinguistic issues that are germaine in the context of COSO. I would strongly recommend that the basic accounting language be standardized not only cross-border but also within one and the same country. Let me explain this through an example.

The accounting system the U.S. Congress approved in 1981 is not GAAP but one known as Regulatory Accounting Principles (RAP). This system differs sharply from the GAAP. Another negative is that RAP permitted worthless thrifts to stay in business and grow at a cancerous pace leading to the savings-and-loans crisis that cost the taxpayer an estimated $180 billion.

To appreciate the RAP-GAAP differences, let's assume that a 7 percent, 20-year mortgage with a face value of $100,000 is now worth only $80,000 because interest rates have risen and reduced the market value of the loan. Also say that the loan is sold at the market and the proceeds used to buy another $80,000 mortgage with a 10-percent yield:

- Under GAAP, the red ink is $12,000, $20,000 lost on market value partly offset by a gain of $8,000 per year in interest income.
- Under RAP, the profit is $7,000: The $20,000 loss is amortized annually at $1,000 plus a gain of $8,000 in interest income.

Forty-two years ago I had a professor of banking at the Graduate School of Business, UCLA, who taught his students that one can prove anything he likes if he is free to choose his accounting system. He can have huge profits or huge losses, as it suits him best. That's what happens today with the differences existing among "standard" accounting systems around the globe. Regretfully, we have to admit that Paciolo's accounting is no more an exact art.

Financial statements by reputable accounting standards bodies try to wave the flagrant differences and close at least some of the loopholes. In the beginning of the new IAS effort, it was decided that IASC should explore the possibility of adopting U.S. standards on financial instruments including derivatives and hedging regulations that finally crystallized in SFAS 133 (see Chapter 10). The idea was to make SFAS 133 clauses part of the International Accounting Standard, as an interim measure.

Accordingly, IASC staff prepared an Exposure Draft based on U.S.-based requirements and put it to the Board for consideration at its Paris meeting in late October 1997. The Board rejected this proposal because it felt that an international organization like IASC should always develop "its own standards"—doing so through its own unconstrained due process and not adopt the standards of any one country. That's the "Not invented here" principle that usually leads to irrational acts.

Another reason given for the rejection of sound derivatives reporting clauses has been that the style of U.S. standards is "different" from the "normal" style of IASC's standards. Also, there might be difficulties in integrating the U.S. literature on financial instruments with the rest of the IASC literature—an argument that does not make much sense, but speaks volumes on how far apart the two parties are, and how silly some of the arguments are.

IASC keeps trying to follow International Accounting Developments. Following the issue of IAS 32 regarding disclosure of financial instruments, IASC issued an exposure draft, E 62. Its objective is measurement and recognition of financial instruments. The main principles underlying E 62 are that:

- All financial assets and derivatives should be at fair value unless they are held to maturity (that's what SFAS 133 says),
- By contrast, financial liabilities should be held at cost.

Some hedging provisions do apply to financial reporting. E 62 says it is important for all parties involved in derivatives to carefully consider accounting and tax implications. Reliable financial reporting in connection to gains, losses, and transaction resulting from derivative financial instruments is indeed a huge subject covered in detail in Chapters 9 and 10.

THE RIGOROUS NATURE OF AMERICAN ACCOUNTING STANDARDS IS GOOD FOR COMPANIES

The existence of major differences in fundamental accounting standards and practices did not deter IASC in its search for a compromise. Released in January 1999 (see Exhibit 2.2), IAS 34 is an interim solution, and IASC is targeting a more permanent solution for right after year 2000. But the differences of opinion among IASC and SEC, as well as among IASC members, will persist rather than subside.

An interim period for financial reporting is one shorter than a full financial year, but there can be exceptions. IASC's IAS 34 contains presentation and measurement guidance for interim reporting, prescribes the minimum, and elaborates the principles for recognition and measurement for an interim period. IASC interim standards—which are in no way binding—cover all companies with traded securities, but exclude insurance companies. The leading concept is that:

- All items in the portfolio are to be included in the balance sheet at fair value.
- The only instruments not to be adjusted to fair value are those held to maturity.

This poses critical problems: First and foremost one of management intent and second, there is an issue about recognizing nonrealized gains and losses with respect to derivative financial instruments (see Chapter 3).

On the other hand, what interim standards state will not necessarily become permanent accounting standards. To appreciate the viewpoint of the SEC and other regulators who wish to see that there is in place a rigorous system able to inspire confidence to investors, we have to keep in mind that the stiff accounting rules and standards prevailing today in the United States have been the outgrowth of two major crises of the twentieth century:

1. The stock market panic of 1909 which shook New York.
2. The depression of 1929, which created a crisis of confidence in the capital market.

While Europe too suffered from the 1929 crash, until quite recently, the reporting and supervisory rules regarding listed companies were lax. For instance, until quite recently insider trading was condoned in continental Europe, while it is a criminal offense in the United States. This is a major difference that goes way beyond accounting.

To track insider trading and other conflicts of interest, the SEC has a colossal database of company directors going all the way not only to their families and business connections but also to roommates in college dormitories. Mining of a vast database is needed because insider trading can masquerade under many covers. SEC has the necessary high technology, but this is not true of regulators in Europe and Japan.

I was therefore appalled when John Mogg, then general of the European Union's directorate responsible for competition, asked in a speech in December 1994, whether it is thinkable that eventually all large European companies will apply U.S. GAAP? Mogg said this is a matter of concern to the European Union's Commission, suggesting it would not be acceptable for Europe to delegate the setting of accounting standards to the United States. It puzzles me how a talented person can make this sort of funny "Not Invented here" statement.

Mogg's lecture indirectly asked for the establishment of a European Accounting Standards Board, but nowhere was there a reference to ironclad guarantees against illegal activities and for a strong capital market supervision. If the European Union is to develop its own standards, these must be *stronger* not weaker than those already prevailing in the United States.

If anybody in the EU bureaucracy has more rigorous accounting standards to propose, he or she should bring them forward. These should include not only accounting rules but also fundamental procedures and associated internal control requirements—a first class example being COSO. Another, albeit more limited example is SEC's Payment for Order Flow disclosure rule which gives investors a very valuable insight on how a company behaves: Brokerage firms must disclose to their customers their policies and practices regarding receipt of Payment for Order Flow. The term stands for any sort of compensation or other consideration paid to a brokerage by:

- A registered stock exchange or association, a regional stock exchange, or the National Association of Securities Dealers (NASD).
- By another broker-dealer, who grants favors in return for directing to him customer orders for execution, hence influencing the opinion of the correspondent broker.

The Payment for Order Flow is a possible conflict of interest. Examples of noncash compensation include reciprocal arrangements, discounts, rebates, reductions, or credits against fees that would otherwise be payable in full by the brokerage firm. Regulators must be doubly careful when money is involved, because many people look for loopholes.

Other types of Payment for Order Flow concern favors the brokerage may receive, such as profit participation from specialists on regional exchanges in connection with the overall profitability of a given specialist unit in those stocks in which it routes orders or a refund or credit against future fees. SEC takes account of the fact that the factors considered by a brokerage firm executing Payment for Order Flow in determining where to send an order include:

- Opportunity for price improvement.
- Reputation of the exchange specialist who makes the market in the stock.
- Size of the order, therefore commissions, and so on.

Another critical factor in the regulatory armory regards the quality of previous order executions, including cost and efficiency as well as likelihood of execution. These decision criteria are important in every exchange, but they become truly vital in a globalized market where orders are increasingly sent from one marketplace to another through networks. So far there is no evidence that IASC addresses *networking,* yet with securities traded on the Internet this should be integral to execution rules.[3]

In the United States, cross-exchange executions are subject to regulations of the Intermarket Trading System and related trade-through rules. On this basis, regional specialists guarantee execution of market orders at a price that is at least as favorable as the best displayed bid (for a sale) or offer (for a purchase) quoted in the public market for that security at the time of execution.

SEC regulations see to it that the investor is informed on how the deal is done. This is not necessarily the case in other countries, where the rules are more lax.

If an exchange has not established clear rules, investors who want to check if a broker executed the order to buy or sell at market price can get data streams for a given stock from Bloomberg and scan through. Technology helps to correct the lack of precise rules, but the job is tedious and therefore few people take the time and effort to do it. I have done this comparison and know what it involves.

The bottomline is that in the United States the SEC is acting as a watchdog that executions don't take place behind the investor's back or to his or her detriment. If a fundamental objective of the EU is the harmonization of accounting standards and disclosure requirements to facilitate the free movement of capital between member states, then the principles which should be obeyed by all parties must come first, followed by common formats and reporting standards—not vice versa. Neither should individual countries have the choice to apply or not to apply the rules.

The issue of uniformity is vital, but it is secondary to culture and to rigorous controls. The speed with which IAS standards are incorporated into the laws of individual countries is highly varied and, in the general case, this process is not satisfactory. The watchdog clauses are missing and there are too many exemptions and local interpretations reducing the usefulness of a common accounting system.

Furthermore, a universal accounting system worth its salt must pay attention to intangibles, including brainpower which for many companies is a key asset. Professor Baruch Lev of New York University has tracked the relationship between share prices and the

43

reported value of a company's equity. His finding is that this relationship has weakened over the last dozen years.[4] Such weakening leads to the hypotheses that a firms' accounts may not be so relevant as indicators of value.

Investors therefore look at a company's *intrinsic value,* estimating future investment grade profits a firm will earn from its assets. Accounting for intangible assets in a global landscape requires much more skill and intuition than the old accounting standards offer. Trying to apply a universal standard without an accompanying cultural change and well-tuned legislation might make matters worse.

NOTES

1. See also Financial Accounting Standards Board, "The IASC-US Comparison Project" (Norwalk, CT: FASB, 1996).
2. D.N. Chorafas, *New Regulation of the Financial Industry* (London: Macmillan, 2000).
3. D.N. Chorafas, *Internet Financial Services: Secure Electronic Banking and Electronic Commerce* (London: Lafferty Publications, 1997).
4. *The Economist* (June 6, 1998).

CHAPTER 3

Why Global Accounting Solutions Are an Integral Part of Capital Markets and Derivatives Markets

Though it is rarely expressed in this way, to a substantial extent the difference in opinion regarding clauses of accounting standards has to do not only with measurement and reporting of *actual exposure* but also if not primarily, with *future exposure*. Transparency includes the ability to give an advance warning about risks to come to capital markets, derivatives markets, and regulators. Any global accounting solution that does not pay attention to warning signals would be useless.

Behind this statement is not only sound management but also the $1 quadrillion experts think will be the size of derivatives markets in less than 10 years. According to some estimates, having passed the $150 trillion in notional principal amounts the derivatives market is headed for the astronomical $1,000 trillion mark. Are the experts seeing gloom and doom in this forecast?

As mentioned in Chapter 1, Nobel Prize winner Dr. Merton Miller suggests that derivatives have made the world a safer place (though he fails to explain how and why this has happened). But George Soros warns that, quite to the contrary, derivatives will destroy society. Both are overstatements, for the following reasons:

- The greater risk comes from the fact that very few people (if any) can see through to the limits of the derivatives business.
- Even these have no hint how far the damage would go if the huge derivatives market crashes or even starts a tail spin.

Precisely because we must be able to position ourselves against oncoming but yet unseen risks, a global accounting solution should focus on both actual and future exposure. *Actual exposure* is also known as replacement cost, actual market risk, or marked-to-market value. In spite of suggesting market-dependent risk factors, the larger chunk in actual exposure is essentially credit risk.

By contrast, *future exposure* primarily targets risks taken because of financial transactions and positions held in the bank's portfolio. Mathematically, *potential exposure* is equal to the sum of actual exposure, and future exposure. Within potential exposure, recognized losses represent the amount of risk inherent in a derivatives transaction—a loan, investment, or any other banking operation—leading to determination of financial condition.

Future exposure, also known as *deemed risk, time-to-decay risk,* or *presettlement risk,* is the amount of potential exposure inherent in financial transactions and inventoried positions. It represents future impact of present decisions and can be estimated through modeling and simulation for internal management accounting (IAMIS) reasons. One of the questions to be settled through global accounting standards is whether or not, and how, it should be reported to regulators.

As COSO explains, reliable financial reporting is a keyword, but the role of models (and of model risk) should not be forgotten, particularly after the 1996 Market Risk Amendment by the Basle Committee on Banking Supervision. Models built to represent future exposure essentially address the potential risk that might be encountered in a transaction kept in trading book or banking book:

- At the inception of a trade, future risk is seen as a reward because practically every transaction is made for profits.
- But eventually, exposure may exceed the reward during the deal's lifecycle, due to market risk, credit risk, or other type of risk.

Market risk does not always have a negative value. Several of the derivatives in a bank's trading book may be in positive territory, because of profits from past deals. But if the market risk is positive, then the banker, treasurer, trader, or investor must be concerned about credit risk. A valid global accounting system should provide the ability to make this switch.

When market risk is positive, a counterparty default will result in loss to the bank if this other party fails to perform. Therefore, it is to the advantage of everybody that accounting and financial reporting rules are both rigorous and able to convey a signal to the market that the management of this or that entity or investment vehicle leaves much to be wanted. One way to answer this requirement is to integrate into P&L accounts rating by independent agencies, as explained in Chapter 11.

ACCOUNTING PROFESSION AND FAULT LINE DIVIDING SECURITIES REGULATION IN DIFFERENT COUNTRIES

Part of the fault line dividing prudential securities regulation in Anglo-Saxon countries from that in continental Europe, Japan, and other countries is in tradition. The accounting profession in the United Kingdom dates back to 1854, when the Society of Accountants was founded in Edinburgh. In the United States, it dates back to 1887 with the founding of the American Institute of Accountants.

By contrast, the German accounting profession, as a body, dates only to 1932; the French to 1942. Also weighting on the scale of standards setting is the size Anglo-Saxon professional bodies have reached over time. Size matters because it means that so many more cognizant people work on critical issues, bring up problems, or try to solve them. For example:

- There are over 260,000 certified public accountants in the United States and 100,000 chartered members in the United Kingdom.
- In France and Germany, the figures are 11,000 and 5,000, respectively.

The size of capital markets is an even more weighty factor. In continental Europe, the stock markets are much smaller and have less influence than in Anglo-Saxon countries. Equally important is the fact that the capital market itself is not so well developed, and individual investors are rare in continental European stock markets. Not only is this gap not closing, but it is growing. As already mentioned:

- The $11 trillion American stock market is now equal to a record 53 percent of total value of all global markets.
- Just 10 years ago, this percent figure was 28 percent.

Such a huge difference in the size of capital markets is one of the arguments for adopting worldwide FASB accounting standards and SEC regulations, rather than watering down the current versions in favor of a compromise (and compromised) IAS. If the different continental European and Japanese rules and regulations were as good as their promoters maintain, why is it that only a tiny proportion of the public invests in the local stock markets?

Alert investors in Europe know that in the large majority of companies there is a collusion of interests—and the private investor is taken for granted or is considered to be an irrelevant entity. Like in America prior to 1932, the big banks, not the capital market, are the main providers of new funds, both debt and equity, to European firms. Therefore, they are often represented on the boards of companies in which they are significant investors. Such close relationships have allowed a high levels of leverage to be hidden from investigative regulators. It has also confused the work done by financial analysts and institutional investors.

It would not be easy to separate the European companies from their banks and vice versa. President Roosevelt did so in 1932 because these were the depression years and resistance was minimal. There is no depression today in continental Europe, only very high unemployment particularly due to ossified social structures and the practices of the nanny state.

Some analysts are of the opinion that the EU will act as a catalyst in changing current practices, because it will create a unique capital market in the 11 countries that joined the common currency on January 1, 1999. I consider this argument half-baked because the larger capital markets of Germany and France currently dwarf the other 9, but surprises could happen if people pull money out of their mattresses and rush to the capital market. There exists a prerequisite business confidence which feeds only on tough regulation and takes years to build.

So far the EU has not substantiated these optimistic scenarios and governments have done nothing to revamp antiquate labor laws. Neither have industrial companies bypassed their traditional banks to get a better break in terms of cost of capital through commercial paper—a move that runs against tradition.

Another impediment that demonstrates the depth of the fault line, is the state of affairs in Asian capital markets. The Japanese do not accept IAS for foreign companies trying to list in Tokyo. And they have also been very slow to disclose detailed information about the composition and financial interdependence of their own industrial firms. The fight against transparency is even more pronounced in Korea.

The irony is that in spite of the fact that in Asian countries accounting finds itself in a foggy bottom, many Western governments, banks, and industrial companies have rushed to do business in that part of the world. This happens on the false premise that accounting information "ought to be comparable to that of the United States or Europe"—and comprehensive. The East Asian meltdown has shown how wrong this hypothesis is.

Another reason American and European banks and companies got themselves in deep trouble after East Asia went into a tailspin in 1997 was the lure of the Pacific Rim and its prospects—in short, fast bucks. But as time went on and the Asian crisis hit, these banks, industrial companies, and investors found out that the booming markets of the Pacific Rim have been—so far at least—a chimera.

To further appreciate the impact of the fault line in accounting standards and supervisory rules, remember that during the last quarter century the capital markets have undergone significant change. In America, a most important factor is the increase in size and influence of institutional investors. In continental Europe, mutual funds are still small and private pension funds are just starting.

The rise of institutional investors who *think globally* makes a difference on how capital markets behave. Unlike the individual investors with minor equities holdings and limited stock market skills, pension funds, mutual funds, hedge funds, and other institutional investors have demanded more and more information from companies in which they invest, including details of future prospects.

Proactive investor attitude changes quite radically the answer to the query: For whom are the accounts? Because the proactive investor wants to know about future exposure. Institutional investors and their financial analysts have sharp pencils, imaginative minds, and can tear to pieces accounting statements that are rotten.

The role of the taxperson, too, should be brought into perspective. Internal revenue services are tougher in the United States and the United Kingdom. This has relevance because one of the traditional purposes of accounts has been to establish the basis for collecting taxes. Consequently, there was every incentive to keep the reported level of profits down as far as the accounting standards and prevailing regulation make this possible.

Differences in accounting rules, supervisory policies, and the way companies are run see to it that in Europe, there has been a general belief that accounts understate both profits and assets. Partly, this is the result of using accelerated depreciation and generous provisioning. On the other hand, the more dynamic a capital market, the more its investors use rocket scientists for rigorous evaluation of P&L and overrunning secretive policies. The more rocket scientists are employed, the more sophisticated become the analytical models and the more far fetching is the use of computers and communications.

Rocket scientists are not yet the order of the day in continental Europe. Therefore, management can be more secretive with the accounts. By all likelihood, SEC will not accept practices that hide information from investors while European governments will resist a large amount of transparency. Daimler's red ink (see Chapter 2) is a lesson that has not been lost for continental European companies and their regulators.

My research in the major continental European countries documents that there is a widespread fear: If GAAP standards are accepted there will be a torrent of red ink all over EU's corporate landscape. Hence, the current policy that it is better to have "weak" standards than no universal accounting standards at all. This policy is wrong.

We shall see how stock markets react if weak reporting standards are made the rule. The way to bet is that investors will not take kindly to wanting accounting standards—and, if they are adopted, these will lead to a very serious market correction worldwide because of lack of business confidence. Bureaucrats should appreciate that in a free economy the market is the critter.

WHY THE NEW ACCOUNTING STANDARDS MUST FULLY REFLECT OFF-BALANCE SHEET EXPOSURE

As already stated, derivative financial instruments include futures contracts, forward rate agreements, interest rate swaps, currency swaps, options written, options bought, resource obligations on receivables sold or long, repo agreements, instruments sold short, and other transactions implying financial commitments. Each of these instruments has an embedded amount of market risk and/or credit risk.

This list of instruments is not all-inclusive. George Soros once said that there are so many derivatives of esoteric characteristics that they present a problem to investors. The risks being involved are not properly understood even by the experts, while in many cases derivative instruments masquerade as low risk.

Dysfunctional behavior and underestimates of exposure permit institutional investors to make gambles that are not allowed by their Statutes. Greed pushes supposedly conservative investors into taking major risks capitalizing on the fact that the majority of derivatives are traded over the counter and they contain varying degrees of off-balance sheet risk, whereby changes in market values may result in losses in excess of the amounts recognized in the consolidated statement of financial condition.

Generally, these derivative financial instruments represent future commitments that a bank, institutional investor, or any other company must face because they constitute a contractual obligation. Assets and liabilities in the portfolio oblige management to purchase or sell underlying financial products at specific terms on specified future dates, to exchange currencies, or to swap interest payment streams.

All derivative products are financial instruments with off-balance sheet risk. Securities sold but not yet purchased represent obligations to deliver specified securities at the contracted price, thereby creating a liability to purchase the securities at prevailing market prices. Accordingly, these transactions result in exposure to market risk, as a company's ultimate obligation may exceed the amount recognized in its balance sheet.

A fairly major problem with the IASC interim standards is that the gains and losses regarding derivative financial instruments in the trading book, as well as other items like interest rate exposure from loans in the banking book, are given a fuzzy home. Assets and liabilities that are recognized but not realized are to be taken:

- Partly to the profit and loss (P&L) statement (income statement).
- Partly to equity—which, to say the least, is an odd choice (see Exhibit 3.1).

The statistics in Exhibit 3.1 are taken from the 1998 income statement of a money center bank. Its equity is $11.3 billion, but its derivatives exposure in notional principal stands at $8.86 trillion. Not everything in this huge sum is pure risk. Maybe the loans-equivalent risk is 4 percent of the derivatives exposure. If so, the $5.66 trillion should be divided by 25.[1]

Exhibit 3.1 Some Frightening Statistics on Equity, Assets, and Derivatives Exposure of a Major Money Center Bank

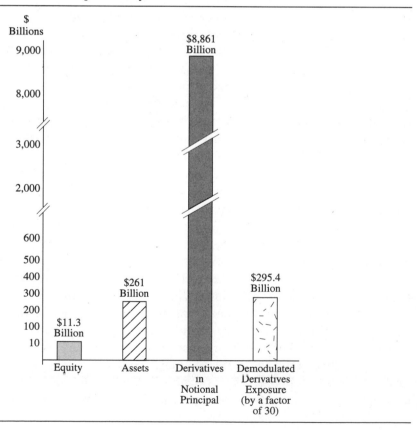

Being conservative, in Exhibit 3.1 I demodulated by 30, which corresponds to a reduced, but still huge, level of risk. After this reduction, the resulting pure derivatives risk stands at $295.4 billion which is over 2600 percent of its equity.

If the IASC compromise carries the day and the recognized but not yet realized derivatives losses are written in equity, the more money a bank loses in terms of trillions the more healthy it should feel—as its equity zooms. Equally unsound is the proposal to mark the realized gains and losses at fair value, then but to use the method of accruals for the future commitments.

Proponents of these highly compromised "solutions" would say that there exist other oddities in accounting. An insurance company, for example, makes a good deal of its profits from float. Float is the cash flow it holds but does not own, arising because premiums are received well before losses are paid—an interval that sometimes extends over many years.

The accounting irony with float is that it is shown in the balance sheet as a liability, yet it has a value to the insurance company greater than an equal amount of net worth—which cannot be said with derivatives.

To bring this argument a notch further, the fact that it gathers cash upfront but disgorges its funds over time, as accidents take place and claims come up for settlement, is part of the power of an insurance company. Some other entities, too, follow the same line, as for instance Blue Chips, the California marketing stamps company, which has the added advantage of not being regulated.

But these examples fade when we talk of derivatives exposure assumed by an entity. Here the rules are different. To estimate potential market risk, companies must prognosticate and quantify future market movements and their impact. For instance in forward rate agreements, several banks simulate the result of a change by 1, 5, 10, 50, and 100 basis points in their FRA portfolio—as well as the impact this exposure will have on their more important counterparties.

The case is no more that of prudential cash flows, as in insurance, but of actual and projected market risk that may run in billions. Hence, the need to write down in the loss side of P+L the difference between original cost and replacement cost, marked-to-market or marked-to-model. It is equally important to compute the actual and future credit loss if the counterparty defaults.

This is particularly important with derivatives deals in that many are longer term, as shown in Exhibit 3.2. For instance, interest rate instruments that in the general case represent more than 50 percent of all trades.

Notice that these are hard core losses, which with derivatives can come at any moment. Posting them in the side equity is a great accounting flaw—a deadly misrepresentation of facts. Some money center banks today have a derivatives exposure that is 10 times or more their equity. This top-heavy capital at risk can swamp all of the bank's equity under its weight and still leave a gapping hole in the treasury. Putting together equity and recognized derivatives losses is tantamount to turning accounting facts on their head, and it would be most misleading to investors, regulators, and members of the board.

Such practice can also lead to heterogeneity in reporting substance, for a number of other reasons. One of the more important is that it brings up the question of management intent to which, as we have seen, most IASC members have objections. Management

Exhibit 3.2 Some Vital Statistics on Derivative Financial Instruments

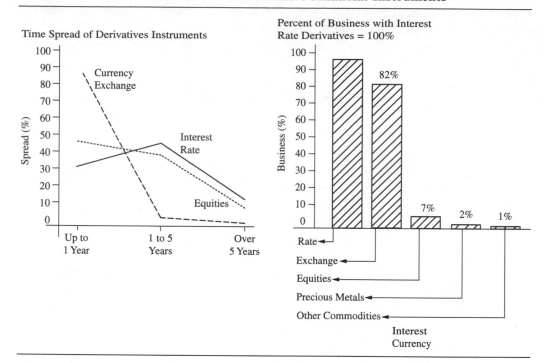

intent, if there is one, is difficult to ascertain and to document when derivatives losses and equity mix. Precisely for this reason, FASB has traced the dividing line through iron-clad rules. The Swiss National Bank did the same, but, curiously enough, FASB's solution was not retained by IASC. The irony is that the first draft by IASC was sound, but it was rejected.

To better explain what I mean by the silly compromise of the "interim solution," I briefly review the very sound Swiss approach. Since 1996, the reserve bank has required that banks clearly differentiate future off-balance sheet gains and losses—reporting recognized but not realized gains as "other assets" and losses as "other liabilities." Both are written, respectively, in the assets and liabilities sides of the balance sheet.

A second major reason for the unsuitability of the "interim" IASC proposal, as it now stands, is that British regulators are dead set against writing recognized but not yet realized gains and losses in equity. They fear that this would open the door to creative accounting practices that distort both the P&L and the balance sheet, leading investors to lose confidence in financial statements.

The solution by the British Accounting Standards Board (ASB) is the Statement of Recognized Gains and Losses (STRGL). Profits and losses that are recognized and realized during the reporting year are written in the P&L statement. Those that are recognized but not yet realized—and may not be realized for several years—are written in the STRGL. This is different than the Swiss solution, but it also leads to reliable financial reporting.

Finally, one of the issues where there should be a global agreement not only in terms of accounting rules but as well in legislation and in supervisory practices, is that of hidden or undisclosed reserves. A hidden reserve may be viewed as a cushion of available liquidity to shore up the balance sheet. At the same time, it may be an opportunity taken by the bank to use the benefits of good results in one year to cushion the impact of poor figures in other years.

Not everyone agrees on this subject. Some analysts caution that hidden reserves can be a warning sign rather than a comfort element because management knows that one year's exceptional results will not be repeated soon. At the same time, in many countries, tax authorities look with suspicion at hidden reserves as a way to legitimize tax evasion.

Yet reserves have a role to play that should not be discarded in a summary manner. Their usefulness becomes evident if we classify credit risks into expected (frequent), unexpected (infrequent), and very infrequent but catastrophic. Also, if we compute the exposure by major counterparty by integrating credit risk and market risk. This being done, the reserve is no more hidden; it is a re-insurance for events that are expected to occur at an unknown date.

DERIVATIVE FINANCIAL INSTRUMENTS AND ANALYSIS OF ANNUAL REPORTS

Business schools should teach 100 years or, at a minimum, 50 years of histories of leading corporations and relate the data to what actually happened in the aftermath of good and bad decisions. This would better focus on major events that have shaped the economy like railroads, automobiles, computers, and telecommunications.

A focal point must be the rise of dominance in one corporation and the fall from dominance of another, including the reasons behind such change. This rise and fall of corporations can be nicely studied by means of accounting, financial statements, critical ratios, cash flows, leveraging, and (more recently) derivatives.

Business schools should base these case studies on real-life data, including the footnotes to accounting treatments and the results of analyses. Students must learn firsthand the negative effects of accounting games some people and companies play. One of the worst is creative accounting: Changing basic information, handling orders that would naturally fall in the next quarter(s) into "this" quarter, and face-lifting the reported P&L.

Both good news and bad news are important in analysis. When reading an annual report, you should be looking both for things that you want and for things that you do not want to see in the financial statement. Both good news and bad news are important, and the same is true of qualitative comments. It is very hard to deal with information if we don't put it in context.

Exhibit 3.3 illustrates the comparison between the accruals method and fair value. The statistics come from the 1998 annual report by Black & Decker—a company quoted in NYSE which does not seem to be badly leveraged. Between 1997 and 1998, Black & Decker retired a significant proportion of its long-term debt. However, in terms of long-term nonderivatives liabilities, the difference between accruals and fair value is indeed

Exhibit 3.3 Assets and Liabilities Reported in Two Consecutive Annual Statements by Black & Decker (Just Note Difference)

	As of December 31, 1997		As of December 31, 1998	
	Carrying Amount	Fair Value	Carrying Amount	Fair Value
Nonderivatives:				
Long-term debt	(1,623.7)	(1,660.4)	(1,148.9)	(1,200.2)
Derivatives relating to:				
Debt liabilities	—	(5.6)	.5	14.2
Foreign currency				
Assets	68.4	82.6	60.1	40.8
Liabilities	(13.2)	(16.5)	(35.2)	(34.9)

small. This difference is most significant in the derivatives chapter, particularly in connection to assets.

In 1997, the fair value of foreign currency derivatives assets is 20 percent higher than that shown as carrying amount (accruals). In 1998, this reverses and fair value of derivatives assets is only $\frac{2}{3}$ that of accruals.

The 1998 annual report by Johnson & Johnson provides another example. To protect the value of currency assets and hedge future foreign currency product costs, the company uses interest rate forwards and currency swaps maturing within 5 years. The result of these hedges, however, seem to be rather significant financial losses as Exhibit 3.4 documents.

On notional principal amount outstanding of about $10.3 billion, the total loss has been $197 million. If the $10.3 billion was demodulated to a credit equivalent of $343 million using a factor of 30 as in connection to the statistics in Exhibit 3.1, then the actual recognized losses would stand at 57.4 percent of potential losses (credit equivalent) represented by the demodulated amount.

In the 1998 annual report of Coca-Cola, management takes care to underline that it does not enter into derivative financial instruments for trading purposes. Nevertheless, the estimated fair value of derivatives used to hedge or modify the company's exposure

Exhibit 3.4 Recognized Claims and Losses with Derivatives as of December 31, 1998 by Johnson & Johnson (in $ millions)

Type of Instrument	Notional Principal Amounts	Gains	Losses
Forwards	$ 0.000	$ 94	$227
Currency swaps	3.422	25	89
Total	$10.270	$119	$316

to interest rates and currency exchange rates fluctuates over time. These reported fair values, management advises, should not be viewed in isolation but rather in relation to:

- Fair values of underlying hedging transactions and investments.
- The overall reduction in company exposure to adverse variation in interest rates, forex rates, commodity prices, and other market risks.

Exhibit 3.5 presents the Coca-Cola's derivatives exposure as of December 31, 1988. Notice the relatively short term to maturity; also the fact that while undoubtedly management exercises great diligence in handling the derivatives portfolio, there is a net loss of $189 million measured in fair value of existing contracts.

This talks volumes about the derivatives risks companies face, as well as of how hedges can turn on their head. If a well-managed company like Coca-Cola has these negative results, think about the derivatives losses sustained by a myriad of companies under an average or below average management—as well as by professional gamblers.

Brokers, too, are in the derivatives game and their off-balance sheet holdings increase from one year to the next. This is documented in Exhibit 3.6 with statistics from 1998 annual statement by Donaldson, Lufkin & Jenrette. Notice that forward contract purchased more than doubled in notional value in one year, while those sold increased by nearly 50

**Exhibit 3.5   Derivatives Exposure by Coca-Cola* as of December 31, 1998
(in $ millions)**

	Notional Principal Amount	Values	Maturity
Interest Rate Management			
Swap agreements			
Assets	$ 325	$ 19	1999–2003
Liabilities	200	(13)	2000–2003
Foreign Currency Management			
Forward contracts			
Assets	809	(54)	1999–2000
Liabilities	1,325	(73)	1999–2000
Swap Agreements			
Assets	344	6	1999–2000
Liabilities	704	(51)	1999–2002
Purchased Options			
Assets	232	3	1999
Other liabilities	243	(26)	1999–2000
	$4,182	$(189)	

Source: 1998 Annual Report.

Exhibit 3.6 Donaldson, Lufkin & Jenrette One Year Growth in Commitments (December 31, 1998 vs. 1997, in $ millions)

	1997	1998
Forward Contracts		
Purchased at notional value	$18,366	$41,254
Sold at notional value	27,028	39,767
Futures Contracts and Options on Futures Contracts		
Purchased at market value	998	1,184
Sold at market value	2,767	1,607

percent. By contrast, the notional value of futures contracts and options on futures contracts sold was significantly reduced.

Accounting standards should permit one to distinguish whether companies like Coca-Cola enter into interest rate swaps to maintain a chosen mix of fixed interest rates and variable interest rates or do so because they run their treasury for profits. Similarly, there should be a way to ascertain if the purpose of foreign currency hedging is to reduce the risk that the firm's dollar net cash inflows resulting from sales outside the United States will be adversely affected by currency rate changes—or if hedges are made as part and parcel of the casino society.

Sometimes the use of derivatives is so bold that it penetrates every aspect of operations and therefore of financial reporting. While few board members and senior managers understand the adage that the only perfect hedge is a Japanese garden.

The Japanese yogurt company Yakult's derivatives losses because of "financial engineering" are a good example of what happens when companies let themselves be drawn into a mess. Indeed, with some enterprises derivatives trading by their treasury is so large that by buying their stock the investor is betting more on the fate of options, forwards, and swaps than that management will perform well in the firm's main product lines.

In March 1998, Yakult announced losses of $810 million in undisclosed derivatives trades that occurred over the previous four years. How could a yogurt firm lose that much in derivative products? On the average, the company lost more than $200 million per year in derivatives, and this should be a good lesson to all firms which venture into financial engineering. It is immaterial if senior management authorizes such silly trades, or they are done down the line by eager employees because internal controls are substandard.

What is important is that financial gambles cannot be hidden under this or that stone because of lax accounting standards. In connection to credit risk, well-managed companies are keen to establish strict counterparty credit guidelines, entering into transactions only with financial institutions of investment grade. They monitor counterparty exposures daily and any downgrade in credit rating leads to an immediate review of counterparty risk.

If a downgrade in credit rating of a counterparty were to occur, there are provisions requiring collateral in the form of government securities for substantially all transactions. Therefore, the accounting system must be tuned to provide timely alarms, so that prudential clauses can be executed without delay and new collateral evaluated in real-time.

Well-managed companies also see to it that to mitigate presettlement risk, minimum credit standards become more stringent as the duration of the derivative financial instrument increases. Also, to minimize the concentration of credit risk, they enter into derivative transactions with different financial institutions. In principle, diversification of credit risk is a good policy, but diversification also has limits: If you diversify to capture the entire market, then you are bound to capture the defaults and increase probability of loss.

INTERNALLY GENERATED INTANGIBLE ASSETS

The argument about internally generated intangible assets is not new. It has its roots in a number of different accounting practices and is used consistently by companies bent on cooking their books. From time-to-time, every 30 years or so, this argument resurfaces in an attempt to become an international standard, but typically (and happily) the effort fails.

Let me take an example on where this practice can lead. When in the early 1960s General Electric bought the French Compagnie des Machines Bull, its accountants had no inkling that Bull management had capitalized research and development costs—which are heavy in a computer company—over several years. This distorted the A&L statement.

The unwarranted capitalization came as a surprise after GE started to run Bull, and its accountants took a close look at the books of the acquired company. A thorough investigation revealed that Bull assets prominently featured in the balance sheet were consumed long ago.

Not only was R&D capitalized as "internally generated goodwill" but also the cement used in the building of a new computer factory in Angiers was carried in the "internally generated assets" chapter. The rationale was that a new factory added to the prestige of the computer maker and therefore it should be shown both as fixed asset and as internally generated goodwill.

Some accounting problems posed by handling of goodwill are at the root of conceptual differences between IAS, U.S. GAAP, and U.K. GAAP. These were briefly discussed in Chapter 2. Goodwill represents the cost of acquired businesses in excess of the net assets purchased. Typically, it is amortized on a straight-line basis, but the three aforementioned accounting standards differ in terms of number of years the amortization can be done.

This has material implications because goodwill is reported in the financial statement net of accumulated amortization, and the recoverability of the carrying value is evaluated on a periodic basis by assessing current and future levels of income and cash flows as well as other factors. The prevailing opinion in the global capital market, and among several industry players, is that amortization requirements for intangible assets and goodwill should be the same.

But other industry players disagree, believing that goodwill and intangible assets should be treated differently. The dissenters from the prevailing opinion view goodwill as a residual. Therefore, there should be a ceiling on its amortization period. Furthermore, according to this school, goodwill should be written off on acquisition either in the income statement or against equity.

The general practice supports systematic amortization of intangible assets and goodwill. Opponents think that amortization is inappropriate for intangible assets with indeterminate useful lives. A way to replace amortization is through regular impairment testing. This concept is gaining ground.

A growing body of opinion now supports annual impairment tests for intangible assets and goodwill amortized over more than 20 years. But the majority does not support annual impairment tests for internally generated intangible assets that are amortized over more than 5 years.

GAAP calls for all research and development costs to be recognized as an expense when incurred. A year's running expenses should never be capitalized. But IAS has proposed capitalizing the costs incurred for an internally generated intangible asset. Opponents to this IAS proposal, known as E60, are mainly from the United States, Germany, the Netherlands, and Switzerland. Their thesis is that there is no reliable way to identify when an internally generated intangible asset should be recognized. They also express concern that the proposed criteria are too subjective, and comparability of financial statements will not be achieved.

Other commentators to the E60 proposal support more explicit requirements and guidance for recognizing internally generated intangible assets, such as those contained in IAS 9, Research and Development Costs, and stricter criteria for recognizing other internally generated intangible assets.

Still others are demanding that costs of all internally generated intangible assets should be recognized as an expense, except for a few items, such as computer software and motion picture films. This too opens loopholes as, for instance, in software there is a difference between producing computer programs for personal use and making them for sale as a commodity. Therefore, a sound approach is to have the costs of all internally generated intangible assets recognized as an expense in the year when they are incurred.

Furthermore, if internally generated intangible assets are recognized, there should as well be provisions for internally generated liabilities. These can go well beyond the profit and loss aftermath because derivatives are a trade with aftershocks in which a company can afford no slip up. The next stop may be disaster. Let's look at an example.

Kidder Peabody alleged that one of its traders, Joseph Jett, left a hole of $350 million by exploiting the inefficiency of the company's accounting system. Kidder's accounting permitted a person to create bogus profits by buying a STRIP (usually Treasuries whose coupon was stripped off the principal) then booking its sale at a much higher price. This was handy because it always led to high commissions for traders.

A derivatives trade might be a boom for the salesperson but poisonous for the firm. The salesperson or trader pockets a huge sales commission, but the company carries an inordinate risk.

At Kidder Peabody, the window of opportunity for fake profits but real commissions was opened by the fact that STRIPS were sold with the face value of the original bond. Since the STRIP is only a piece of the original bond, its value is much less than that of the whole bond, but there is no sure formula for exact pricing. Into this crevasse came the make-believe profits.

Kidder's accounting system made matters worse by failing to disclose the $350 million of losses from skewed STRIP trading. Neither was Kidder Peabody the only investment bank to pay for this accounting failure. It appears that prior to unearthing the creative accounting practice, some of the $350 million—a guestimated $50 million—had miraculously migrated to Credit Swiss First Boston.

Accounting standards should as well be able to capture and report model risk whether this is due to assumptions coming into the model, or algorithms, deficient databases, or the way the model is implemented. Model risk is a new concept that followed the euphoria that mathematical representation of exposure is the best thing that happened since penicillin.[2]

Here is an example of chances taken with the implementation of models. In the case of the highly leveraged portfolio of Orange County, prior to the December 1994 meltdown, most of the repo desks at investment banks which acted as counterparties to the county's treasury were not calculating daily price change of the collateral—as should be done for a realistic estimate of exposure. Instead, they were marking to market this collateral *once per month* because they did not know how to value the structured notes in an accurate manner.

Even after the publication of the 1996 Market Risk Amendment this anomalous practice continued, in fact, it extended itself penetrating many financial institutions despite the fact that regulatory requirements imply daily computation of value-at-risk. Because of model illiteracy, senior management is not in a position to challenge such biased practice—and as Warren Buffett warns. If you don't know who the sucker is, it is you.

MANAGEMENT ACCOUNTABILITY AND THE NEED FOR A RIGOROUS GLOBAL ACCOUNTING SYSTEM

In spite of differences in opinion and in accounting procedures prevailing among countries, a global accounting system makes sense. This is attested by the fact that several countries, including Japan, are moving toward adopting International Accounting Standards. In April 1998, major Japanese companies produced fully consolidated accounts, which were until then provided by only a few of them.

Financial analysts believe that even if SEC sees the IAS rules as wanting, the cultural change resulting from their implementation in most of the Group of Seven countries and in some others, will by all likelihood be significant. Today, in countries where shareholders are an afterthought, accounting methods have degraded to the point of rendering the existence of profit, or lack of it, somewhat meaningless. In the post-World War II years, most company accounts in Japan, Italy, and other countries have been characterized by a reverse process. Management decides what profit it wants to report, then the accountants fill in the numbers accordingly.

There are many ways in interpreting double booking. Not all of them are tax evasion. Frequently, the background is hidden reserves which themselves have several reasons:

From having an egg nest for a rainy day to illicit contributions to political parties and greedy pockets.

Losses threatening P&L reporting can be covered by either creating or cashing hidden reserves. Significant surpluses can be allocated to research and development or other worthy cases—leading to tax evasion.

Another questionable aspect of this sort of account is the treatment of subsidiaries. In Japan, for example, subsidiaries were left off the parent company's accounts if its shareholding was less than 50 percent. As long as they own below the 50-percent mark, parent companies in Japan can hide information from both shareholders and tax inspectors; doing so with impunity.

By contrast, the introduction of consolidated accounting forces companies to take on their books subsidiaries in which they have effective control, even though they may have only a minority stake. They also have to adopt marked-to-market valuations for all tradable securities. Such changes oblige the management of firms to reveal unpleasant truths—which, for many of them, is a new practice.

The implementation of new policies and practices that are alien to a jurisdiction's current culture cannot be done only by changing the accounting rules. The problem is cultural and the board must understand that more transparent standards are urgently needed. The other leg is regulation, but it usually takes many years to build regulatory agencies capable of coping with today's volatile private capital flows, and highly geared financial markets.

The unpleasant truth is that unless a cultural change takes place and sound accounting principles are established, many of the advances in prudential management of the financial industry may be reversed. If repeated financial shocks happen, they will widen the gap between well-run companies—which play by the rules—and those who fail to anticipate change, hence they have to improvise.

Sound accounting principles require a well-tuned system of regulation able to use both carrot and stick. This dual role is of fundamental importance to the good functioning of markets. Equity is, after all, a call option on the value of a company's business. Therefore, investors are entitled to know everything about the business in which they own a stake.

There is a close relationship between the likelihood of default and a decrease in the ratio of a company's total equity value to its total debt. A public company defaults when its commercial value drops below its obligations, and investors run away to cut their losses.

To appreciate the impact of these concepts on disclosure, we must look at cultural and accounting issues at the same time. Both are vital in connection to the standards IASC is due to present to IOSCO. Let's keep in mind that, if accepted by all supervisory authorities of stock exchanges—including SEC—these accounting standards would become *listing standards* of stock exchanges worldwide.

Will the Americans follow lax standards which are the result of horse trading? The sure bet at this time is that the SEC, which is a key player in IOSCO, will not commit itself in advance to the acceptability of new accounting standards in-the-making which might compromise the current disclosure rules in the United States—and for good reason.

American regulators remain deeply distrustful of European and Japanese standards. They believe that continental European stock exchange rules allow the building up of secret reserves and the recording of excessive depreciation. American tax authorities think the same way. Also, continental European and Japanese standards and, by extension, IASC's:

- Do not allocate tax acceptably,
- Tend to omit certain assets,
- Do not always consolidate group companies, and
- Allow some off-balance sheet financing to go undetected.

This brings our discussion back to the reference made in the introduction to the $1 quadrillion. The role of derivative financial instruments in gearing the global economy, and most particularly the financial sector, should under no condition be underestimated. Exhibit 3.7 shows this exponential growth which at the end of 1997 for the first time exceeded the $100 trillion in notional principal amount and by the end of 1999 might reach $160 trillion or more.

In this highly leveraged environment, both *transparency* and *management intent* become cornerstones to *accountability*. Accounting is essentially the set of rules and measures which permit us to gauge accountability as FASB Statements suggest.

In the United States, since the Securities and Exchanges Commission, established in the aftermath of the depression of 1929, has delegated its statutory right to set standards through independent professional bodies. The Financial Accounting Standards Board (FASB) is the practical example. While it works by consensus through discussion papers, the board of FASB is the final judge.

In England, progress in establishing a common set of standards has been much slower. It has been carried out by joint committees established by the major professional accounting bodies. But with the creation of the Accounting Standards Board this has changed, and prudential accounting standards carry the day.

There is a fault line between the Anglo-Saxon countries and continental Europe—while Asian countries try to escape stiff accounting controls that would bring to light

Exhibit 3.7   Thirteen Years of Exponential Growth in Derivatives (in Notional Principal Amounts) to over $150 Trillion

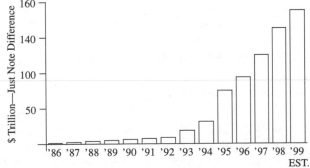

their supergearing. But withholding information is counterproductive. In both the United States and the United Kingdom, serving the needs of investors has been the driving force in the development of accounting standards, which is an alien concept in other countries.

TECHNOLOGY, DERIVATIVE FINANCIAL INSTRUMENTS, AND THE NEED FOR REAL-TIME RESPONSE

The use of derivatives often serves to modify market risk and credit risk embedded in financial transactions, by exchanging one for the other and by passing either or both to other parties. The concept of hedging rests on this notion. But while the disclosure of notional principal amount of derivative financial instruments is indicative of the extent of involvement in a particular class of financial products, it is not necessarily the only assessment of overall exposure.

A bank's or any other company's exposure to market risk is influenced by various factors. Key among them is the relationship between derivative financial instruments and the company's proprietary securities inventory. For instance, as a writer of options, a bank receives a premium in exchange for bearing the risk of unfavorable changes in the price of the underlying security, commodity, currency, or index. Part of this risk can be covered by being long, short, or actually owning the assets.

This facility is crucial to all underwriters or market makers and those who maintain a substantial trading inventory with positions in off-balance sheet instruments. Because such trades are leveraged, they may well include an inordinate amount of risk, new accounting standards must make it possible for every banker, treasurer, investor, and regulator to monitor all exposures through the use of:

- Interactive computational finance.
- Real-time analytical reporting.
- Interactive visualization of risk estimates.

These few lines merge trading and technology into one system at the banker's service. They also bring under perspective the need that accounting standards include ways and means for computer-based representation. The tools used when Luca Paciolo published his seminal work were paper and pencil. This has radically changed. Now management, investors, and regulators should be able to analyze and experiment on financial instruments and their exposure in real-time.

Experimentation and real-time response are important because with many derivative products, ideas spring unpredictably from searching a more efficient way for doing something else (in Chapter 7 see the discussion on quality control). Given the number of unknowns, the curve of market risk should be tapered by establishment of trading limits and ad hoc auditing of trading activities. Inside the financial institution, this should be done by both the management of trading areas and by a centralized risk management group.

New accounting standards must be in place to help all professionals in pursuing their risk control action, rather than disguising the longer term losses as equity or hiding them in some dark corner. Advanced technological solutions should assure that timely and accurate information is at the banker's and the investor's fingertips allowing them to make well-searched decisions.

To appreciate the role played by analytics let's remember that Luca Paciolo who in 1495 established the rules governing accounting practice was mathematician by profession (and a Benedictine monk). To help in senior management decisions by means of analytics, all positions must be valued daily through quoted market prices, when available, or through the use of properly tested pricing models. All inventoried values are affected by change in the following:

- Interest rates.
- Currency exchange rates.
- Credit spreads.
- Market volatility.
- Market liquidity.

The polyvalence of factors affecting fair value helps to document another major objection to the contemplated mixing of recognized but not realized gains and losses with equity. *Equity* and *uncertainty* are different concepts. Mixing them risks destroying market confidence. Yet, business is based on confidence. Other issues raised in connection to new standards are:

- Global acceptance of accounting definitions that promote transparency.
- An unambiguous expression of management intent regarding every transaction.
- The strengthening of concepts such as value and materiality.
- The value of auditable information versus non-auditable, hence not dependable.

The auditability of records is currently in a process of redefinition which will have significant impact on the work and responsibilities of certified public accountants (CPA). For instance, recent regulation in England, Germany, and Switzerland sees to it that external auditors also have the responsibility to audit a bank's internal controls.

This is good news, but it also lifts the issue of requirements to a level of greater sophistication. Without doubt, any new accounting standards must pay full attention to the suitability of a company's internal controls because accounting is the quantitative expression of economic events.

Internal control and materiality correlate. While any valid accounting solutions must support the principle of materiality, some types of fraud may involve trivial amounts per operation but mushroom because millions of such operations are performed daily.

Here is an example: A programmer working for an Italian credit institution had modified the computer software rounding out amounts whose value was equivalent to a few U.S. cents. These amounts were credited to an account opened by his wife in her maiden name—a practice which went undetected for years. The books balanced out nicely, each client was cheated only a little, but the rogue programmer made a small fortune.

As we saw in Chapter 2, the principle of materiality includes all aspects related to the presentation of information whose omission or misstatement could influence the economic decisions mapped into financial statements. But in cases, internal control and the principle of materiality may correlate negatively. All *events* and *non-events* are important for internal control, while the materiality of information is a function of the size of the item, of the firm's business and associated error.

It is important to rethink the concept of value, as far as accounting information is concerned. By comparing cost to benefit, the principle of value implies that the usefulness of information published in annual reports and other financial statements should be commensurate with, and preferably exceed, the cost of producing that information. Accurate costing is therefore a prerequisite.

This accounting principle can be best served through technology—whose specification should also be part of the new accounting standards. Interactive computational finance and intraday virtual balance sheets is not just the better way for an efficient internal control—it is the only one.

I emphasize these points because of my firm conviction that many errors in business, and in life at large, are the result of forgetting what we really want to do.

NOTES

1. On demodulation of the notional principal amount to credit equivalent, see D.N. Chorafas, "Credit Risk Management," *The Lessons of VAR Failures and Imprudent Exposure,* vol. 2 (London: Euromoney, 2000).

2. D.N. Chorafas, "Credit Risk Management," *The Lessons of VAR Failures and Imprudent Exposure,* vol. 2 (London: Euromoney, 2000).

PART TWO

COSO, Behavioral Analysis, Quality Control, and Statements of Financial Accounting Standards

CHAPTER 4

The Work Done by the Treadway Commission

Fraudulent financial reporting and the problems associated with it are not new. But as business expands in a globalized landscape, in number of transactions and in value represented by these transactions, the opportunities for fraudulent financial reporting increase. This fact has not escaped the attention of regulators.

The Treadway Commission was constituted in the late 1980s to deal with ways and means to control fraudulent reporting. After some years of incubation, the implementation of its recommendations has been undertaken by the Committee of Sponsoring Organizations (COSO). These recommendations have turned into rules and they are now in the process of being implemented throughout the American banking system.

A brief background would help to better appreciate the scope of COSO and the most likely extent of its impact on the financial industry. The Treadway Commission has been an initiative of James C. Treadway, Jr., a former commissioner of the Securities and Exchange Commission (SEC). The other members of the Treadway Commission were William M. Batten, William S. Kanga, Hugh L. Marsh, Thomas I. Storrs, and Donald H. Trautlein. The Treadway Commission was jointly sponsored and funded by the:

- American Institute of Certified Public Accountants (AICPA).
- American Accounting Association (AAA).
- Financial Executives Institute (FEI).
- Institute of Internal Auditors (IIA).
- The National Association of Accountants (NAA).

In the mid-1990s, the Federal Reserve Board took the initiative of implementing COSO. Three regional Federal Reserve Banks: New York, Boston, and Chicago have been the first to apply and test Part One of the Treadway Commission's recommendations, which are:

1. Reliable financial reporting.
2. Effectiveness and efficiency.
3. Internal controls and compliance.

According to a decision by the Federal Reserve Board and the other regulatory agencies in the United States, all banks with $500 million or more in assets must implement the control environment defined by COSO. These rules have passed the feasibility test: Their 1998 application by the Fed of New York, Fed of Boston, and Fed of Chicago was successful; in addition they have also shown good results among the nine other Federal Reserve Banks. Financial reporting impacts nonbank companies, too, since many of the COSO recommendations have been adopted by SEC.

THE CONTROL ENVIRONMENT DEFINED BY COSO

The control environment defined by COSO includes integrity, ethical values, competence, organizational structure, management awareness, philosophy, operating style, assignment of authority and responsibility, and human resource policies and practices. COSO's definition of *risk assessment* incorporates:

- Risk analysis because of external and internal sources,
- The study of exposure associated with innovation and change, and
- The ability to manage change in a successful way.

Control activities defined by COSO are associated with policies and procedures established by management to meet financial, operational, and other objectives. Information and communication prerequisites are also part of the control environment. They concern the ability to capture and disseminate relevant information to ensure people carry out their job responsibilities in a responsible manner.

COSO places emphasis on monitoring stress in connection to activities that supervise and measure the effectiveness of the internal control system over time. Monitoring, recording, and data analysis must allow management to ensure it meets objectives and to take corrective action as necessary. In brief, the five interrelated control components defined by the COSO model are:

1. Control environment.
2. Risk assessment.
3. Control activities.
4. Information and communication.
5. Monitoring and recording.

Fraudulent financial reporting is a serious problem and by all indications one that is increasing. While fraud is difficult to detect and even more difficult to eradicate, fraudulent reporting can be reduced through rules, regulations, and supervision.

In principle, the ways and means taken by fraudulent financial reporting are influenced by the institution's size, exact nature of its business, lack of transparency, and management culture. Opportunities to commit or conceal fraudulent activities exist in all firms. These involve accounting policies and practices as well as:

- Slack in internal control procedures or even absence of rigorous control structures.
- The existence of transactions involving contentious, difficult, or evolving accounting issues.
- The presence of significant assets, with valuation problems when marked-to-market.
- Extreme events that impact on the entity's usual way of doing business.
- The occurrence of very large transactions or unusual adjustments at or near year-end or quarter-end.

The Treadway Commission addressed all five issues. The principles of sound management underlying every one of them have been elaborated into a system of rules by the Committee of Sponsoring Organizations. COSO published the "Internal Control—Integrated Framework Report" in September 1992, intended to provide management with:

- Practical, broadly accepted criteria for the elaboration of internal controls systems and procedures.
- A framework to evaluate its effectiveness, both during an audit and over time.
- Principles promoting transparency in financial reporting and management accountability.

The more transparent a financial reporting structure, the easier it is to understand the nature of transactions and appreciate the net worth embedded in banking book and trading book. Also critical is whether gains and losses are recognized during the reporting period. The bottomline is what COSO is all about.

Transparency makes it possible to access the right information and be sure the financial data is factual and documented. Transparency is the cornerstone in developing a navigation map that is well-founded rather than depending on rumors, personal connections, and data which cannot be verified. For this reason, practically no one would disagree on the benefits of correct disclosure. Practically, everybody accepts that the more timely and reliable the finance information, the better the markets work and the more efficient is the management of exposure.

Rigorous internal control is instrumental in assuring transparency. In the United States, COSO's internal control recommendations have been widely accepted as state-of-the-art for the evaluation of management's ability to be in charge. After it became public, the COSO report was viewed by many knowledgeable parties as having achieved, at least on paper, its stated objectives.

The main critique came from the SEC, which said that COSO does not adequately address controls relating to safeguarding of assets. Therefore, it would not fully respond to the requirements of the Foreign Corrupt Practices Act of 1977. As a result, an addendum to "Reporting to External Parties" of the COSO report was published in May 1994. This discusses the issue of, and provides a vehicle for, expanding the scope of financial reporting. It also focuses additional attention on internal control, particularly relating to the safeguarding of assets.

To reach factual conclusions about fraudulent reporting, the Treadway Commission advised that it is necessary to examine whether the bank's sales and profits forecasts *can be* achieved and *are* achieved; how sales and profits compare to other banks in the industry; and the adequacy and status of reserves, as well as provision for bad debts. Today, it would be necessary to add to this list exposure to derivative financial instruments.

ISSUES INVOLVED IN FRAUDULENT FINANCIAL REPORTING

According to the conclusions of the Treadway Commission, when assessing the risk of fraudulent financial reporting, it is important to consider not only the bank's business but also its current and future financial status. The study of trading book and banking book should encompass liquidity, profitability, cash flow, and capital adequacy.

One of the key observations made by the Commission is that fraudulent financial reporting has traditionally been associated with companies experiencing financial difficulties. However, there is also evidence that fraudulent activity sometimes starts during good economic times and under rather favorable financial conditions.

Fraudulent acts are discovered more often during economic and financial stress, because a favorable economic environment tends to mask illegal facts. Another reason for finding more fraudulent reporting under stress conditions is the increased scrutiny a company receives from regulators when it finds itself under financial adversity. Specific factors to be considered in both good and bad times include:

- The profitability of the bank.
- Its liquidity and cash flow.
- Quality of receivables.
- The need to obtain borrowing.
- Compliance with restrictive debt covenants.

A thorough analysis of the institution's profitability involves, among other factors, trends in sales, profits, and new product development. A decrease in the quality and quantity of sales may indicate potential for lower profits in future periods and can be evidenced by:

- Liberalization of the company's credit policies.
- Introduction of unusual discount and payment programs.
- Other changes loosening up prudent business practices.

The study of the bank's liquidity considers the adequacy of working capital and trend in cash flow. Significant differences between net earnings and cash flow may indicate the use of improper revenue or expense recognition policies. Inadequate cash flow may result in less-generous credit terms, or even bankruptcy proceedings forced on an otherwise profitable company.

These are situations leading to fraudulent financial reporting. It is also important to consider the quality of the company's accounts receivable. Significant increases in the aging of the receivables, or slowdowns in average daily receipts, may portend serious economic difficulties. Connected to this is the ability to borrow in the money market under competitive terms. An analysis of trend in additional borrowing will consider the:

- Need for funds.
- Credit rating.
- Current debt-to-equity ratio.
- Amount of unrestricted collateral.
- Marketability of existing collateral.
- Evolution in debt restrictions.

Other factors critical to an evaluation are a projection of likelihood for noncompliance, particular covenants attached to loans, and extra premium paid to obtain loans in the interbank market. These factors may be of even greater concern in situations where some of restrictive covenants already have been violated.

The previous section made reference to transparency connected to financial transactions. COSO recommends that whether or not an institution's procedures for identifying and recording related-party transactions are adequate must be examined under two types of circumstances:

1. Operations under normal conditions.
2. Operations under stress.

The Treadway Commission emphasized the need to test under both normal and stress conditions, which is a forerunner of the stress testing adopted by many institutions in the aftermath of the 1996 Market Risk Amendment by the Basle Committee on Banking Supervision.[1] This test must also include the overall quality of the institution's accounting records. Another recommendation regards testing whether:

- Transactions are processed in a systematic manner.
- Accounting procedures are performed in a conscientious fashion.

The Commission also underlined that more opportunities are present for fraudulent financial statements when the bank employs exceptionally aggressive, controversial, unusual, or liberal interpretations of accounting principles, particularly with regard to revenue recognition—the so-called *creative accounting*.

Another sign of troubles with financial statements, COSO advises, is the case of disputes between the institution and its independent public accountants, concerning the company's application of accounting principles. Internal control should capture the existence of such disagreements at an early stage.

Furthermore, the Treadway Commission strongly advises that in evaluating the quality of an institution's internal financial reporting system, auditors and examiners should consider matters such as whether:

- Senior management consistently uses financial reports in controlling the operations of the bank.

- Factual financial statements are submitted to the board of directors both at regular intervals and by exception.

As Benjamin Graham used to say to his students at Columbia University, it is quite possible to decide by inspection that a woman is old enough to vote without knowing her age, or a man is heavier than he should be without knowing his weight. As Chapter 8 will explain, the modern tools for deciding by inspection are statistical quality control (SQC) charts. They provide:

- A visual appreciation of exposure.
- An inference based on trend.
- The ability to assure a margin of safety by adjusting control limits relative to tolerances.

The Treadway Commission has underlined that the existence of elements in the financial statement that depend heavily on the exercise of subjective judgment or unusually complex calculations is an indication of pockets of potential conflict of interest or fraud. While many of these issues and their aftermath are known, most banks do not apply required prudence. COSO's implementation in the banking industry will see to it that in the future what needs to be done for reliable reporting is done in an appropriate manner.

INTERNAL CONTROL AND THE TREADWAY COMMISSION

The Treadway Commission report emphasized the importance of an institution's internal control structure, particularly the command and control environment and the "tone at the top." These were characterized as deterrents to fraudulent financial practices. It also called for a rule by the SEC to require all public companies to include in their annual reports a management section acknowledging their responsibilities for the preparation of:

- Reliable financial statements.
- A rigorous internal controls audit.

The Commission sought to qualify and quantify the problems associated to fraudulent financial reporting, outlining the corrective measures to be taken. Quantification, however, proved most difficult as the Commission found no way to gauge the amount and significance of undetected fraudulent financial reporting. (See Chapter 8 on the use of statistical quality control charts as a solution.)

An interesting hindsight has been the finding that there are a number of cases where fraudulent activities are detected but, for a variety of reasons, they are not pursued by senior management or law enforcement officers. This was characterized by the Commission as one of the most explicit cases of internal control failure at the top management level.

One of the best examples where the internal control system was clogged with top management's complicity is the Salomon Brothers affair of 1990. It started with the manipulation of Treasury bonds sales by Paul Mozer, head of the broker's government bond desk, and eventually engulfed the investment bank's top management.

For starters, U.S. Treasury securities are the world's biggest market with over $100 billion in daily trading. This is an order of magnitude more than the $10 billion or so traded daily on the New York Stock Exchange. Salomon was a primary dealer in U.S. Treasuries and Mozer's job was bidding for bonds at Treasury auctions, trading them after they were issued.

Fearing an attempt by big brokerages to corner the market, the Treasury had imposed a 35-percent limit on awards to each account. But there was a loophole. Primary dealers were allowed to also bid for their clients and Mozer bet for Mercury Asset Management and Quantum Fund *without* client authorization or even post-mortem information. This was illegal and before too long, John Gutfreund, chairman, Thomas Strauss, president, John Meriwhether, star bond trader and boss of Paul Mozer, and Donald Feuerstein, general counsel, were informed of the impropriety.

In a securities business where confidence is of enormous importance, nothing was revealed to the Fed and SEC in a timely manner about this happening. "(Gutfreund) had a *duty,* which at the extreme resembles fate," says Roger Lowenstein.[2] In the aftermath, after the news finally broke, Gutfreund found himself obliged to quit.

Estimating the true extent of the problem posed by this type of business practice is not simply a matter of counting how often such improprieties happen—or of comparing the number of fraudulent financial reporting cases brought by the SEC with the total number of publicly filed financial reports. As the Treadway Commission has found, the truly prevailing relation is much more complex than a simple ratio.

The Salomon Brothers case is an internal control failure at apex of the organizational pyramid. An interesting aftermath of this and similar bypasses of internal control is the fact that the resulting fraudulent financial reporting has not one but many victims. Typically, these victims are counterparties who look to the company to perform on its contracts, including:

- Government authorities who confer the status of primary dealer.
- Investors in the company's equity and/or debt securities.
- Depositors who entrust their wealth to the institution.
- Banks and other institutions lending funds to the company.
- Suppliers who extend credit which gets jeopardized.
- Merger partners who may enter into agreements based on inflated values.
- Financial analysts who give investment advice about the issuer and its securities.
- Independent rating agencies evaluating the company's creditworthiness.
- Underwriters who distribute securities.

Victims can also be the company's independent public accountants, attorneys, and insurance companies that write directors' and officers' liability insurance and then experience large claims.

If these are the immediate victims of the breakdown of internal controls and of ethical standards in a financial institution, there are others who are more remote victims, suffering from the harm created when investor confidence in the stock market is shaken, such as the bank's employees who suffer job loss or diminished pension fund value.

The Treadway Commission has brought attention to another aftermath of fraudulent financial reporting. When the wrongdoing comes to light, people within the bank who reported the existence of unreliable financial information are often injured. Also, the company's senior management and directors, may suffer loss of money as well as of reputation and standing; and holders of large blocks of company stock, such as estates or family trusts, may suffer because the value of their holdings can drop dramatically.

For these reasons, the Treadway Commission placed a great deal of emphasis on prevention of fraud through appropriate controls. It also called for senior management to analyze and describe how internal control responsibilities were met—and to assess the effectiveness of the internal control structure.

While the Treadway Commission report did not recommend auditor attestation to management reports, it did say that the ASB provides guidance to an auditor when he or she disagrees with management's assessment of internal controls. Such disagreement is usually based on information obtained from the audit of financial statements, but may also come from personal interviews.

Some of the characteristics and functions of auditors have also been called into question. Is the chief auditor preparing a plan to help in allocating his time and that of his examiner? Are plan versus actual analyses used as a guide in planning control activities? Does the depth coverage of the audits appear to be sufficient? Is the chief auditor a member of an executive systems planning committee?

Auditing procedures, too, have been brought under a magnifying glass. Do current procedures employ statistically valid sampling techniques, with acceptable reliability and precision? Is the content of the audit independent of adverse influences of other interests? Has it been approved by the board of directors? Does it provide for resolution of exceptions and deficiencies?

In response to a related Treadway Commission recommendation, COSO funded a project to develop integrated guidance on internal controls, including the development of criteria to assess the effectiveness of an entity's internal control structure. The COSO report, "Internal Control-Integrated Framework," was issued in September 1992 after public exposure and a significant amount of debate.

This COSO document takes no position on whether management reports on the effectiveness of the institution's internal control structure should be required, or whether auditors should attest to those reports. However, it does recommend that when management reports are issued, they should focus on internal controls over the preparation of published financial statements, rather than spending time on relatively secondary subjects.

IMPLEMENTING THE COSO SYSTEM

Seen in retrospect from the viewpoint of its findings and recommendations, the contributions of the Treadway Commission led to practical tools able to ascertain the dependability of financial and accounting information in regard to the operations of a company.

Particular emphasis has been placed on understanding the impact of financial reporting, and on principles to make a better business scrutiny which permits auditors to gain confidence when working with financial information.

Reliable reporting has been characterized as the means to communicate effectively with the accounting staff, obtaining insight on financial performance measurements that drive the business, and identifying areas needing internal control. Reliable reports make it possible to use financial data with confidence, in making decisions which impact on profitability and survival of the institution.

In its "Overview of Financial Examination Program Objectives," the Federal Reserve directs its examiners to evaluate compliance with principles and prerogatives established by COSO. They should do so while reviewing in their evaluation staffing, training, productivity, work flow, computers, communications systems, forms, files, and records storage.

Internal control should be examined to assure proper maintenance of depository institutions accounts associated to requirements and penalties. The examiners are directed to review the appropriateness of access to the computer systems and perform an assessment of current status as well as recommend improvements.

Among the issues to which attention should be paid is audit staff qualifications, as well as the critical mass necessary to perform due tasks adequately. Is the staff experienced in auditing and banking? Is a training program in effect? Are members of the staff able to handle specialized areas such as derivative financial instruments? Interest rate products? Currency exchange trading? Loans? Trust? Information technology?

One of the issues discussed during the research meetings with cognizant executives of the Federal Reserve, Office of the Comptroller of the Currency (OCC), Office of Thrifts Supervision (OTS), Federal Deposit Insurance Corporation (FDIC), and Securities and Exchange Commission (SEC) has been the relationship between GAAP and COSO. In the United States, the GAAP was established by the Financial Accounting Standards Board (FASB). It is followed by every American firm and any foreign company that wishes to be listed in a U.S. stock exchange.

GAAP, and its relationship to International Accounting Standards, is discussed in Chapters 2 and 3. The following paragraphs address themselves only to the relationship between COSO and GAAP, which is the regulatory accounting language of the SEC. This is the lower level general accounting set of rules while, as Exhibit 4.1 suggests, the accounting principles and procedures promoted by the Committee of Sponsoring Organizations (therefore, COSO) is the *metalanguage*. A metalanguage is a language which acts as abstraction and control of lower level linguistic constructs. Application-specific aspects of accounting problems can best be formulated in a higher level language of rules and constraints.

COSO is to become the topmost framework for internal control in the financial industry. Not only is there no contradiction between GAAP and COSO, but they complement one another.

- GAAP addresses standardized accounting procedures.
- COSO focuses on management controls and responsibilities.

Exhibit 4.1   The Standardization of a Metalanguage Assists in the Reliability of Financial Reporting

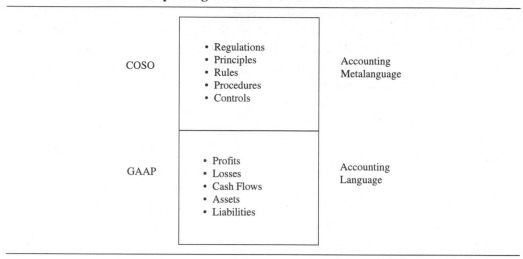

This is the reason why the Fed is so interested in the implementation of COSO. It is also a direct aftermath of the fact that a crucial part of the work of the Treadway Commission concerned the responsibilities connected to the correct management of an institution and the dependability of its financial statements.

The framework the Commission is based on is the principles the top management of a public company must use in identifying what may cause the entity's financial statements and reports to be fraudulently misstated. Senior management accountability requires:

- Understanding the factors that can lead to fraudulent financial reporting, including factors unique to the company.
- Assessing the risks of fraudulent financial reporting that these factors create within the entity and its accounts; also, in regard to its partners.
- Designing and implementing internal controls that provide reasonable assurance fraudulent financial reporting will be prevented or at least detected in a timely manner.

The introduction made reference to the 1998 implementation of COSO by the Federal Reserve Banks of New York, Boston, and Chicago. The results confirm that the assessment process enables an entity to design and apply internal controls able to minimize the risks of misrepresentation. Rather than suggesting a separate effort or department for internal control, the Treadway Commission brought to regular management activities a heightened awareness of and sensitivity to the potential for fraudulent financial reporting.

The Commission underlined that individuals at all levels of the company, including operating management, financial managers, internal auditors, and attorneys participate in the assessment. The chief executive officer, chief operating officer, and chief financial officer must not only supervise this process but also be personally responsible for its correct functioning.

COSO strengthened the federal legislation that existed since 1977 and required each SEC registrant to devise and maintain a system of internal accounting controls sufficient to provide reasonable assurance that fraud is under control. COSO contributed to this process through the framework which it provided.

"Transition to COSO has been easy," said David L. Robinson of the Federal Reserve Board, "but the banks needed some education on its rules, procedures, and systems." If three major Federal Reserve Banks in America have done it in record time, other central banks can do it. This will provide a good motivation to commercial and investment banks to go the COSO way—and therefore strengthen their structure of senior management control.

BENEFITS FROM IMPLEMENTATION OF COSO

"What we do in the COSO implementation," said William McDonough, executive vice president of the Federal Reserve Bank of Boston, "is to go through the COSO-defined process of 'Risk Assessment and Communications.' We also implement risk management tools and decide the sort of mechanism which will serve best these goals. In this, COSO serves as a framework which permits us to look into different types of risk and check the mission-critical processes."

According to this, internal control is the big goal in which credit risk, market risk, and other risks is integrated, as shown in Exhibit 4.2. Reliable financial reporting is strengthened through this integration. Every risk the bank faces in its operating environment, as

Exhibit 4.2 COSO Provides the Framework Which Permits Better Control of Exposure

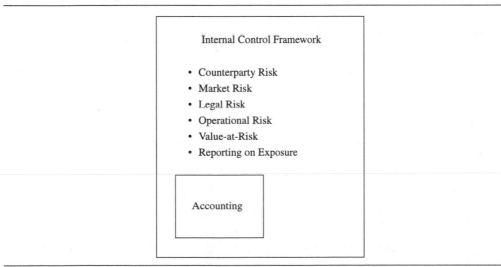

well as its reporting on exposure, fits into the internal control framework defined by COSO.

A direct result of these experiences is that rigorous auditing procedures today characterize the examination of the 12 Federal Reserve Banks (FRB) by the Fed Board. In accordance with the Federal Reserve Act, sections 11.2 and 21.7, the Board of Governors orders an annual examination of each Federal Reserve Bank. At its discretion, it examines the accounts, books, and affairs of each bank. COSO has been implemented in connection with these examinations.

Historically, the Fed has executed this responsibility by means of an annual balance sheet analysis and control, conducted by the Financial Examination Program, which includes a review of FRB operations for compliance with regulations, policies, and procedures. The examiners also review the bank's expenses. The objectives of the examination are to determine:

- Reliability of financial reporting.
- Effectiveness and efficiency of operations.
- Compliance with applicable policies and procedures.
- Adequacy of safeguards to prevent the unauthorized acquisition, use, and disposition of assets.

The Board also initiates tests of new methods and procedures in collaboration with the Federal Reserve Banks. As a metalanguage of accounting standards for financial reporting, COSO has acted as rigorous internal controls framework. The principle is that improved systems will make management fraud and manipulation of accounting information more difficult, while financial events will become more transparent.

A better control of exposure and reliable financial reporting are key reasons why the Fed requires that banks with over $500 million in assets must submit to regulators COSO-based financial statements. The Federal Reserve also asks external auditors to attest and report on management statements, which can be seen as an audit of the institution's internal control system.

Much has been learned in this connection from a 1991 study by the General Accounting Office (GAO) which concluded that internal control weaknesses lead to banks filing inaccurate call reports.[3] GAO underlined that one aspect of the importance of internal control to the health of the banking system was to "ensure that . . . accounting principles are properly applied in the preparation of bank call reports and financial statements."

The GAO also found that rigorous internal controls can be an "early warning" of practices affecting banks' safety and soundness—as well as of breakdown in an institution's system of corporate governance. Subsequent to this, GAO's requirements for management and auditor reports were adopted in 1991 as part of the Federal Deposit Insurance Corporation Improvement Act.

The rules spelled out by FDIC specify that examiners should have full and timely access to a supervised institution's internal audit resources, including personnel, work papers, risk assessments, work plans, programs, reports, and budgets. Delays in the execution of this work require examiners to widen the scope of their examination, and subject the institution to follow-up supervisory actions.

Like the Fed, FDIC examiners evaluate whether the activities of internal audit are consistent with the long-range goals of the institution and are responsive to its control requirements. Here again, COSO acts as main line of defense against the likelihood of fraudulent reporting.

FDIC examiners assess the quality and scope of internal audit and consider whether the board and the audit committee promote the internal audit manager's impartiality and independence. Also whether the institution's internal control plans and programs are appropriate for its activities.[4] Examiners focus on whether or not the internal audit function is adequately managed to ensure that:

- Audit programs are appropriately carried out.
- Audit plans are met in timely fashion.
- Results of audits are promptly communicated to the board and senior managers.

A basic criterion is whether the institution has promptly responded to identified internal control weaknesses. Senior management and the board are expected to use rigorous standards when assessing the performance of the internal audit. Internal audit activities must be adjusted for significant changes in the business environment the institution's business, structure, and risk exposure.

In conclusion, the metalanguage provided by COSO permits the examining regulatory agencies to ask a lot of focused questions to capture the pattern in other people's minds—not only the pattern of records. This is a most significant assistance to examiners.

NOTES

1. D.N. Chorafas, *The 1996 Market Risk Amendment. Understanding the Marking-to-Model and Value-at-Risk* (Burr Ridge, IL: McGraw-Hill, 1998).
2. Roger Lowenstein, *Buffett, the Making of an American Capitalist* (London: Weidenfeld and Nicolson, 1996).
3. General Accounting Office, *Failed Banks: Accounting and Auditing Reforms Urgently Needed*, GAO/AFMD-91-43 (Washington, DC: GAO, 1991).
4. FDIC, *Internal Audits*, FIL-133-97 (Washington, DC: FDIC, 1997).

CHAPTER 5

Control of Fraudulent Financial Reporting

In June 1993, a few years after the work of the Treadway Commission was completed, a White Paper published by the Board of the American Institute of Certified Public Accountants (AICPA) stated that the internal control system is the main line of defense against fraudulent financial reporting. It also underlined that a key AICPA preoccupation is the investing public deserves an independent assessment of the internal control line of defense.

Who should provide the needed assessment? In the American banking industry, external auditors play a somewhat lesser role than in Europe because the Federal Reserve, Federal Deposit Insurance Corporation, and Office of the Comptroller of the Currency, who are responsible for the supervision of commercial banks, use their own examiners. Certified public accountants, however, still maintain an important position in detection and reporting of fraudulent practices, and bear a major responsibility in bringing to light lack of compliance in financial reporting.

In the United States, regulatory reporting dates back to the 1860s, when institutions were periodically required to file and publish statements of financial conditions. At the time, the Office of the Comptroller of the Currency was the sole bank supervisor.

Today, the domain of commercial banks in the province of the Fed, OCC, and FDIC; the SEC regulates investment banks, mutual funds, and the securities industry at large; the Commodity Futures Trading Commission (CFTC) is responsible for certain types of commodities-based financial instruments and entities; the National Credit Union Administration (NCUA) regulates credit unions; and the Office of Thrifts Supervision looks after the savings and loans.

The increase in the number and structure of supervisory agencies has not been the only change in the U.S. landscape. Over the years, compliance rules and the regulators' duties have evolved. COSO is the latest step in this evolution.

The Group of Ten countries do not follow the same policies and procedures in regard to supervision. In contrast to U.S. practices, in the United Kingdom (during the years it was responsible for supervision), the Bank of England did not carry out on-site exams on a regular basis; and the Financial Services Authority (FSA) which succeeded the Bank of

England follows the same policy. To a substantial extent, supervision is based on reports made by external auditors who detail their findings.

In Germany, the Federal Banking Supervision Bureau, that depends on the Ministry of Finance, does the supervision of financial institutions, in collaboration with the Bundesbank. But, as in the case of Britain, it relies on external auditors to analyze the information in annual financial statements and to check for compliance.

In Switzerland, the Federal Banking Commission, that also depends on the Ministry of Finance, licenses the external auditors. A commercial bank's board appoints its external auditors among those licensed. This firm can only be changed with the Commission's approval. In 1988, however, the Federal Banking Commission instituted a new department: Big Banks, with its own examiners, for UBS and Credit Suisse.

In all G-10 countries, the regulatory agencies are statutory bodies authorized by law to supervise the financial system in order to assure that banks and other financial institutions operate in a sound manner, with safety, without fraud, and without taking exposures that contribute to systemic risk. In principle, violations of the law or reporting irregularities typically lead to penalties and corrective action. But as markets get globalized and products are innovated at a rapid pace, the rules and regulations as well as the financial reporting standards must become increasingly more sophisticated. An example is COSO.

THREE PHASES OF COSO'S CONTRIBUTION TO RELIABLE REPORTING

An old proverb says that it is not worth mounting a high horse unless one is willing to perform some acrobatics to remain safely in the saddle. If one gets thrown off because of lack of skill or imprudence, it was hardly worth trying in the first place. This is also true for the effort to catch fraudulent reporting practices.

Reliable financial reporting is a pragmatic consideration that is doable. If financial reports are manipulated by those who prepare them, they are hardly worth being done in the first place. To appreciate what it takes to develop and maintain dependable financial reporting practices, the Treadway Committee examined the three stages through which a business system moves:

1. *Study, analysis, and design.* Financial reporting is not invented overnight, though overnight it may be massaged. It is important that the existing financial reporting system be reviewed to gain understanding of how it works: Norms must be specified, reporting solutions designed to meet the prerequisites of reliability, and tests made to assure the specifications are observed as well as being sure there is compliance to rules and regulations.

2. *Evaluation, system testing, and implementation.* In principle, the way a financial reporting system is recast may be sound, but this is not necessarily an assurance that in practice it will work as intended. Only a live test will tell if the revamped

financial reporting solution is valid. Live evaluation must be done step-by-step at rapid pace. While those parts already tested are put into action, it is necessary to perform systems tests.

What many institutions are missing today is the ability to display in a dependable manner the dynamic mechanism of an activity—doing so in a way that provides a fairly detailed operational view. The methodology implied by COSO permits a critical look at operations, as well as it facilitates observation and analysis of information inputs, outputs, and database resources.

3. *Online operation and steady upkeep.* The operation of a financial reporting system is the day-to-day applications routine. Reporting chores must be done accurately, and those responsible for them must be ready to correct deviations without delays, and adjust their practices as new rules emerge. This brings attention back to the first stage: Study and design.

Study and design of a financial reporting system is no one-time affair. It is continuous and it should be done with the greatest care. This is seldom fully appreciated in the banking industry, neither is it appropriately described in accounting literature.

A careful examination of what has been available prior to the norms advanced by COSO demonstrates that while many isolated bits of specific information relating to particular financial reporting problems did exist, a total approach commensurate with advancements in the banking industry was not in place. This gap between old rules and new financial realities has been closed by COSO by specifying that:

* Before a new reliable accounting system can be implemented, it must be architectured.
* Any prior solution that may form the basis of the new system must be completely understood in terms of strengths and weaknesses.

Hidden between the study and design functions is another major task that has been frequently overlooked: Analysis of requirements that satisfy responsibilities of several groups of people: The institution's board, senior management, shareholders, analysts, and regulators. If any of these responsibilities is skipped, the new system will often be just a bigger, faster way of repeating existing mistakes—and fraud.

By way of restructuring the study and design prerequisites of a reliable accounting system, COSO brings attention to three aims:

1. To understand what the current accounting solution does and does not do—as well as to which degree it can be manipulated by people ready and willing to do so. This is expressed in terms of activities that thread through the business, and of records connected to these activities.
2. To analyze current procedures comparing them to what is specified as necessary for a dependable management of accounts. This needs to be done with a view to accomplishing the goals of reliable financial reporting within the tolerances specified by regulators.

3.   To analyze and design accounting and reporting procedures to assure not only that the institution's accounting system can meet reliability requirements, but also that these are described in a manner capable of displaying different levels of detail in facts and figures regarding input data streams, supporting databases, and regulatory financial reports.

Another contribution of COSO is that the emphasis placed on reliability enhancements helps to assure that different accounting tools can work together to provide a coherent description of financial condition. Moreover, because they can be used at several levels of detail throughout the bank, these enhancements should constitute an inspecting instrument of magnifying power at the disposal of senior management.

TREADWAY COMMISSION'S GUIDELINES FOR THE AUDIT OF MANAGEMENT REPORTS

The investing public, the company's clients and suppliers, tax authorities, and regulators are most interested in the way an entity's management carries out its financial reporting responsibilities. A reliable implementation of management reports, able to represent individual company circumstances and reflect its financial pulse, significantly improves the linkages with users of accounting statement about the nature of financial information being communicated to them, and the processes and responsibilities that surround data preparation and presentation.

The Treadway Commission recommended that all annual reports to stockholders be required by rules set by the SEC to include a management report signed by the company's chief executive officer, chief financial officer, and chief accounting officer who may be the controller. This report should:

• Acknowledge management's responsibilities for financial statements and their content.
• Discuss how these responsibilities have been fulfilled.
• Provide management's assessment of the effectiveness of the company's internal control.

The part reflecting on management's accountability for financial statements must specifically acknowledge responsibilities in connection to preparing the presentation of facts and figures. These must be fairly stated in accordance with Generally Accepted Accounting Principles, and not misstated due to material fraud or error.

The Treadway Commission also specified that senior management carries full responsibility for providing assurance as to the integrity and reliability of the entity's internal control system. In line with this requirement, COSO extends senior management's accountability to include:

• Protection of the entity's assets.
• Prevention of reasons leading to fraudulent financial reporting.

COSO places on the auditors the responsibility for assuring that management performs the stated functions in a factual and documented manner. It recommends that the Auditing Standards Board revise standards to restate the independent public accountants' responsibility for detection of fraudulent financial reporting, requiring them to:

- Provide guidance for assessing risks and pursuing detection when risks are identified.
- Take affirmative steps in each audit to assess the potential for wrong reporting.
- Design and implement tests to provide reasonable assurance of fraud detection.

The Treadway Commission has taken notice of the fact that the degree of responsibility for designing the audits to detect fraudulent reporting has been a source of continuing debate. Early auditing texts set forth three objectives for the audit:

1. The detection of fraud.
2. Technical errors.
3. Errors of principle.

However, both internal and external auditors experienced increasing difficulty in detecting carefully concealed frauds. Therefore, pressure built within the profession to modify auditing standards relating to responsibility for detecting fraud, and its disavowal.

According to the Treadway Commission, part of the problem has been a statement made in auditing literature which stated that the auditor's responsibility for fraud detection was limited and therefore financial statement users should not rely on the audit for assurance of fraud detection. In 1975, however, an AICPA committee determined that failure on the part of auditors to detect massive fraud in the widely publicized Equity Funding case pointed to a need for revised standards.

The AICPA committee's work as well as that contributed by a Commission on Auditors' Responsibilities led AICPA in 1997 to issue Statement on Auditing Standards (SAS) No. 16, "The Independent Auditor's Responsibility for the Detection of Errors and Irregularities." Beyond SAS No. 16, the Treadway Commission recommended that independent public accountants' responsibility for the detection of fraudulent financial reporting is restated to include:

- The need to assess the risk of fraudulent financial reporting.
- The requirement to design tests able to provide reasonable assurance of fraud detection.

COSO states that a strong corporate ethical climate is necessary to assure the risk of fraudulent financial reporting decreases. Also, that auditors should be responsible for actively considering the potential for fraudulent financial reporting in a given assignment (see the discussion on behavioral controls in Chapter 6).

Exhibit 5.1 presents in a snapshot a financial reporting system defined by the Treadway Commission and gives appropriate weight to the role played by the auditors in connection to the assurance that an entity's financial reports are reliable. In planning the

Exhibit 5.1   Players Contributing to the Production and Distribution of Reliable Financial Reports

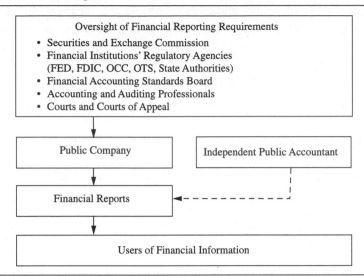

audit, new standards require the auditors to assess the company's control environment, including management and its internal control system.

The Treadway Commission further suggested that to aid auditors in designing audit tests, there should be available guidance able to present illustrative audit objectives along with examples of audit tests that may achieve those objectives. Guidance should recognize the difficulties in:

- Assessing risks.
- Designing tests.
- Evaluating audit evidence.

Further, the Treadway Commission has observed that fraudulent financial reporting usually follows a predictable path often in response to the presence of certain institutional and individual pressures. A firm opinion was expressed that this pattern differs from that of unintentional errors, which may occur randomly in the reporting process.

Reference has also been made to the fact that most fraudulent financial reporting cases unearthed by SEC show significant management involvement and include improper revenue recognition, overstatement of assets, and faulty deferral of expenses. Frequently, the Commission suggested, these improprieties were accomplished through unusual transactions near the end of a reporting period. They also occurred most frequently in industries characterized by rapid change which made the manipulation of accounts more easy, while the detection of fraud became more complex.

THE NEED FOR RELIABLE FINANCIAL
INFORMATION MADE PUBLIC

The principles advanced by the Treadway Commission have been adopted by the Fed, the SEC, and other U.S. regulators. Some of these principles have been periodically integrated in Statements of Financial Accounting Standards (SFAS) by FASB. When a company wishes access to public capital markets and credit markets, it must accept and comply by financial responsibility principles, and it must fulfill a number of obligations necessary to protect the public interest.

A good way to look at the work of COSO is that it does the utmost to maintain an environment which inspires business confidence. The current environment does not induce to business confidence, because it is characterized by:

- Creative accounting.
- Wanting ethical standards.
- Speculative derivatives trades.
- Deficient risk control methods.

Given the background of its members in reporting practices and the control of fraud, the Treadway Commission realized that one of the basic principles in building confidence in the financial markets is to assure the existence of full and fair public disclosure of corporate information, including all sorts of financial results.

The company's own board and senior management are not the only parties responsible for accuracy of financial statements. The U.S. Supreme Court has recognized that, when an independent public accountant expresses an opinion on a public company's financial statements, he assumes a public responsibility that transcends the contractual relationship with his client. The regulations and standards for auditing public companies are there to safeguard public trust, and auditors must adhere to those standards. The certified public accountant's responsibility extends to the corporation's stockholders, creditors, customers, the investing public, and the regulators.

COSO is not alone in pressing the chartered accountants accountability in these terms. In the United Kingdom, too, new accounting rules bring to bear a wide-ranging reform of the current liability regime. This is affecting both companies and their auditors and is expected to form part of a longer term, wider review of company law.

Released in mid-September 1998, one of the first installments of these new U.K. regulations sees to it that directors of companies are to lose one of the most popular tools of creative accounting that allowed them to smooth profits and disguise poor performance. New rules published by Britain's Accounting Standards Board (ASB) govern the so-called "big bath" provisions, in which companies bundle together vaguely disclosed liabilities often amounting to billions of pounds. The rules governing such provisions are now being tightened.

The Accounting Standards Board has also limited the discretion given to directors on provisions linked to acquisitions. This new financial reporting policy is the culmination of a long campaign against companies which manipulate their results by setting aside money in the accounts to cover hypothetical costs, then boost profits later on, when all or some of this money is not needed.

Like FASB in the United States, Britain's ASB, is concerned about the effect of these practices on capital markets. Share prices often rise after this sort of provisions are made, on the assumption that the money will be used to add to shareholder value. But most often creative accounting actions give a false impression of future profits.

The new ASB standard constitutes a significant step forward in the plans to define liabilities and assets in balance sheets much more strictly than in the past. The rule means that a provision can be made only when a clear obligation exists, and such obligation can be measured.

The new ASB rules do not only severely limit companies from providing for future operating costs, but also see to it that some provisions often avoided by companies will now have to be made early and in full. Failure to enact such necessary provisions has also been one of creative accounting's tools.

The implementation of both COSO among financial institutions in the United States and that of new ASB rules in Britain help to shape up a new and more rigorous internal control environment. They assure a better focus on management accountability leading to a different corporate culture. New responsibilities are added to the board of directors and to the executive committee. The lines of accountability are shown in Exhibit 5.2.

Within the landscape described by the preceding paragraph, mid-November 1998 SEC Chairman Arthur Levitt stepped up pressure on American companies to improve their financial reporting. In a speech to the Financial Executives Institute, Levitt reiterated a theme he has raised on other occasions:

• Companies increasingly are manipulating their earnings to meet Wall Street analysts' quarterly estimates.

Exhibit 5.2   The New Lines of Accountability Drawn by COSO for Financial Reporting by Public Companies

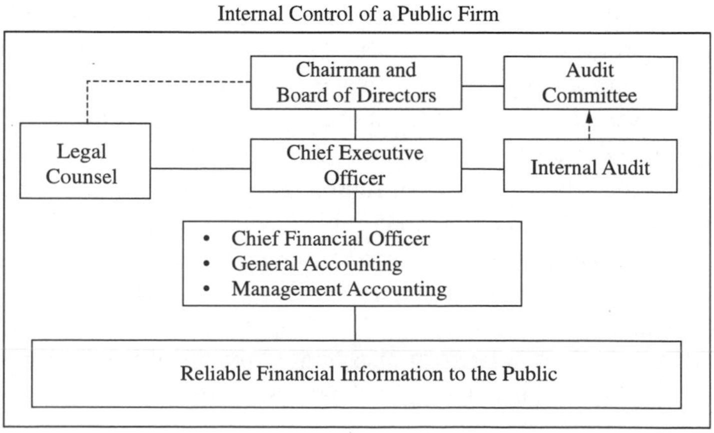

- Fearful that any shortcoming will trigger a sell-off in their stock, company management looks favorably on creative accounting.

As a result, financial reports are descending into "the gray area between legitimacy and outright fraud," with unnecessary special charges or loss reserves and inflated or improper revenue. Therefore, SEC will target inflated corporate earnings accounting.[1]

To improve financial reporting, SEC issued new accounting rules that force companies to make more disclosures on certain items, including restructuring charges, ongoing research and development write-offs, as well as loss reserves and revenue. Shareholders should be dearly interested in these issues because, in the last analysis, they answer a basic query: "What am I expecting from my investment?"

SEC also plans to present stricter rules on what items are material and thus must be disclosed to investors. For this purpose, the SEC has set up an earnings management task force, within its division of corporation finance, to crack down on improper accounting gimmicks. (See in Chapter 6 the emphasis IOSCO places on behavioral controls.)

THE COMMAND AND CONTROL SYSTEM OF FINANCIAL OPERATIONS

Whether in technology or in finance, command and control of large scale projects and processes must follow-up all events associated with day-to-day operation. This concerns a variety of issues, whether routine or extraordinary. Clear-eyed management now appreciates that for command and control reasons it is important to establish the distribution characterizing the time and frequency of occurrence of all events whose complexity:

- Necessitates a finely tuned process of internal and external supervision.
- Gives rise to increased reliability guarantees connected to financial reporting practices.

Technology plays a role in this process. The complexity associated with financial reporting by medium to large financial institutions militates against classical data processing methods and suggests the use of real-time systems. While the Treadway Commission did not enter into detail about the merits of real-time data collection and reporting practices, or the production of virtual balance sheets in 5-minutes notice, this is the conclusion reached by tier-1 banks.

The Treadway Commission did, however, consider issues associated with computer fraud. One of the studies that was undertaken documented the growing exposure to fraud created by computer systems, and explored the implications of this finding for the prevention and detection of fraudulent financial reporting. The Commission pointed out that it is difficult to segregate frauds:

- Some are aimed at manipulation of financial statement information.
- Others have as primary objectives the misappropriation of assets.

In both cases, financial results are materially misstated. The Commission also recognized an increasing potential of fraudulent reporting because of software manipulations. Based on its findings, it stated that computer fraud will increase in frequency and sophistication if:

- Corporate management, with oversight from board of directors and the audit committee does not establish and maintain adequate systems of internal control over information technology (IT).
- Internal auditors as well as independent public accountants fail to regularly review, monitor, and report on possible IT-connected fraud—as well as to suggest corrective action.

These recommendations led to a number of considerations regarding IT. Today, for instance, in many computer-run financial environments, detailed audit trails exist for only a short period of time. Therefore, the internal and external auditors find it difficult to move close to accounting transactions at their entry point into the system.

While online access to the institution's database helps in solving some of the organizational challenges facing a rigorous risk management practice, it also offers new opportunities for manipulating information elements. To improve control over financial operations, from input to processing and reporting, the Treadway Commission recommended that internal auditors need to:

- Get involved in systems development to assure needed controls.
- Integrate fraud prevention and detection measures into the IT system.

Another recommendation by the Treadway Commission, integrated into COSO, is that professional auditing standards should clarify the minimum procedures independent public accountants should perform to evaluate the computer-based part of the institution's accounting system. They should no longer take a classical approach to audits which considers mainly:

- Accounts receivable.
- Inventoried items.
- Accounts payable.

But should follow an integrative approach because of the interdependence of financial data among various functional areas. To be effective in this mission, auditors should understand the overall business environment and how the various accounting aspects relate to one another, by interactively exploiting the entity's databases.

Because of the growing complexity of financial operations, the classical analytical methods no longer provide the necessary guarantees in finding flaws in risk management practices. A rigorous solution implies the use of Monte Carlo simulation. In the longer run, most elements of modern banking resist the attempt to deal with them by traditional accounting methods. Yet, few audit departments have so far recognized the need for using both quantitative and qualitative techniques for auditing and risk analysis.

The Treadway Commission underlined that management, internal auditors, and independent public accountants all face an urgent need to become more computer literate. This was seen as critical to being better able to:

- Make decisions about the desired level of (physical and logical) security.
- Take measures to prevent, detect, and limit the potential for computer fraud.

The Commission underscored that companies need to adopt formal codes of conduct that include policies related to computer resources. Also, that internal and external auditors should make greater use of computer technology in performing online tests and audits.

The Treadway Commission also recommended that colleges and universities, as well as professional organizations like the American Institute of Certified Public Accountants, the Institute of Internal Auditors, the National Association of Accountants, the Financial Executives Institute, and the EDP Auditors Association, must do all they can to increase the computer literacy of professionals. It suggested a heavier emphasis on IT issues during professional certification examinations.

The advent of derivative financial instruments and the emphasis placed on global finance in the years following the work of the Treadway Commission, have given rise to further projects to promote command and control, with a scope greatly exceeding that of more classical banking operation. The pace of innovation in the financial industry sees to it that new products and processes are being created virtually ex novo.

Such projects evolve rapidly and their milestones of progress cannot be set without the assistance of high technology. An extensive study of organizational issues is necessary because of the impact of such processes on the institution. Organizational studies typically try to discern critical chains of business activity, anticipate adverse events, and guide action. If internal and external auditors are not able to cope with organizational changes and with technology, then fraud in financial reporting will reach an unprecedented level. Lying through models and using undocumented hypotheses will become a leveraged way of cooking the books.

SETTING STANDARDS AND CONTROLLING COMPLIANCE THROUGH OFF-SITE INSPECTION

Because it appreciated that it is impossible to set at once all rules that should in the future constitute the standards for reliable financial reporting, the Treadway Commission elaborated a hierarchy of standards-setting operations. At the top was the SEC which:

- Sets disclosure rules and standards.
- Oversees private sector standard setting processes.

For its part, FASB establishes Generally Accepted Accounting Principles for all reporting entities. But, as we have already seen, the rules established by COSO are equally important to the Federal Reserve, Office of the Controller of the Currency, Office of Thrift Supervision, and Federal Deposit Insurance Corporation.

The National Association of Securities Dealers (NASD) and stock exchanges also elaborate standards, rules, and regulations for dealers and member firms. The state government securities commissions and legislatures interpret as well as set state laws and regulations. They also address disclosure issues at state level.

An example of regulatory action regarding specific reporting requirements is off-site monitoring of thrift holding companies established by OTS. In addition to on-site examinations of thrift holding companies, OTS analysts and examiners monitor the thrifts financial condition and operations through daily reporting requirements.

The OTS is particularly interested in how ongoing changes may affect the safe and sound operation of savings and loans. The focus on off-site monitoring is to analyze changes in the thrift holding company's structure, management, assets, and liabilities.

The basic data source used in off-site monitoring are the reports thrift holding companies file with OTS, which provides information regarding changes in the corporate structure, management, and activities of the holding company, over and above the annual audited financial statements. Holding companies are required to notify OTS of significant changes to their financial condition.

OTS believes that this off-site procedure is crucial in evaluating the thrift's operation and safety. The analysis taking place complements the on-site inspection by its examiners. Based on this information submitted by the thrifts, OTS classifies the holding companies as:

- *Above average,* which indicates a clear source of financial and managerial strength.
- *Satisfactory,* corresponding to a neutral effect on the thrift's survivability, and
- *Unsatisfactory,* indicating a detrimental or burdensome effect on the thrift's operations and soundness.

Statistics on thrift holding companies are shown in Exhibit 5.3. Off-site monitoring by OTS may result in requirements for explanations and more detailed information

Exhibit 5.3 Examination of Ratings of Thrift Holding Companies and Nonbank Activities by the Holding

Rating	% of Total of Holding Companies Being Examined	% of Total of Holding Companies Involved in Nonbank Activities
Above average	13.4	37.7
Satisfactory	86.0	62.3
Unsatisfactory	0.6	—
Total	100.0	100.0

concerning certain transactions or changes in financial condition. It may as well trigger a special examination of the holding company and/or in changing the timing of the regular full scope on-site examination.

A similar concept to the outlined off-site examination is followed regarding compliance in connection to financial reporting. The method advanced by the Treadway Commission is that SEC reviews filings and interprets standards. Then, depending on the results, it enforces compliance. Similarly, NASD and stock exchanges review and enforce compliance with standards, rules, and regulations from their operational viewpoint.

A significant role is played by the courts which adjudicate government and private actions for noncompliance. In doing so, they interpret laws and rules. Both the regulators and the courts may decide on enforcement actions. A good example is the initiatives in connection to thrift holding companies by the OTS. Typical enforcement actions include the following:

- Supervisory agreements.
- Cease and desist orders.
- Removal and/or prohibition orders.
- Civil money penalties.
- Capital directives.
- Injunctive actions.

According to established policy, supervisory problems identified in examinations and off-site monitoring must be corrected in a timely manner by thrifts and thrift holding companies. OTS takes format enforcement measures for those problems *not* corrected to the satisfaction of its examiners. In addition, OTS will take formal enforcement actions when warranted by violations of statutes.

As an example of enforcement statistics, from January 1, 1993, through June 30, 1997, OTS initiated a total of 898 enforcement actions against thrifts and thrift holding companies that it supervises. Fifteen of these actions, or 1.7 percent, were initiated against thrift holding companies. Another 25 actions cited a thrift or individual as the primary cause for the action, but also involved a holding company. Of this total of 40 enforcement actions involving holding companies, only 3 were against holding companies engaged in nonbanking activities.

NOTE

1. *Business Week* (December 28, 1998).

CHAPTER 6

The Emphasis COSO, COCO, and IOSCO Place on Behavioral Controls

The acceptance of risk is an integral part of any business, but risk must be kept under control. Reliable financial reporting is a cornerstone to the management of exposure. Its able execution requires a properly functioning internal control designed to report in a dependable manner the result of operations on assets and liabilities, as well as the aftermath of all transactions that are committing the company.

While decisions should be based on reliable information, the study and analysis of behavioral patterns is equally crucial because it indicates the bank's ability to steer itself toward prudential reporting practices, without jeopardizing profitability goals. Wrong incentives see to it that risks are underestimated while returns are imaginary. Quoting Roger Lowenstein on the conditions prevailing at Salomon Brothers in 1990 prior to the change in management:

> Not a nickel of value had been built for stockholders, yet bonuses had risen every year.
>
> [Warren] Buffett and [Charles] Munger were aghast at the chaos within the firm. They and other directors did not even get an up-to-date balance sheet.[1]

In behavioral terms, Buffett feared that an irrational pay scale was not a containable problem. Lopsided rewards tend to produce irrationalities throughout the firm leading to the wrong behavior. Disincentives also exist if an institution gets its capital at risk ratios wrong, eventually running into insolvency. Effective controls, including behavioral controls, are of great importance to capital management.

The U.S. Committee of Sponsoring Organizations of the Treadway Commission is not the only entity working to revamp internal controls and behavioral processes. Another initiative in Canadian banking was known as *Criteria of Control* (COCO). It was elaborated by the Canadian Institute of Chartered Accountants in 1995. Like the U.S. initiative, the Canadians realized that adequate reporting systems can effectively assist in reducing the risks being run.

Because human nature is what it is, both COSO and COCO heavily emphasize behavioral controls necessary to manage an organization and ensure effectiveness. As we will see in this chapter, behavioral control has a dual target: Behavior as a combination of reputation, virtue, and inner strength; *and* behavior reflected in experience, clout, and effectiveness. Both in COSO's and COCO's definition, the foundation on which a behavioral system rests includes:

• Integrity and ethical values.
• Competence and operating styles.
• Management philosophy and corporate culture.
• Methods and procedures for corrective action.
• Authority, responsibility, and accountability.

This chapter goes beyond accounting principles for reliable reporting practices and into issues that connect to the second major target of the Treadway Commission: efficiency and effectiveness. Behavioral controls are an integral part of this process which is currently under study at the Federal Reserve.

The best way to describe the sense and mission of behavioral controls in financial reporting is through cross-fertilization from other fields of activity, along with a reference to the work undertaken by the Canadian financial supervisory authorities. This presentation is followed, in Chapter 7, by the bold steps now taken to assure quality control in banking—and in Chapter 8 by the principle underpinning statistical quality control (SQC).

DEPENDABLE FINANCIAL REPORTING AND BEHAVIORAL CONTROLS

Cornerstone to both COSO and COCO is the notion that organizations are as reliable as the people whom they employ. Also, quite often the question of motivation is obscure, and internal culture may play a major part in what happens. For this reason, a financial institution must provide itself not only with a suitable structure and technology but also with a qualified and ethical staff supported by a system of behavioral control.

The emphasis on behavioral science is an integral part of the rationalization of labor. Both the composition of human effort and its impact on the aggregate output of goods and services—as well as their quality—is changing, while the proportion of *intellectual capital* to other inputs, including skills, materials, and money continues to increase. This intellectual capital takes freedoms which labor did not have previously. There exists, as well, a strong correlation between intellectual capital and technological change. This works in two ways:

1. Steady innovation promotes the relative importance of intellectual capital.
2. Intellectual capital helps in accelerating technological change.

Pioneering acts of intellectual capital can be kept in control through *virtue;* but virtue, Socrates suggested, is knowledge which cannot be taught. Its outward expression is sustained through demonstration of good faith—apt to be returned in kind if not undermined by conflicting behavior.

Internal control can help in sustaining good faith behavioral patterns, by ensuring compliance with the law as well as the entity's own principles, bylaws, and regulations. Management culture plays a key role because, in the end, the spirit of compliance is as important or more so than the content of financial reports.

Globalization and networking make behavioral control more complex than it ever was. Distance sees to it that qualities of generalship such as confidence, perspective, and ability to focus on an issue become more abstract, hence less controllable. By contrast, the importance of ease in communicating, and of the gifts this might confer, increases.

One of the results of end-to-end connectivity provided by the Internet is making the products of information technology widely available and more successful, provided the benefits they offer can be effectively communicated. The other aftermath is that well-placed individuals capitalize on networked resources to propagate valuable information or, alternatively, fraudulent financial reports. Hence the need: to evaluate whether the human resources have been adequately trained, properly supported, and are of ethical standards, and to institute corrective measures based on detected behavioral patterns and their steady upgrading.

COSO advises that reliable financial reporting and human performance correlate. Like a human failure, a failure in financial reporting can intervene at any point in operations. Therefore, prudent management would seek and examine all causes of failure, including those due to personnel. If it is determined that the failure cause was human error, then it becomes necessary to decide whether:

- That error was by all likelihood random.
- There is evidence leading one to suspect that, most likely, it was intended.

If auditing establishes that by all probability a failure was due to a systematic human error, *then* senior management must not only apply penalties but also see to it that the institution's accounting and reporting systems are revamped so that this and similar intended errors can no more be repeated.

The able execution of this recommendation requires addressing both human issues and technical subjects. This dual approach is in essence implied by the behavioral aspects of reliable financial reporting advanced by the Canadian COCO.

But is it really possible to change human nature? "Now the SEC and the government think they are going to legislate human nature . . ." says John D. Spooner.[2] "Let me give you examples of why we're heading down the drain and why you've got to make your pile soon, before it's too late." Nobody can legislate human nature, but without regulation there would be anarchy.

Some financial experts look at COCO's behavioral recommendations as the banking world's equivalent of having "human components" specialists go back to the laboratory and run the suspicious sequence of events. The reason for this "back to basics" action would be to study the role played by human performance and decide on a system fix.

A system fix could conceivably be anything from making minor or major procedural changes to the reassignment of personnel to strengthen weak financial reporting nodes. This determination, COCO suggests, would be made by employing behavioral pattern trade-offs, including appropriate consideration of relative risks to be incurred under different hypotheses:

- No change to the status quo.
- A weak change scenario.
- A strong change scenario.

A strong change scenario would question the dogma of the institution's rules and by-laws. People, or at least some people, are not the purely economic creatures depicted in company statutes. Some could be motivated by loyalty; others by glory leading themselves to certain acts which end by breaking the law.

Big egos are often confronted with the dilemma between being good and making money. Then, they get into trouble by trying to kill two birds with one well-placed stone.

Any reasonable expectation of reducing the incidence of fraudulent financial reporting caused by humans requires that senior managers understand behavioral patterns and make decisions accordingly. One school of thought maintains that the performance of human components is functionally equivalent to that of machine components:[3]

- The burden of success or failure clearly rests on the correct execution of specified task(s).
- A main difference, however, is that while any machine component can fail, it is not doing so willfully.

Behavioral studies teach that there is a very simple criterion for deciding when human performance fails in carrying out the sequence of events that culminates in accomplishment of a given mission. Many elements in this approach are imported from psychology and the social sciences. Other elements have their origin in statistical quality control (see Chapter 8).

COCO pays particular attention to those tasks that are functionally critical to financial reporting, and whose accurate performance is essential for successful mission accomplishment. A vital issue in the implementation of both COSO and COCO is that of establishing a clear-cut mission profile. To help in this effort, Exhibit 6.1 portrays the complex interaction between critical mission subsystems whose input affects financial reporting policies and practices.

Each of the subsystems identified in Exhibit 6.1 is responsible for specific event(s), or a sequence of events, which contribute(s) to mission accomplishment. Each subsystem is dependent on the contribution of its human components. This goes all the way from the institution's strategies and policies, which provide the guidelines, to the advanced technology layer—therefore, the infrastructure.

Exhibit 6.1   Typical Interactions of Complex Systems, with Reliable Financial Reporting the Target Profile

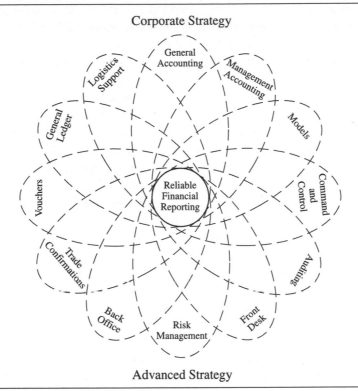

IOSCO EMPHASIZES THE INFLUENCE OF HUMAN FACTORS

The Treadway Commission and Canadian Institute of Chartered Accountants are not the only entities placing emphasis on behavioral controls. A report by the Technical Committee of the International Organization of Securities Commissions (IOSCO) aptly suggests that a control structure can only be as effective as the people who operate it. Therefore, a strong commitment by all managers and professionals within a financial institution is a prerequisite to the good functioning of an internal control system.[4]

In connection to the management of exposure, IOSCO suggests that in developing the lines of authority and accountability for internal control, a primary consideration should be the separation of responsibility for the measurement, monitoring, and evaluation of risk from the execution of transactions giving rise to the risk.

There should be segregation of duties and personnel must not be assigned conflicting responsibilities. The internal audit function must be independent of trading, lending, and other revenue side business.

IOSCO particularly emphasizes the influence of human factors in connection to the role of internal audit in analyzing accounts, evaluating qualitative business aspects, and expressing an opinion on the bank's financial statements. In executing these functions, the auditors, IOSCO suggests, should form a view on the effectiveness of the system of internal control, including behavioral patterns.

Within the framework presented in Exhibit 6.1, reliable financial reporting is ultimately dependent on the correct performance of a relatively few but crucial human tasks that should attract a great deal of attention. At the same time, precautions must be taken so that errors or fraudulent activities taking place in the execution of less critical tasks do not pass through undetected.

Because many behavioral issues exist not only in operations but also in interfaces, Exhibit 6.1 must be enriched through a third dimension to describe the multitude of interactions that actually take place. For instance, some of these interfaces may be filtering events taking place without authorization or events hiding other events.

Human factors in finance and banking also impact the reporting structure's reliability by means of incorrect assumption, lack of data, or the wrong algorithms used in modeling. In all likelihood, no one will ever learn enough about all of the details of how humans react to adverse financial conditions to build a valid prognosticator model. But what we know is that the manipulation of expected results, sometimes done through modeling, is a process just beginning.

Modeling can have a multitude of impacts. For one, it serves in using the computer as a laboratory by running simulations of the behavior of complex systems. This permits us to optimize, find the best solution, or expose possible snafus and work around them before the critical mission of the system is compromised.

But models can also be misused, sometimes intentionally so because of behavioral reasons. While there are risks arising from chronic software woes, as the year 2000 (Y2K) problem, and fiascoes associated with large computer systems, a potentially worse sort of technological risk comes from using modeling for overleveraging. This has been well demonstrated in September 1998 with the near-bankruptcy of Long-Term Capital Management (LTCM).

The misuse of models is a behavioral issue rather than a mathematic problem. Behavioral sciences teach that, in any system, human components have a much larger physiological and psychological functional capacity than the one normally required to perform an assigned task.

This reserve acts as a motor behind the self-adaptive capability possessed by humans. But it can also have *unintended consequences* if ingenuity is applied to socially unacceptable aims.

Adaptation makes human elements most valuable in the performance of certain missions. A critical question, therefore, is how to preserve human ingenuity and adaptation while blocking ways and means leading to fraudulent financial reporting. This challenge is present in every banking environment, as well as in other fields, such as engineering, manufacturing, and merchandising.

Exhibit 6.2 presents a summary of considerations that govern the choice of human components and machine components in system design trade-offs. While engineering experience has been a primary criterion in this classification, the listing can just as well serve other industries. We can appreciate the relative strengths of men and machines in regard to key performance criteria.

Exhibit 6.2 Performance Criteria and Relative Strengths of Men and Equipment

Humans	Machines
• Discriminate differences in, and patterns of, stimuli.	• Are sensitive to finite stimuli.
• Store and recall critical information.	• Are capable of continuous monitoring.
• Have inductive reasoning.	• Exhibit accuracy and precision.
• Do variable tracking and control.	• Execute very well routine and repetitive tasks.
• Perform fine manipulations.	• Are capable of status control.
• Have adaptability and variability.	• Exhibit accessibility and serviceability.
• Have physiological limits.	• Feature stability control functions.
• Have psychological limits.	• Have quick compensatory responses.
• Could escape from stress and recover.	• Can be designed with redundancy for greater reliability.

A system design team concerned with predicting human errors and with avoiding the occurrence of intended deviations can learn a great deal from behavioral sciences. Exhibit 6.2 reminds us that men and machines have relative strengths and weaknesses in achieving a prescribed level of effectiveness that contributes directly and without equivocation to final results.

APPROACHES TO THE PREDICTION OF HUMAN RELIABILITY

Some 40 years ago, based on his work at Aerojet-General of Sacramento, CA, A.B. Pontecorvo suggested a method for predicting human reliability. Though this work was connected to liquid rockets, its fundamentals are applicable to internal control in banking. This case is an applications example with significant potential and an excellent reference in behavioral analysis.

One of the notions underpinning the Pontecorvo method is the ability to grade human dependability and evaluate the degrees of unreliability as well as its likelihood. This is vital to an accounting system where conditions can be greatly affected by human components and interfaces.

COSO, COCO, and IOSCO promote the application of behavioral controls, but this type of study is still in its infancy among financial institutions. However, there exists a wealth of knowledge on behavioral controls in engineering. We can therefore benefit from an interdisciplinary approach.

The need for constant vigilance is a common ground between engineering and some areas of banking operations, characterized by the requirement to maintain readiness to face potentially severe conditions. The method we will study sees to it that long and complex procedures can be analyzed by keeping under perspective the factors that tend to reduce overall dependability.

Every financial institution has a number of domains that should be evaluated for the implementation of the Pontecorvo method. To do so, procedures must be analyzed to isolate error-prone nodes and links. Once the weaknesses are identified, it will be possible to handle the actual cause(s) with greater accuracy than has previously been possible.

Important to the dependability of human factors is accuracy in translating information into meaningful terms so that current and potential problems can be effectively solved in a pragmatic way, applying corrective action that leads to meaningful results. The problem with behavioral approaches is that, by and large, their outcome has been limited to qualitative statements. This is true regarding a number of issues, including those that concern man-machine interfaces. What is now needed is:

- Practical methods for providing a reliable measure on how the human interface functions.
- A dependable way of predicting the performance of the financial reporting system.

In terms of behavioral factors, for example, it is important to know what kind of incremental improvement—or degradation—accrues as a result of human intervention. When this information is lacking, management decisions tend to emphasize the nuts and bolts of accounting rather than how these nuts and bolts can be, or are, manipulated by human elements.

Behavioral scientists ascertain that many gaps in supervision can be closed by directing attention to tasks that are facilitated, hindered, or altogether altered through personnel behavior. According to this school of thought, behavioral science also indicates factors that permit us to understand and improve the design of a financial system, leading to increased accuracy and dependability of human contributions to reporting and other practices.

Critics of this thesis suggest that a much more crucial factor is the qualitative and quantitative analysis of failures of human performance, whose aftermath is unreliability of results and fraudulent financial reporting. These two viewpoints might be reconciled if we keep in mind that behavioral studies try to determine the:

- Estimation of level of dependence on successful human performance, judged by clearly set criteria.
- Allocation of functional requirements to be accomplished by personnel at a pre-established level of dependability.
- Systematic collection of qualitative and quantitative data on the adequacy of human task performance in relation to defined mission(s).

Central to the convergence of the two schools of thought is that the attainment of qualitative goals should be complemented by quantitative evaluations. For instance, recording and observing human performance in daily operations; analyzing antecedents to specific failure events in order to determine whether human error is a primary or secondary cause; evaluating detectable trends to fraudulent activities, and so on.

A good example on how these principles can be applied in finance is *pay-for-performance*. Well-managed institutions have no problem with extraordinary pay performance, but quite often an initially sound system of rewards degenerates to share-the-wealth—subsidizing everybody, even the mediocre at shareholder's expense.

At some Wall Street firms, earnings before compensation and taxes are available for bonuses at the rate of 55 to 80 percent, and sometimes this ratio hits 100 percent, leaving very little in terms of stockholder value. The equity, therefore shareholders, take the risks, but managers and traders collect the rewards.

THE IMPACT OF HUMAN FACTORS ON ERROR RATES

At the conceptual level of a financial reporting system design, behavioral scientists maintain that they can anticipate a high degree of success by specifying the profile and qualifications of human components. This should include the virtues and skills of personnel to be employed in accounting and financial control functions. After the general gross level system decisions are made, an analysis is undertaken to:

- Derive detailed behavioral characteristics.
- Project likely behavior in specific applications areas.

The analysis done by Pontecorvo at Aerojet-General was outstanding because it combined qualitative and quantitative approaches along the frame of reference outlined in the previous section. The procedure described in the following paragraphs combines task ratings with empirically based data, in the derivation of a regression line regarding error rates associated to human factor dependability.

While this method was principally developed to study and quantitatively assess man-machine interactions, it also provides data on task analysis which is important to internal control and financial reporting missions. The core of this study has been the human element as a systems contributors relating the necessity of engineering human factors solutions concurrently with the development of machine components, rather than waiting for a laborious and often costly trial-and-error postmortem solution to problems posed by human unreliability.

The motivation behind this study has been the increasing criticality of error consequences to the proper functioning of man-made systems, and the crowding of human capabilities beyond anything previously experienced. This state of affairs often leads to functional defects. Similar factors are present in modern finance.

Among the criteria Pontecorvo used were human physical tolerance to stress, matters concerning intellectual functions, and the ability to transform information in a meaningful manner. The latter issue was judged through observable events. One of the findings from this behavioral study was that it is not sufficient that a human factors analysis has specific data on separate and distinct human capabilities. There should also be a practical method for describing functional relationships that exist in the system.

In terms of behavioral science, these functional relationships could be used to predict performance with sufficient validity so that costly errors might be eliminated, or at least controlled through precise knowledge of what can be expected from human performance in the longer run. Let me add some hindsight to better explain this reference.

In the years that followed World War II, there were several attempts at resolving the problems posed from negative effects connected to human interactions, particularly regarding weapons systems. Researchers attempted to identify and quantify human errors that might result from different ways of performing a given task. Task reliabilities, however, were:

- Either so discrete that they could not be combined into a meaningful whole.
- They were composed of several subtasks difficult to identify and analyze individually.

One of the challenges was that the number of errors related to one task may exceed the number of subtasks to be performed. A.B. Pontecorvo developed a method by which it was possible to predict the effect of man as a systems contributor. Although made initially to prognosticate degradation resulting from periodic maintenance performed on rocket engines, its value extended to reliable accounting and financial reporting.

This behavioral approach derives a mathematical relationship between a previously quantified observation of one small segment of human performance, in terms of its dependability, and a judged or predicted value of a like segment of behavior. The method utilizes similar system configurations applied to a specific condition. It then combines the observed event and the judged event.

This integration takes place through a mathematical formula that helps to foretell the dependability with which a human element will perform a given task. The method's procedural aspect has been divided into the following seven steps:

1. Identify each of the tasks to be performed.
2. Divide each task into its elements (subtasks).
3. Collect empirical performance data for each subtask.
4. Establish the error rate of each subtask.
5. Develop a regression equation based on error rate and sum of ratings.
6. Compute task dependability based on human dependability.
7. Account for human redundancy in the execution of a given task.

Similar to the method used in engineering and the physical sciences, in banking the first step is to identify the task to be performed at gross level, so that each task represents one complete operation. For instance, "perform a functional check on derivative positions in connection to interest rate exposure."

This gross system mission is made up of subtasks which need to be executed either sequentially or in parallel, to complete the operation. Analysis into subtasks should take place in a way that it is possible to observe if the person responsible for this mission has performed what was expected in a dependable manner, or, the work raises questions about the quality of output.

Let's take, as an example, risk control associated to the late September 1998 meltdown of Long Term Credit Management (LTCM). The United Bank of Switzerland, a money center bank found itself with both feet in the sea of LTCM's red ink and lost $1.04 billion in the hedge fund's near bankruptcy. It also had to pour into the wounded company another $300 million because of the salvage by the Fed of New York. This event indicates a significant level of human unreliability at two levels: Risk control and top management.

The executive vice president of UBS in charge of risk management, who was subsequently fired along with the chairman and two other senior executives, explained his approach to the control of exposure in the following way: "To include the LTCM monthly data into daily calculation of the consolidated value-at-risk (VAR) at Group level, we always input to the model the last available intrinsic value of LTCM supplemented by artificial data computed by us."[5] The "last available intrinsic value" was provided to UBS by LTCM once per month:

- The VAR model, its daily calculation, and the computers on which it ran was the machine component of the risk control system.
- Using obsolete monthly information as input to a daily run and "artificial data" was part of human unreliability.

When such incomprehensibly silly statements are made by highly paid bank executives, it is unnecessary to proceed with Step 2 of the Pontecorvo method: The identification of finer task elements. If the gross system level is rotten, this provides full evidence on the lack of human dependability. But it is necessary to look into further detail to assign precise accountability. This is done through steps discussed in the next section.

AN ANALYTICAL APPROACH TO PERFORMANCE MEASUREMENTS

COSO states that the degree to which an institution is likely to succeed in its objectives is dependent on the extent to which it regularly creates a clear and compelling focus for its activities. This is done through vision, clear goals, proper planning, leadership, and an informed reading of the results being obtained as well as the deviations.

Other factors, too, impact on the reaching of objectives. One of the most crucial is the degree to which it secures the commitment of the organization's principal players, focusing their efforts through a supportive culture and appropriate merits (rewards) as well as demerits (penalties):

- Merits and demerits are the proverbial carrot and stick.
- Rewards can be so much more effective when they are specific and awarded in a factual manner.

Merits and demerits work best when they identify themselves to the finer task elements: Once the gross task has been rated, it must be broken down to its basic components or subtasks necessary for its completion. In finance, subtasks may correspond to functional checks consisting, for instance, of carefully estimating current exposure on all interest rate, currency exchange, equity, and commodity-related positions. Performance information should be available for each subtask being rated:

- From data capture.
- To information handling by the accounting system.
- Reliable financial reporting.

Empirical data should reflect the ultimate conditions under which the rated subtask will be performed. Because in-house operations take place to a very large extent online involving computers and databases, information elements are generally available on human performance dependability—even if they are rarely used in reliability studies.

To assure objective reporting of errors versus performance, strict attention must be given to the method by which this data is handled. Every effort must be made to assure objective reporting of errors. If need be, human performance data being acquired online can be enriched by experiments under controlled conditions. The concept underpinning this process is that to arrive at element reliability each subtask must be rated in accordance with its level of difficulty, likelihood of being manipulated, and error potential.

The rate to be used should be based on the evaluation of a sufficient number of units to permit an adequate judgment of degree of unreliability. A ten-point scale, from least error prone to very error prone, is recommended because it permits sufficient breadth for a statistical evaluation.

Pontecorvo advises that no attempt should be made to predetermine the exact type of error that might evolve during performance. But the analysis should specify that there might be an error as a result of task difficulty or, in finance, of both the difficulty and likelihood of unreliability of the task. Under this principle, each subtask must be rated in accordance with its judged error potential. Typically, the ratings are statistically summarized, and a pooled rating is assigned to each element of the task under evaluation.

The next analytical step is based on the statistics being collected, and it consists of developing a regression equation. This provides the means with which subtask dependability could be predicted. Empirical data and judged ratings must be expressed in the form of a regression line which is tested for goodness of fit.

This approach reflects the functional relationship between an established value and the prediction of that value. It also provides a measure that describes the precision with which human performance dependability could be prognosticated.

The regression line shown in Exhibit 6.3 is based on the work Pontecorvo did at Aerojet-General. It is the line of best fit and is expressed in logarithmic form as:

$$Log\,E = -2.9174 + 0.006122\,R$$

where E = Error rate = 1 − Empirical dependability
R = Pooled rating of error likelihood

Exhibit 6.3   Error Regression Line Based on Ratings and Error Rates from the Aerojet-General Application on Human Factor Dependability

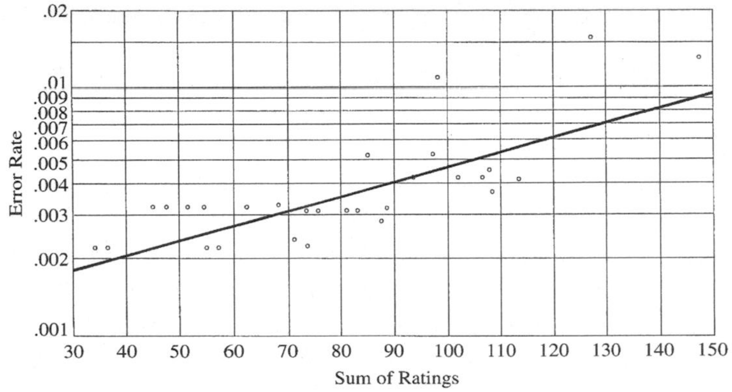

Once developed, a regression line similar to that in Exhibit 6.3 can be used to help in making subtask dependability estimates for which there is no empirical data. A sound approach is to see to it that a regression line is developed for every task and for every critical subtask.

Note that this is not a risk measurement system connected to derivatives financial instruments, loans, or any other banking product. It is a system oriented to the measurement of human dependability associated to the task which must be executed. As such, it is different than other methods available so far, which target different objectives than the behavioral aspects I am describing.

Because behavioral studies like those advised by COSO, COCO, and IOSCO have not yet been done in banking in any significant amount or depth, we should be eager to learn from what has been achieved in other domains, transforming, adapting, and applying the results to our work. The following section emphasizes this aspect of cross-fertilization which can provide an implementation based on interdisciplinary approach.

LEARNING THROUGH INTERDISCIPLINARY CROSS-FERTILIZATION

The next step is to establish task dependability. One of the challenges in this step is to assign dependability estimates to subtasks, as suggested or derived from a regression line similar to the one in Exhibit 6.3. Total task dependability can be obtained as the product of the subtask dependabilities—combined to provide an estimate of human contribution to system performance.

In connection to this last statement, there is an interdisciplinary contribution: The reliability algorithm known from missile studies. A.B. Pontecorvo advises the use of the reliability equation for the estimate of human dependability. Reliability theory states that system reliability is the product of component reliabilities:[6]

$$R = R_1 \cdot R_2 \cdot R_3 \text{K } R_i$$

where R = Systems reliability

R_i = Reliability of each component i

The reliability equation is based on the Weibull distribution, which is a modified form of the Poisson distribution. Both the Weibull distribution and the Poisson distribution are currently being used in connection with rigorous analytical studies in finance, for instance, in the analysis of risk derived from derivatives exposure.

Let me first take an engineering example to explain this concept. There are four different ways for connecting points A and B. One alternative is to have one link. Another, to have two links connecting A and B in parallel. At equal level of component reliability, this second alternative is more reliable than the first. If one of the two links fails, but the second functions, the message will be transmitted from A to B.

A classical example from banking, in ways and means for improving reliability, is the requirement that two executives sign important checks. These two components must work in parallel to produce a throughput. Contrary to the engineering case, they complement one another in a control sense. This is so embedded in daily practice that it often is taken for granted.

The reliability equation, which we just saw, and whose usage was suggested for human dependability, needs to be modified to account for this sort of redundancy. Such modification should bring into the picture the predictability of increase in dependability of task elements based on redundant subtasks.

A careful look at accounting procedures and principles of COSO will help in effecting such modification. Accounting can profitably learn from other professions who faced dependability problems in the past. This reference brings our discussion back to the principle of redundancy as used in engineering design to provide equipment back-up in the event the single component fails completely or fails to operate as projected.

In technical terms, a connection from A to B through an intermediate node C is less reliable than the examples preceding it because it features two limits in series. Both of them must be functioning for a message to be transmitted from A to B or for a banking operation to be executed, requiring the services of both the account manager and the teller.

Another way to interpret the meaning of this engineering reliability estimate when applied to trading, investing, loans, and accounting, is that the greater the number of important subtasks given to the same person, the lower is the overall dependability connected to this person. An example is combining front desk and back office functions under the same executive—as it happens in so many institutions, a flagrant example being the Barings operations in Singapore.

These are simple examples, while real life is much more complex. Instead of two links: A to C and C to B, there may be 10, 20, or 100. Reliability curves with n components ($n = 1 \ldots 400$) as shown in Exhibit 6.4 help you appreciate the rapid deterioration in

Exhibit 6.4   System Reliability Is a Function of the Average Reliability of the Components and the Number of Components

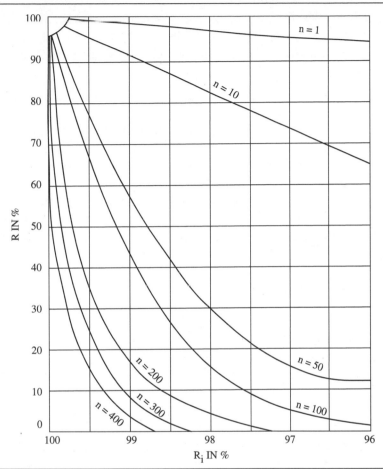

reliability of a given system when the number of serially connected component parts increases.

You will further notice that the outlined method of calculating human reliability can as well be applicable to the evaluation of the performance of one person acting alone. The seventh step in the Pontecorvo list accounts for this case. Where operator backup exists or is anticipated for some or all of the subtasks, the algorithm should be modified to account for it.

Converting the reliability concept discussed in this section into a tool applicable to banking operations at front desk or back office, the backup system based on a second, independent human component assigned to a given task or subtask can be expressed as a function of four variables:

R_1 = Reliability of one person

R_r = Redundant reliability

t_1 = Time (in %) a second person is available for the redundant effort

t_2 = Time remaining wherein the second person is unavailable for this specific subtask $(-t_1 + t_2 \leq 1)$.

In those cases where a task or a subtask is critical and incremental reliability improvements cannot be achieved through procedural design, task element redundancy may be investigated as a valid solution. This, too, is a concept that has been applied in engineering, hence with a precedence in successful applications.

It is proper to add to this procedure the necessary means for validation. To do so, I will revert to the original work by Pontecorvo. The method he outlined has been validated through performance data obtained during reliability studies on the basis of the ratio of the number of successes to total attempts. In Aerojet-General, the number of attempts reported for the various subtasks ranged from 12 to 2820, with confidence intervals being a function of sample size.

For those results which were statistically significant, a rank-order correlation and a chi-square test were performed to assess the relationship between predicted and observed reliability estimates and to test the adequacy of predictions.

Results indicated a significant relationship between predicted and observed reliabilities. This promoted the method's potential usefulness as a predictive tool for the early identification of potential problem areas.

The method just described permits an analysis of human functions inherent to a system. It also makes feasible a predictive measure of performance. As such, it provides the means whereby existing data may be used to extrapolate on conditions or procedures not previously observed or recorded, to provide for system dependability incorporating the behavior of human factors.

NOTES

1. R. Lowenstein, *Buffett, the Making of an American Capitalist* (London: Weidenfeld and Nicholson, 1996).

2. J.D. Spooner, "Smart People," *From Members Only,* David T.W. McCord (Ed.) (Boston: St. Botoloph Club, 1980).

3. D.N. Chorafas, "Man Is a Machine Component," *Product Engineering* (New York: December 30, 1957).

4. Technical Committee of the International Organization of Securities Commissions. *Risk Management and Control Guidance For Securities Firms and Their Supervisors* (Montreal, Canada: IOSCO, 1998).

5. *CASH,* No. 40 (Zurich, Switzerland: October 2, 1998).

6. D.N. Chorafas, *Statistical Processes and Reliability Engineering* (Princeton, NJ: Van Nostrand, 1960).

CHAPTER 7

Measuring and Managing the Quality of Financial Services

The second major milestone suggested by the Treadway Commission for the reliability of financial statements is efficiency and effectiveness. A good way to distinguish between the two terms is that *efficiency* is doing things the right way, while *effectiveness* is doing the right things. This is Peter Drucker's definition we quoted in the Preface.

The exact issues included under the headline of efficiency and effectiveness, and the tools that are necessary, are still under development—but there is a major decision by regulators that the measurement and control of the quality of financial services should be at center stage. As explained in Chapter 6, the Canadian authorities have already focused on Criteria of Control.

No company can hope to keep its customers if they are provided with less than the best available quality, or a quality inferior to that offered by its competitors. This is true all the time and for all firms—particularly so in banking as the industry moves from traditional to highly innovative products.

There is no lack of formulas that can be used in conjunction to a quality control program. Some of these formulas have the added advantage that they make it possible to customize the solution to an institution's individual requirements. As we will see in this chapter and in Chapter 8, statistical quality control (SQC) methods and tools have this characteristic.

Many of the SQC tools were developed during World War II in conjunction with the Manhattan project. At that time, Monte Carlo simulation, which found a great applications domain in finance, was developed.

While statistical methods are widely used today in finance and banking, statistical quality control charts are not yet a household item—yet they provide invaluable assistance to management because they demonstrate both analytically and graphically the evolution of quality assurance and/or of internal control findings. To capitalize on this tool, an institution must develop a program that focuses on data collection from ongoing operations, identifying the tolerances within which, in principle, such data should fall.

From the manufacturing industry to banking, long runs can benefit from standard statistical quality control charts. Where runs are short, it is often better to individualize SQC charts adapting them to characteristics of each case.

An integral part of a statistical quality control process is the need to install a sound sampling program, also determining desirable quality levels. The institution must select one or more sampling plans in a way able to meet quality levels for different lot sizes.

Not everything, however, is quantitative. The right quality control program would be designed to handle qualitative information, as well. Exemplified by quality circles used by Japanese banks, management should hold regular statistical quality conferences with personnel and during these conferences evaluate the quality picture and quality problems.

An equally crucial issue is the ability to steadily refine applications of all quality control tools being used, to obtain greater accuracy and make the results more meaningful to senior management. Top management, too, must make a contribution by assuring that quality control operations are run by people with ability and integrity—people senior executives are very comfortable with.

FINANCIAL INSTRUMENTS WHOSE QUALITY MUST BE CONTROLLED

The discussion on qualitative and quantitative disclosures by financial institutions, and on associated quality assurance procedures, will be so much more rewarding, if we first define the type of financial instruments subject to such disclosures and the transactions affecting them. Exhibit 7.1 presents a comprehensive display of instrument types and transactions:

- *Spot, forwards,* and *options* are the types of transactions.
- *Interest rates, currency exchange rates,* and *equities* are the instruments.[1]

Exhibit 7.1   Types of Instruments and Transactions Whose Quality Is Subject to Control

Transaction / Instrument	Spot	Forwards	Options
Interest rates			
Currency Exchange rates			
Equities			

Plain cash in base currency (the primary currency in which the institution establishes its balance sheet), as well as cash in equities and other currencies, are *spot* positions. With *future cash flows,* we enter the domain of *forwards.*

Forwards include future cash flows not just in base currency but in any pair of currencies, as well as when equity or other commodity is exchanged for a currency. Forwards address not only currencies but also interest rate agreements and all commodities in which the entity trades. Futures are exchange-traded forwards. The difference between forwards and *options* is:

- With forwards the instruments *will* be owned some time in the future.
- With options it *may be* owned at some time in the future.

This freedom of choice between "will" and "may be" is conditioned by the future market price of the instrument. To gain such freedom of choice, the option buyer pays a price to the option writer, which is largely determined by the likelihood that the buyer will exercise the option.

While cash comprises only a small fraction of the assets of any entity (as well as of the monetary base),[2] it is the common denominator of all financial instruments whether spot, forwards, or options. This is true whether transactions and inventoried positions concern interest rates currencies, equities, or other commodities.

In the balance sheet, a much larger segment of assets and liabilities consists of contractual obligations to deliver cash, and of rights to receive cash from the counterparty. Discharging these obligations and honoring the contractual rights is done by means of cash flows.

In contractual terms, in the framework of Exhibit 7.1, interest rate instruments like bonds represent a sequence of future cash flows. Bonds are forwards, and the same is true of forward rate agreements (FRAs) and interest rate swaps (IRS). Bond options and swaptions are classified at the options column of the interest rate class.

All transactions in Exhibit 7.1 have characteristic risks. Basic currency cash may be subject to inflation or other sovereign risks like a decree taxing cash holdings (Greece, 1922; Italy, 1994). Bonds are subject to the uncertainties of the yield curve, spread risk, duration, liquidity, and specific risk. Swaptions face an important volatility risk as well as the risk that the closer the spot price is to exercise price, the more difficult it is to anticipate whether the option will or will not be exercised.

Foreign forwards, cross-currency swaps, and forex options are graduations of currency exchange products. Notice that every time there is a change in the reference framework, going left to right in Exhibit 7.1, the level of risk increases. Foreign cash has currency risk and sovereign risk, but cross currency swaps have both foreign exchange and interest rate risk.

Commodity prices fluctuate and the same is true of shares. In a way, shares could be seen as options on commodities. Shares of gold mining companies, for example, are options on gold bullion. All options, whether interest rate, currency exchange, equities, or other commodities have volatility risk and curvature risk (gamma risk). Curvature is the volatility of an option's sensitivity to spot market risk (price of the underlier).[3]

If we are able to develop and use a dependable model, we can employ it to study a number of crucial factors connected to future gains and losses because of the contents of our portfolio, including the aftermath of volatility on our holdings. For instance:

- The aftermath of movements in spot exchange rates taken one at a time (interest rate, currency rate, equity index).
- The effects of decay in options as we move forward one day, week, or month while volatility, interest rates, and other parameters remain constant.
- The way volatility affects portfolio value, under different hypotheses of change from one day (or other period) to the next.

Frank Partnoy gives a good example of quality control in banking:

Morgan Stanley imposed strict quality controls on the new MX trade (a derivative instrument designed specifically for Japanese investors). The rocket scientists . . . couldn't afford even slim margin of error. Initial test results were positive, but the derivatives gurus at Morgan Stanley continued to tweak and fine-tune this turbo-powered trade. It had to work perfectly.

Quality control awareness has came into the mainstream of finance. It started with derivatives and became a major issue practically overnight. If quality control tests are passed successfully the instrument is marketed with confidence—without a day's delay. Says Partnoy, "Once the trade had been tested, the preparation for launching would require *only a few hours* of actual work. Properly executed, the MX trade would not expose Morgan Stanley to any unwarranted risk. Just a few days and it would be over."

Modeling and simulation help to increase the quality of exposure management in *our* bank, in connection to both market risk and credit risk. The proper handling of counterparty accounts would look not only on collateral the customer posts, but also how exposed this customer entity is elsewhere, and how the value of its collateral changes with the market.

A crucial issue in quality control associated with loans is what kind of collateral *our* bank takes and what haircut it applies. A sound principle is to take only first class securities when extending credit. One should never accept nonliquid collateral, and steer away from the counterparty's own shares offered as collateral. UBS broke this rule in its highly leveraged deal with LTCM.

Models can help to experiment on risk and return with projected transactions, as well as to study modifications to specific deals to find out if future policy concerning such deals should be altered. For instance, we could do a test of hypothesis marking options to their theoretical value, displaying the difference between this and current market value or other chosen parameters.

Depending on the technology supporting this data mining, experimentation, and visualization, the method just described can be adopted for intraday trading and intraday control of exposure. In principle, risk management should move as fast as the trading process. We can as well:

- Test our estimates of correlation and volatilities with these outstanding in the market,
- Reset limits that have gone out of tune with prevailing market conditions, and
- Detect on intraday basis the violation of set limits by branches, desks, and traders.

Because technology plays such an important role in the quality control of banking operations, institutions using the best in software, computers, and communications are ahead of the curve. Therefore, a key question in judging the level of technology is to ask: What exactly is top management expecting?

QUALITATIVE AND QUANTITATIVE DISCLOSURES BY FINANCIAL INSTITUTIONS

The same query is valid in connection to financial reporting to the authorities, and the reliability attached to such disclosures: What do you expect to get from the established solution? Classical reporting requirements for banks have been accounting-based, hence quantitative. More recently, regulators also demand qualitative disclosures. These provide an overview of:

- Business objectives.
- Risk-taking philosophy.
- Management intent.
- How well lending, investments, trading, and derivatives activities fit the objectives.

An integral part of qualitative disclosure is the types of internal control procedures that are in place for managing the institution's day-to-day business, watching over possible violations, and preserving its assets. This provides the bank's management the opportunity to elaborate on, and provide depth to, quantitative disclosures in the annual report. According to the COSO philosophy of reliable financial reporting, this meets a dual goal:

1. It co-involves the board and the institution's senior executives in restating and affirming management's policies and plans.
2. It provides regulators a better understanding of the quantitative part of a financial report, comparing it to the institution's objectives.

This dual approach of quantitative and qualitative reporting goes beyond COSO. Within the Basle Committee framework (see Chapter 3), credit institutions are encouraged to include an overview of key aspects of the organizational structure and their policies, which are central to the institution's risk control process for lending, investing, and trading.

Another Basle Committee guideline is the inclusion of a description of each of the major risks arising from an institution's derivatives and other business activities, including credit risk, market risk, liquidity risk, operational risk, and legal risk. Also, the methods used to measure and manage these risks. For instance, polices that limit exposures to market risk and credit risk, and an explanation of how value-at-risk measures are used to control market risk.

In the Group of Ten countries, regulators increasingly require a discussion of how the institution assesses its performance in managing the risks that it faces. Equally important is information about the overall objectives and strategies of trading activities, involving all on-balance and off-balance sheet components.

The added value with COSO comes from the new quantitative forms of internal control and regulatory reporting that are being devised within the framework of the effectiveness and efficiency target, which employs quality control concepts. Let me briefly elaborate on this approach. Whether in banking or in the manufacturing industry, we are typically concerned with two aspects of quality:

1. Determining the quality of an individual item or unit of product, for instance, an account, a watch, or an automobile.
2. Determining the over-all quality of a process or of a given group of individual items, products, or accounts, which are parts of the same process.

Statistical theory and quality control practice based on this theory provide a number of plans for evaluating and describing the quality of an item. We can use one of several types of inspection, our choice depending on the product or process, the characteristic being measured, the method most appropriate for making such measurements, and the approach which can provide the more reliable results. For example:

- Inspection by variables.
- Inspection by attributes.
- Percent defective.
- Number of defects per unit.

These inspection plans provide a descriptive approach answering the question: "How well?" and (if there are deviations) "By how much?" This approach is quantifiable and leads to visualization of results. By contrast, an explanatory approach along qualitative reporting lines answers the question: "Why?"

Both with the descriptive and the explanatory approaches, the answer given involves an element of causal inference. That's why statistical quality control charts used in the financial industry help to merge qualitative and quantitative characteristics. The transition moves from quantitative reporting through classical accounting to qualitative reporting by means of management disclosure to qualitative and quantitative reporting through charts that aid in quality control.

In industrial statistics, for instance, we use the control chart to focus on a certain element of operations in parts manufacturing or in connection to the output of the assembly line. The chart improves the production process by removing the disturbing influence of some nuisance factor. It provides a good explanation. This process of interfacing between qualitative and quantitative description has its counterpart in finance.

THE QUALITY CONTROL INQUIRY COMMITTEE AND USE OF PROCESS CONTROL IN BANKING

In the United States, there is a Quality Control Inquiry Committee (QCIC). Its activities are promoted by the Securities and Exchange Commission Practice Section (SECPS). A goal of this committee is to enhance the opportunity of identifying information elements relevant to quality of audits performed by companies and certified public accountants.

The objectives followed by QCIC are very close to the use of quality control charts in the banking industry, and more generally in financial reporting practices characterizing other industry sectors. SECPS member firms must report to the QCIC all litigation or regulatory proceedings involving:

- Audits of public companies.
- Compliance issues concerning financial institutions.

Quality control is the main theme highlighting this approach to reporting that must be done within 30 days of receiving a complaint. The QCIC has the responsibility to determine if the allegations suggest:

- An aberrational error.
- A defect in the firm's quality controls.
- Matters concerning compliance.
- A shortcoming in professional standards.

All of these are excellent domains where statistical quality charts could be applied (see Chapter 8). Statistical theory is rich both in control procedures and in investigative tools. Graphic plots can be instrumental in visualizing the quality of outcome of a certain product or process.

Contrarians might say that while such practice may be beneficial in the process industry, it has little to do with banking. But banking has many of the process industry's characteristics. An example from process reengineering as it has been implemented by Deutsche Bank will illustrate this.

Under controllership, Deutsche Bank has created a department of *process re-engineering* with four main functions: Quality assurance, business processes re-engineering, financial system architecture for control purposes, and a task force for global key projects. Quality assurance concerns itself with products, processes, and people, with the goal of improving standards and quality of the output. Business process re-engineering defines core businesses, addresses the adequacy of IT and maps key operations into the computer.

Applications domains of statistical quality control are being tested by the Federal Reserve in collaboration with major American banks. There is a trend toward tighter quality control standards and the use of statistically based inspection procedures.

This approach to quality assurance supports the mission of the Public Oversight Board (POB) in the United States that looks after all QCIC inquiries into alleged audit failures involving public companies. Auditing results can be nicely mapped in statistical quality control charts, thereby providing an enhanced capability of inspection.

Quality control procedures can be combined with algorithms permitting behavioral analysis, explained in Chapter 6. Behavioral states may be decomposed into underlying substates. Transitions are the means through which an entity changes state. Normally transitions have an explicit event trigger, time elapsed, or the effect of parameters describing actions associated with a transition.

Transition matrices (Markov chains) are often used in banking, particularly in connection to the rating of counterparty risk by independent agencies, as shown in Exhibit 7.2. Transitions may have guards, or clauses, that are evaluated when an event occurs. However, the same event trigger may occur on multiple transitions with different guards.

Alternatively, a state machine can be expressed through state charts defining submachines, nested states, conditional transitions and their occurrence, actions on state entry or exit, and activities within states. The behavior of each of these submachines or processes can be mapped into a statistical quality chart, permitting to visualize the output as a function of time and of its observance of tolerances and control limits.

Transitions pertaining to a financial instrument, transaction, or process may have multiple sources and merge into a single outgoing transition. They may also bifurcate going from a single source state to multiple targets. Actions may as well be associated with transitions. They are executed if, and only if, a specified event takes place.

Critical to reliable financial reporting is the fact that the expression of behavioral patterns through transitions provides a strong base for modeling concepts concerning human behavior. It may also help in modeling structural views, which are important to the analysis of systems with compliance characteristics.

The synergy of behavioral transition matrices and quality control charts can help in mapping a financial institution's response over time to issues concerning regulation and supervision. The staff of the Public Oversight Board, for example, reviews both the plaintiff's allegations and the QCIC's staffs analysis of them leading to values that can be effectively plotted in a chart. Board members or staff attend meetings between firms

Exhibit 7.2   Average One-Year Rating Transition Matrix, 1920 to 1996

Rating From:	Rating to:								
	Aaa	Aa	A	Baa	Ba	B	Caa-C	Default	WR
Aaa	88.32%	6.15%	0.99%	0.23%	0.02%	0.00%	0.00%	0.00%	4.29%
Aa	1.21	86.76	5.76	0.66	0.16	0.02	0.00	0.06	5.36
A	0.07	2.30	86.09	4.67	0.63	0.10	0.02	0.12	5.99
Baa	0.03	0.24	3.87	82.52	4.68	0.61	0.06	0.28	7.71
Ba	0.01	0.08	0.39	4.61	79.03	4.96	0.41	1.11	9.39
B	0.00	0.04	0.13	0.60	5.79	76.33	3.08	3.49	10.53
Caa-C	0.00	0.02	0.04	0.34	1.26	5.29	71.87	12.41	8.78

Source: Courtesy Moody's Investors Service.

reporting litigation and QCIC task force members, and participate in discussions about committee recommendations and the way these have been carried out.

Statistical quality charts can play a significant role in both cases. They can also constitute permanent quality control records since the sensitivity of the QCIC proceedings and concerns about litigation see to it that the only documentation retained by the committee is a copy of the complaint and the staff's analysis of the allegations.

Statistical quality control charts and transition matrices can be effective for another reason. Because most cases are not adjusted the way it has been recommended, it is difficult to accumulate data relating to the outcome of reported failures through verbal reports, particularly data relevant to the determination of audit failures. It is even more difficult to subsequently exploit these verbal reports to develop a pattern. It these cases, quality control charts are the answer.

In this and similar cases where quality control is very important, both regulators and the bank's senior management may use SQC to obtain and retain the pattern of process behavior. This is doable during study and subsequent evaluation of obtained results. Two fundamental issues must be resolved to make reports on internal controls meaningful to external parties:

1. A determination of what kind of controls should be reported constituting the system's *boundary,* and
2. A decision on what level of weaknesses should be acknowledged in these reports, forming the *threshold.*

Part of reporting on the threshold is the answer to the query: To what extent should quality and its variations be described? This is a complex issue to be resolved from several viewpoints—regulators, auditors, shareholders, lenders, the board, and senior management—paying attention to the data needs of each party and the bank's ability to derive meaningful information from pattern analysis.

WHAT MANAGEMENT SHOULD APPRECIATE ABOUT CONTROL OVER QUALITY

Auditing the financial books is a control process well embedded into banking culture. Process inspection is the initial step forward from the old technique of sorting faulty accounts from good ones, after the damage was done. The adoption of process inspection by both internal and external auditing greatly improved the quality of accounts. Many reasons underpin the wisdom of this approach, and how fast economies rebound often depends on the speed with which they fix their banking systems.

In banking, as everywhere, careful planning is necessary to see that all data of value as well as quality information are handled efficiently. The quality history of any item, product, transaction, or account must be clear, valid, and available for immediate control. Only then can we derive the maximum benefits from an inspection. Financial reporting must be realistic. That's why in 1999 the SEC targeted inflated corporate earning accounting.

The use of statistical methods in conjunction with process inspection in banking is a major step in solving the problem of controlling quality of financial reporting. Implemented within the context of COSO, methods based on mathematical statistics are providing the modern financial industry with a powerful tool.

This is synonymous to saying that decisions must be based on verifiable data. There is a wealth of information occurring every day from financial transactions, accounting records, and other processes, which can be put to work to make better quality products in the banking industry.

An efficient system of collection, organization, and analysis of data can economically provide the necessary information for making quality decisions. But the board's and senior management's understanding and appreciation are required, *before* any technical tool can be used with maximum value.

The principles, methods, and tools of statistical quality control should be carefully explained to all people who make the program successful. This is true all the way from board membership to the rank and file in the organization.

The foundation and success of a quality control program lies in its ability to sell itself to those that must use it and/or should base their decisions on it. The value of a chart for controlling quality, for example, is greatly enhanced when there is an appropriate attitude, which helps in its interpretation. Without it, the quality program could well be working in a vacuum. This means that everybody in the institution should understand the principles and tools of statistical quality control, and its objectives. Only then can real progress be made as data is accumulated and graphs are plotted.

One of the questions often asked is: "What about the cost associated to quality control?" An easy answer is that nothing is as expensive as poor quality. A more precise answer is that the same data collection process needed for accounting serves in quality control. Quality is remembered long after costs are forgotten. The variation inherent in any process, which is tracked by accounting, is the crux of statistical quality control. Because variation is inevitable, it helps in focusing on possible problems.

As long as variation is inside acceptable specifications, the system is in control, but when variation is excessive, an investigation should be made followed by corrective action.

Unlike accounting which records variation in financial data in the books, but reports only final figures, SQC tracks variation tick-by-tick. The basic problem of any quality control process is to determine whether variation is normal—that is, kept within pre-established tolerances—or excessive. The statistical tools for solving quality problems rest on three fundamentals:

1. Chance causes of variation exists in any process, product, transaction, or account.
2. Acceptable limits of this variation must be defined.
3. Variation outside a stable pattern indicates a change in the system. This change must be discovered and corrected.

The role played by sampling plans, frequency distributions, control charts, and statistical evaluation techniques (see Chapter 8) is to target the pattern of chance variation, as well as its deviations. Accounting systems do something similar, but in a different way, in a different time frame, and for a different purpose.

The tool for determining the pattern of variation for a given variable as a result of the system of chance causes is the frequency distribution (see the following section). The normal frequency distribution, or bell curve, is shown in Exhibit 7.3. Important characteristics of any frequency distribution are the mean and the spread:

- The *mean* $\bar{x}$ is the measure of central tendency of the pattern of variation.
- The *variance* S^2 indicates the pattern of the distribution around the mean.
- The *range,* or *spread,* R is a measure of the amount of variation inherent in the process under investigation: $X_{max} - X_{min}$.

The square root of the variance is the standard deviation, s; it is also the second moment of the normal distribution. The first moment is the mean. The third moment is skewness and the fourth is kurtosis.[4] We will not concern ourselves in this text with skewness and kurtosis because they are not so important in the implementation of SQC in banking, though they are crucial in other types of analysis.

The spread of a frequency distribution must be less than the total tolerance allowed by the specifications. If this is not true, then a certain percentage of failures will result in terms of observing the tolerances. *Confidence limits* are multiples of the standard deviation that play a dual role.

Exhibit 7.3 indicates the values at the tails of the frequency distribution within which is contained the 90 percent, 95 percent, or 99 percent of all recorded events. While the complement of this percentage—10 percent, 5 percent, 1 percent—tells what's the level of confidence that the values of events would fall within stated limits.

In connection to a two-tailed distribution, the 99 percent of all measurements fall within 2.60s; within 2.34s is the 98 percent of all measurements. But with a one-sided (transacted) distribution (when we are interested only on a higher or only on a lower value), the 99 percent of all measurements are within 2.34s.

Exhibit 7.3   The Bell-Shaped Curve of the Normal Distribution

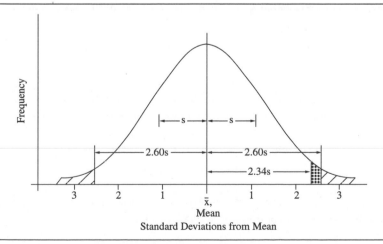

By using the frequency distribution as a tool for comparison, a wealth of information can be obtained from a statistically valid sample of data. This is done with the 1996 Market Risk Amendment by the Basle Committee and the use of value-at-risk (VAR). It is also one of the reasons why quality control charts can provide a high degree of assistance to the financial industry, as we will see in the following sections.

THE ROLE OF STATISTICAL INVESTIGATION IN QUALITY ASSURANCE

The concept of using mathematical statistics for quality control purposes was introduced in 1924 when Dr. W.A. Shewhard—who often published under the pseudonym Student— wrote a memorandum on techniques for obtaining better homogeneity of products. This memorandum resulted in the control chart which, in 1929, was enriched by sampling tables published by Dr. Harry Roming and Harold Dodge.

During the World War II years, the Columbia Research Group at Columbia University, developed sampling plans for the U.S. Navy which resulted in MIL-STD-105A. This document and its more recent versions constitute the Bible for quality control.[5] Such sampling plans, statistical tables, and quality control procedures are based on the hypothesis that process data are normally distributed as discussed in the previous section.

This assumption is consistent with the fact that the most common pattern of variation shown by a frequency distribution is the bell-shaped curve (Exhibit 7.3). Classically, the use of statistics in connection to financial information tends toward the hypothesis that many, though not all, frequency distributions in banking approximate the normal curve. Its popularity rests on the fact that the theory underpinning it is of much practical value particularly because of the existence of rich statistical tables.

Knowledgeable analysts neither accept wholeheartedly nor reject outright the hypothesis of the normal distribution. They accept or reject this hypothesis only after tests done on the population (or sample) of data they work with. If the hypothesis of a normal frequency distribution is accepted, then the bell-shaped curve presents an excellent opportunity for understanding the basic theory underlying statistical quality control.

The normal distribution does not apply to all situations. A similar statement is valid about the hypothesis concerning linearities. For this reason in banking, we increasingly use nonlinear models for financial analysis. Such models are not addressed here but can be found in other references. The application of chaos theory in the financial markets is an example.[6]

The basic notion behind the use of mathematical tools for quality control reasons is that while a statistical investigation may have no purpose other than description, it leads to an explanatory scenario since the latter is always an integral part of a description. At the beginning of any statistical investigation is the orientation and facts collecting phase, which provides material for causal analysis. Typically,

- *Description* includes primary measurements, tabular and graphic presentation of facts, and the assessment of collective characteristics.

- *Explanation* targets the specification of causal hypotheses and their testing against empirical data, permitting meaningful conclusions.

These pillars of a rigorous statistical analysis should be followed by the application proper which includes some element of prediction: The inference drawn from the observed sample is extended to some other sample, different in time, space, or otherwise. This is the notion underpinning the use of confidence intervals.

Statistics permit us to formalize the process of analysis and offer an algorithm for the computation of confidence intervals. This process of inference is an integral part of business life.

When the population of events is large, inference is usually based on conceptually defining, and/or physically drawing, a *sample*. Let me briefly explain the notion of a sample, though this will be discussed in greater detail in Chapter 8. The total transactions our bank did in a month is the population. Though we might like to audit the whole population transaction by transaction for quality assurance reasons, this is time consuming and costly. Instead, internal audit takes a sample through the use of a table of random numbers or by means of stratified sampling.

Auditors and other examiners often do stratified sampling taking a sample from the subset of larger transactions. The inference on the quality characterizing the population is based on the results of inspecting this sample and drawing a conclusion.

Experience from the manufacturing industry that is now being transferred into banking indicates that statistical quality control tools and methods apply best when units are produced in quantity. This premise is fulfilled in banking using transactions and accounts. Also, when the quality characteristics, and their measurement, vary, all financial transactions and all accounts, like all processes, exhibit variation if we take fine enough measurements. When this variation increases, we may have a quality control problem, hence, the wisdom of using statistical charts.

When I make this statement at the senior management level of financial institutions, the answer I typically receive is: "But we have always made money using the system we have. Why change?" This might sound logical, but it is not so. My response is: "You will not be making a radical change. All the know-how and experience with the current method will still be needed. Quality control charts are tools enabling senior management to go further in being in charge of the situation, because they sharpen the decision-making process."

Management which is worth its salt should always be eager to improve its ways and means for process control. The performance of a financial institution, like that of any other company, is variable. Nothing works on a straight line. Therefore, statistical charts can be used to advantage. The control of any variable or attribute can benefit from the use of statistical evaluation methods, if there are too many variables to control, this is one more reason for applying SQC.

Used in a complex environment such as banking, a statistical quality control plan will help determine which of many possible causes is really affecting quality, and by how much. What is more, the implementation of SQC is flexible. The economics of the situation and the length of runs help determine the exact approach to be used.

Banks, which have tested statistical quality control, comment that it can be applied to as few as ten pieces of an account or event. As for the argument that the methods and tools of statistical assurance are too technical and involve something of a revolution in thinking, the answer is that they are not more complex than other tools used in finance.

TYPES OF STATISTICAL QUALITY CONTROL PLANS

Some people argue that the theoretical model on which statistical analysis is based can be specified with less exactness and detail when passing from experimental to observational data. They also suggest that this shift in emphasis leads to only a partial reorientation of current techniques. These arguments, however, forget the critical role played by the hypotheses which we make, the estimation procedures we adopt, and the testing of our hypotheses, which must be based on facts.

The conclusion(s) reached with statistical analysis of observational data is dependent on rigorous statistical theory, sampling methods, and reality tests against evidence that can only be provided through formal inspection plans.

Inspection by *attributes* sees to it that a chosen characteristic is observed or checked with a measuring device that serves as a standard. Then, it is classified as either satisfactory or unsatisfactory depending on the outcome of such go/no-go gauging. In manufacturing, inspection by attributes is very helpful for checking dimensional properties of parts. In banking, this method includes attributes of accounts as defined by:

- The law.
- Regulators.
- The bank's own policies.

In an inspection by attributes, units, products, or accounts are classified as acceptable or not acceptable.

For instance, an account may be correct (go) or show some type of deviation from norm (no-go). Attention should be paid to the fact that in an inspection by attributes a unit, product, transaction, or account is classified as "defective" or "nondefective" with respect to a given requirement or set of requirements. In principle, it does not matter how small the deviation from norm may be. What matters is the existence or nonexistence of a deviation.

Inspection by *variables* is different. The metric system is not a go/no-go gauge but one permitting continuous measurements to, say, four digits of accuracy. Such process makes it feasible to evaluate the quality of an item on a continuing measurement basis. The actual measurement of the quality characteristic we are after is taken and recorded.

In a sample, we compute the mean and standard deviation. In a chart, we plot these means against the mean of the means, x, its tolerances, and its quality control limits (see Chapter 8).

Typically, the continuous scale against which a chosen characteristic is measured may be one of many. For instance, in industry it may be grams, inches, volts, or seconds.

In finance, it may be an inhouse score system of counterparty rating used for loans.[7] (See also the discussion on operating characteristics curves in Chapter 8.)

As its name implies, *percent defective* is a statistical quality control plan which focuses on the percentage of defective items in a defined lot. These may be accounts, violations of prudential limits set by management, or other criteria, processes, or events. Such a method is most commonly used in describing lot quality and is the basis on which many sampling plans have been constructed. A great number of financial applications can benefit from percent defective statistical plans.

Statistical percent defective is the ratio of identified defective items to the total number of items in the sample, times 100. A variation of this quality control plan is the number of defects per 100 units of any given product, type of transaction, or account, which was described as number of defects per unit.

Counting *defects per unit* is the approach chosen when quality characteristics of many transactions, accounts, or other items are evaluated by literally counting the number of a given type of defect. This is different than measuring the quality of a lot that will be described in terms of percent defective or an average number of defects. By and large, the choice depends on the nature of the product, and the ultimate use of the chart.

Where sampling inspection is used, the choice may also depend on the nature of the sampling procedure that is available, as well as the average number of defects per item. For instance, item quality is measured by counting the defects per unit for each item, then averaging out among the items in the sample.

Whether the inspection is by attributes, variables, or any other, there is no simple magic formula for a statistical quality control program. Each application, each plan, each chart must be tailored to fit the particular problem at hand. But there is a common concept behind the benefits that will appear through:

- Increased efficiency.
- Reduced costs.
- A lower exposure.
- Improved product quality.

On these basic concepts rests the use of statistical quality control banking and finance. It is only reasonable that the board and senior management should expect returns on investment (ROI). Therefore, it is vital that all levels of management are thoroughly sold on statistical quality control to ensure enthusiasm behind the program all the way down the line. It is just as important to select the most appropriate type of SQC plan.

The goal of every one of the plans we have considered is to show the prevailing pattern of variation. In any quality control process, the pattern of variation describes the value at which the quality characteristic has been measured under certain conditions, the central tendency (expected value), standard deviation, and frequency distribution characterizing the pattern of variation.

Statistical methods are so deeply embedded in banking today that it would be irrational not to benefit from the best that are currently available. The notions detailed in this chapter are fully applicable in banking, just as they have been widely used in the manufacturing industry. Everything handled through transactions, whether spot, forwards, or options can benefit from statistical quality control.

The effects of volatility on interest rates, currency exchange rates, and other commodities can be effectively visualized through SQC charts.

Trend graphs, scatter diagrams, and regression lines are a less controllable means or procedure which do not provide a crisp pattern. The value-added characteristic of SQC charts is the ability to apply limits that make more meaningful the direction of the trend line; hence, the element of decision-support.

Financial applications of statistical quality control can greatly benefit from cross-fertilization—which is one of COSO's goals. In Chapter 8 we will examine how to apply the statistical tools whose concepts have been described in this chapter. Readers with a scant background in mathematical statistics may wish to skip the next chapter and go directly to Chapter 9 which focuses on regulatory guidelines.

NOTES

1. Other commodities are included with equities since, with the exception of specialized firms, they represent a small part of the bank's trading business.
2. D.N. Chorafas, *The Money Magnet: Regulating International Finance, and Analyzing Money Flows* (London: Euromoney, 1997).
3. D.N. Chorafas, *Advanced Financial Analysis* (London: Euromoney, 1994).
4. D.N. Chorafas, "How to Understand and Use Mathematics for Derivatives," *Advanced Modeling Methods,* vol. 2 (London: Euromoney, 1995).
5. Available from the U.S. Printing Office (Washington, DC).
6. D.N. Chorafas, *Chaos Theory in the Financial Markets* (Chicago: Probus, 1994).
7. D.N. Chorafas, "Credit Risk Management," *Analyzing, Rating, and Pricing the Probability of Default,* vol. 1 (London: Euromoney, 2000).

CHAPTER 8

Using Statistical Quality Control in Banking

Fifty-five years of experience in applying statistical quality control in the manufacturing industry demonstrate the flexibility and adaptability of SQC methods. As Chapter 7 underlined, each application can be tailored to the particular situation at hand. The prerequisite is that of building a framework through which the financial institution can find its way to fit statistical quality assurance plans to the particular problems with which it is currently confronted. Prerequisites are:

- Selling to senior management the concept of quality control of financial services and of expected benefits.
- Establishing a procedure for standardizing, collecting, databasing, and datamining quality data pertaining to inspection.
- Using frequency distributions in connection to critical variables, for comparison purposes and for determining whether operations are in control.

"When we look at the future of business," says Warren Buffett, "we look at riskiness as being a sort of go/no-go value. If we think that we simply don't know what is going to happen in the future, that does not mean it is risky for everyone. It means *we* don't know that it's risky for us."[1]

This go/no-go concept can be extended to the test of inventoried positions in a portfolio of shares, debt, or derivative financial instruments. All portfolios must be frequently evaluated in terms of recognized gains and losses (see Chapter 13), therefore of exposure. For every evaluation, the more so for one made by means of models (therefore with some degree of approximation), it is most helpful to have a pattern that can be checked at all times and deviations corrected before it is too late.

There exists significant synergy between auditing, the assurance of quality of services, risk control, and senior management decisions, particularly those concerning corrective action based on internal control findings. This synergy can be fully exploited through patterns developed by means of statistical quality control plans:

- Auditing identifies defaults in accounts and measures fraud. It does so through appropriate description.
- The methods and tools of SQC provide a comprehensive visual image of variation that characterizes the bank's quality of services, and also serves auditing.
- Risk management plans, algorithms, charts, and procedures bring to attention the level of exposure and help to keep it under control. SQC is a tool in this effort.
- Rigorous investigation by senior management seeks to find out the reasons and assign the responsibilities. This is the job of explanation and decision assisted by SQC.

A frequent situation is that description by auditing serves to maintain some modus vivendi by focusing on the control of transaction pattern, comparing it to established standards for accounting (see Chapters 11 and 12). By contrast, the visualization of variability and trends provided by SQC serves this purpose of accountability as well.

When internal control is executed in an able manner, it sees to it that quantitative visualization is employed as an aid in the adjustment to given conditions, while explanation is a vehicle for qualitative expression of conditions prevailing in the environment. The use of statistical quality control methods and associated mathematical tools, which are examined in the present chapter, should be seen under this dual perspective. Exhibit 8.1 lists the symbols used in SQC.

CONCEPTS UNDERPINNING THE APPLICATION
OF SAMPLING PLANS

Sampling has been briefly described in Chapter 7. Sampling plans are the foundation of a sampling inspection procedure. Typically, such plans are classified by sample size, a measure of the amount of inspection required, and acceptable quality level (AQL) of the lot (or sample). This is the percentage of defects for which the probability of accepting a lot containing that percentage of defective items has a given level of significance. The concept of level of significance, or confidence, has been introduced in Chapter 7 and is further explained in the following section. Indeed: Bankers are well acquainted with the 99 percent level of significance from reporting value at risk (VAR) to supervisors. This same notion underpins sampling plans and SQC tools, as well as the contents of this chapter and any application based on operating characteristics (OC) curves.

Whether we talk of financial accounts or manufactured products, satisfactory quality levels cannot and should not be based solely on individual units—and quality metrics judged through the attention a craftsman gives to each part. Because mass production of goods and service and mass handling of transactions and accounts is the order of the day, it is no longer practical to sort item-by-item and review each one's quality after they have been made.

The answer in terms of assurance of satisfactory quality without examining everything being made, is the use of sampling plans and statistical inference. The first step in utilizing sampling plans is to realize that this is a reasonable compromise and not an absolute guarantee.

Exhibit 8.1   Symbols and Abbreviations Used in Statistical Quality Control

SQC	Statistical Quality Control
P_A	Probability of a lot being accepted by a sampling plan
AOQ	Average Outgoing Quality
AOQL	Average Outgoing Quality Limit
AQL	Acceptable Quality Level
LTPD	Lot Tolerance Percent Defective
OC	Operating Characteristics
OCC	Operating Characteristics Curve

Sampling:

ASN	Average Sample Number
N	Number of items in lot (or population)
n	Number of items in a sample
c	Acceptance number (i.e., maximum number of defective pieces allowable if sample is to be considered satisfactory)
p	Percent defective

$\bar{x}$ and R Charts:

x	Measurement of one item in a sample
$\bar{x}$	Mean value of a sample
$\bar{\bar{x}}$	Mean of mean values
R	Spread, or range, of a sample
$\bar{R}$	Mean range
$UCL\bar{x}$	Upper Control Limit for sample averages
$LCL\bar{x}$	Lower Control Limit for sample averages
UCL_R	Upper Control Limit for sample ranges

A sampling plan works in accordance with statistical laws and its results are always subject to probabilities. But over a period of time, a sampling plan will give desired protection, even if there are risks associated with any variable.

A standard or normalized sampling inspection procedure is a procedure for selecting and using sampling plans in accordance with statistical theory. With a standard procedure, the range of choices is narrowed to relatively few alternatives, with detailed prescriptions becoming available for choosing among them. A normalized approach leads to quality control decisions through established evaluation steps.

Typically, a random sample is taken from a lot and a decision is reached to accept or reject it based on the number of defectives found in the sample. This critical number of defectives is specified through available statistical tables based on the normal distribution (see Chapter 7).

There exist different sampling methods and choice among them is usually influenced by intended use. This choice should take place at the beginning of a quality control program, in full consideration of the dynamics of the statistical inference we are after. A postmortem choice is like betting on a horserace after the horses run their course.

One of the critical questions with sampling plans is that of sample size. Neither a constant percent sample from a given population, nor a constant sample size are sound policies. Constant percent samples have proven disastrous to many production activities and, though a better method, constant sample size is not as sophisticated as other alternatives to single sampling, for instance:

- Double sampling.
- Sequential sampling.

In a single sampling plan, only one sample is taken and a decision is made to accept or reject the lot. Single samples are typically based on a desired quality assurance and lot size, as well as the process average for the past several lots. As we will see in the following section, the operating characteristics curve is instrumental in providing the necessary level of assurance.

With a double sampling plan, the lot may be accepted if the first sample is good enough, or rejected if the first sample is bad enough. The definition of what is "good enough" and what is "bad enough" is part of the statistical sampling plan. If the results of testing the first sample are between these two values, a second sample is taken and a decision to accept or reject the lot is then made. The criteria for designing an appropriate double sampling plan are:

- Lot size.
- Desired quality level.
- Process average.

While it is possible to accept or reject on the first sample, a more informed decision could be done by taking another sample. Depending on the circumstances of the application, double sampling can save inspection costs, because the first sample is smaller than the sample needed for a single sampling plan. If the quality of the lots being sampled is good, the lot will pass on the first sample. There is also the psychological factor of a second check.

Sequential or multiple sampling plans are, as the name implies, an extension of double sampling with some variations. Sequential sampling and multiple sampling are terms that are used by most people interchangeably, but in reality multiple sampling is a truncated sequential plan. It may have four, five, or six steps similar to those we saw with a double sampling plan.

The Risk Adjusted Return on Capital (RAROC) by Bankers Trust is a good example of a sequential sampling plan. Scoring substitutes for percent defective. A prime rate corresponds to the best score. Every successive column in Exhibit 8.2 has a lower score but a higher interest rate. To the bank, this interest rate differential provides a sort of reinsurance policy. This is an example of quality control by attributes.

Exhibit 8.2   A Sequential Sampling Plan Permits Avoidance of Inflexible Yes/No Decisions Taking a Reinsurance for Higher Risk

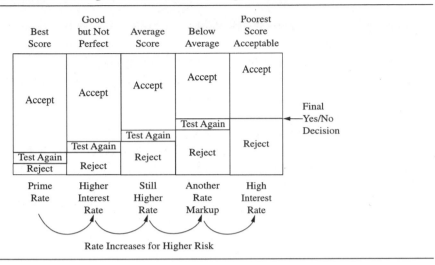

The sampling sequence with a sequential plan is ended by an accept or reject decision on the final sample. This is fundamental with any plan leading to a financial decision. Because a decision must be made to accept or reject, the sample size on which this decision is based should be statistically sound reflecting:

- Process average.
- Desired quality level.
- Lot (or population) size.

The theory of sampling requires that the sample taken be random. This means that each part in the lot has equal chance of being in the sample. There may, however, be stratified sampling plans, where some strata require a larger sample because of the value of the items they contain, or the (lower) quality of these items. (An example was given in Chapter 7.)

Stratified sampling is used with auditing, and it should not be confused with the way we define the population of items or accounts subject to SQC. Take a bank's accounting books as an example. If the quality is found to vary appreciably from one accounting book to another, it is desirable to sample each book as though it were a separate lot. If some of the books present problems while others are up to standard, then a larger sample will be taken for auditing from the defective books—all the way to 100 percent inspection.

Some practices of an inspection process sometimes followed by auditors, such as taking most of the items from the first transactions in the general ledger, can lead to non-random sampling. If so, the results will be misleading in deciding acceptance or rejection. Statistical sampling is characterized by rules which must be followed. This contributes to the effectiveness of financial controls.

BENEFITS PROVIDED BY THE OPERATING CHARACTERISTICS CURVE

Typically for every sampling plan there is an operating characteristics curve, which shows how the plan will perform as lots of different quality levels are submitted to it. The shape of an OC curve is a function of both sample size and percent of the population. It indicates the likelihood that a lot of a given level of attributes or percent defective may be rejected while, overall, it is of acceptable quality.

This is known as an α, Type I error, or producer's risk, and it is shown in Exhibit 8.3. It defines the level of significance in VAR and other tests by presenting the likelihood of a happening—therefore the confidence attached to test results. Without this error, the lot under statistical inspection may be accepted as satisfactory, when it should have been rejected.

This is known as β, Type II error, or consumer's risk. The β in Exhibit 8.3 should not be confused with β indicating volatility, though both volatility and Type II error are conditioned by the standard deviation of the normal distribution.

One way of improving the operating characteristics of a test is to decrease the standard deviation of the statistic being tested. The variance around the mean represents variability in the measurements that we make. Therefore, high quality production has a small standard deviation:

- High quality usually results in fairly uniform items, but not in clones.
- Low quality is characterized by significant differences among items and their measurements.

Exhibit 8.3   Operating Characteristics Curves for Sampling Plans

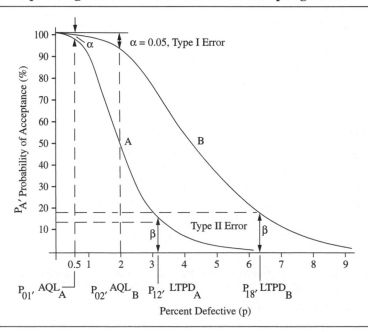

There are statistical means for decreasing the standard deviation, and different plans exist for this purpose. One of them is to take a lot size half as large as the original. Another is to double the size of the sample, but while the OC curve steepens and β shrinks, there will always be present α and β. If n is the size of the sample and N of the population, it is possible to reduce the variance by:

- Decreasing N, while holding n constant.
- Increasing n, while holding N constant.
- Increasing n and N, while holding constant the ratio n/N.

In general, the effect of varying the sample size n is more important than the effect of varying N. Also, the absolute size of the sample is more critical than its relative size. These notions should always be kept in mind not only in designing a sampling plan but, also, in all financial applications of statistical measures.

OC curves help in calibrating sample size in regard to lot size, because they visualize the effects of lot size and sample size on operating characteristics. Type I and Type II errors exist because the percent defective in a sample may be more or less than the actual proportion of defective items in the lot. Under any lot-by-lot inspection plan based on statistical sampling:

- A lot with a higher percentage of defectives than that wanted will occasionally be accepted.
- Conversely, because of α, a lot which is acceptable will occasionally be rejected.

After all, which are our alternatives? The concept a 100 percent inspection provides 100 percent protection is a chimera. Because of a number of reasons, a 100 percent inspection would not correct the aforementioned failures, while significantly increasing the cost. With sampling, the number of the lots that would be accepted and the number that would be rejected would depend on both:

- The nature of the inspection plan used.
- The actual percentage of defective items in the lots under inspection.

Furthermore, never underestimate the power of the hypotheses that are made and of the sampling plan being chosen. The reason for a questionable outcome in a statistical test and in modeling at large, may be the assumptions that were made, unwarranted simplifications, or erroneous data.

Incomplete and inaccurate information is often at the origin of test failures and of model risk. Considering questionable information elements as *defects,* in the sense of statistical quality control theory, we can plot the go/no-go in a c-chart of percent defective. Thereafter, as go/no-go tests accumulate, we can visualize the quality of our data resources.

A similar plan can be used in testing for *anomalies,* a term which became popular among many financial analysts. But other experts are critical of it. "I have always found the word 'anomaly' interesting," says Warren Buffett. "What it means is something the academicians can't explain, and rather than re-examine their theories, they simply discard any evidence of that sort."

When a truly analytical mind finds information that contradicts existing beliefs, he or she feels the obligation to look at it rigorously and quickly. The problem with the majority of people is that their mind is conditioned to reject contradictory evidence, or simply to express disbelief. An ingenious use of statistical theory can turn anomalies into extreme events with a certain likelihood. This is very useful for risk management and other reasons.

As we will see later in this chapter (Developing and Using Quality Control Charts by Variables), an SQC chart is characterized by an expected frequency, upper and lower tolerance limits, as well as upper and lower quality control limits which fall *within* the tolerances. A process which is *in control* behaves within the quality limits—though there may be from time to time outliers.

If these outliers are frequent, and if there is a trend outside the limits, *then* we must search for cause and effect in order to correct the origin of the failure. The cause may be a radical change in the process or an unsuccessful assumption about normality. Hence, an out-of-control trend can be a prognosticator of extreme events.

The hypotheses we make, the quality of our database and the assumptions about outliers and extreme events correlate. COSO concentrates on accounting connected to reliable financial reporting, but the notions discussed in this section came into banking following the 1996 Market Risk Amendment[2] and have been strengthened after the LTCM meltdown. Capitalizing on what has been learned because of lightweight hypotheses and rather incomplete models of LTCM, regulators increasingly require banks:

- To rethink their internal risk management and internal controls systems.
- To disclose more about their exposure to hedge funds, both as investors and lenders.

As we will see in Chapter 16, while still a discussion paper the New Capital Adequacy Framework by the Basle Committee emphasizes *transparency* as a condition for eventually allowing banks to use their internal risk management models in calculating how much capital they need to put aside. A greater emphasis is placed on the accuracy of hypotheses and of information elements.

Many of the assumptions made about anomalies also may be dented. Most institutions assume that hunting for anomalies across a wide range of markets increases their profit potential and reduces their risk. But, as recent events have shown, it is possible that the identification of anomalies is nothing but an illusion—while the market has surprises shown as extreme events that can be effectively tracked by means of statistical quality control charts.

There is still another field where OC curves can be helpful. Regulators now worry that technology and the growth of global institutions that rely on risk models may boost the chance of further storms. Therefore, they would like to audit internal controls and associate the results to the amount of capital that financial firms hold to protect themselves against extreme conditions, such as events that trigger a vicious liquidity-draining circle.

THE NOTION OF AN ACCEPTABLE QUALITY LEVEL

In selecting a sampling plan, one should have specific knowledge of how each of the available alternatives differentiates between good and bad lots. Such information can best be presented as an operating characteristic curve: Each point on this curve shows on the ordinate the frequency of accepted lots, while the corresponding rating in percent defective, p, is found through the projection of this point on the abscissa.

The OC curve is a vital instrument in quality analysis and should be carefully studied in deciding the sampling plan to be used. An OC curve incorporates the assumption that lots rejected by the sampling plan will be sorted out for control action.

In Exhibit 8.3, the acceptable quality level (AQL) is the percent of defective items in an inspection lot. Two OC curves are shown. In curve A, $\alpha = 0.01$. The corresponding acceptable quality level gives a 1 percent chance of rejecting a submitted good lot containing 0.5 percent defective. This corresponds to the 99 percent level of confidence, whose notion is embedded in the 1996 Market Risk Amendment by the Basle Committee.

If the lot acceptance plan accomplishes its full purpose, the process average will become at least as small as p_{01}. The probability of this happening is α. The counterpart to this plan is the lot tolerance percent defective (LTPD) which corresponds to β and identifies a lot of sufficiently bad quality that we do not wish to accept more than a small portion of items.

No two OC curves are the same. In Exhibit 8.3, curve A provides a better protection than curve B. The careful reader will notice that in operating characteristics curve B, $\alpha = 0.05$ at AQL. Correspondingly, the percent defective is 2. At that level, 5 percent of good lots will be rejected.

Banks that tend to cut corners with the 1996 Market Risk Amendment should take good notice of what has been explained in the preceding paragraphs. By choosing the 95 percent level of confidence rather than the 99 percent stipulated by regulators, they are heading for trouble.

Quite often, decisions on level of confidence are made without good understanding of the fundamentals. As a result, plans for control of exposure are wanting and in real life they don't pass the feasibility test.

Let's now look more carefully at the β component. The way to interpret the OC curve in Exhibit 8.3 under plan A, is that if lots of 0.5 percent defective are submitted to this sampling plan, the consumer has a 12 percent risk of accepting bad lots. Under plan B, which features lots with 2 percent defective at AQL, bad lot will be accepted 18 percent of time—which is high. Usually this share should be below 10 percent. The 18 percent level and even the 12 percent level that are admitted, can be improved (reduced) by steepening the OC curve. As explained earlier, this can be done by increasing the sample for the same population, reducing the population for the same sample, or both.

The previous section also posed the question every manager should ask: What are our alternatives? The alternative to accepting a certain level of risk is a 100 percent inspection, and this is not a good solution. A properly studied sampling plan presents a better protection, which costs less and the risk is measurable. The range between outgoing quality level and lot tolerance percent defective (LTPD) shown in Exhibit 8.3 represent the better overall solution that is currently available.

To appreciate the statement I just made, we should look more carefully into two more terms associated with statistical sampling: The average outgoing quality (AOQ) and the average outgoing quality limit (AOQL). Both are used in connection to operating characteristics curves:

- AOQ is the expected fraction defective after substituting good items for bad ones in rejected lots (or correcting the identified account errors), and in samples taken from accepted lots.
- AOQL represents the value of AOQ for lots that are at best average outgoing quality—or, the best average quality that can result over a period of time under the chosen sampling plan.

AQL and AOQL correlate. Among them, they help define the worst quality at which we are willing to buy most or all of the lots. Its likelihood is defined by α, whose meaning has been explained. Alternatively, LTPD defines the best quality at which we wish to buy almost none of the lots. This is the sense *lot tolerance percent defective,* and its likelihood is defined by β.

In Exhibit 8.3, AQL and LTPD are, respectively, indicated by percent defective p_0 and p_1 (p_{01}, p_{02} for OC curve A, and p_{12}, p_{18} for OC curve B). The best examples on how to use p_0 and p_1 for quality assurance reasons come from manufacturing. However, the concepts are just as applicable in banking and finance.

Of critical importance is the procedure to be used in connection with transactions and accounts. A hard-hitting successful program of statistical inference based on outgoing quality level must be carefully planned, kept simple, and have clear-cut directives. It must be accompanied by an understanding and appreciation of the method just explained, as well as have positive cooperation and participation of all personnel: from top management to lower levels of supervision.

What this and the preceding sections have outlined are basic statistical techniques. Conceptually more complex are the test of hypothesis as well as significance tests such as the chi square, t and F tests, which serve as indices on variation from a standard.[3]

Financial analysis can greatly benefit from experimental design, particularly targeting analysis of variance through Latin squares and Greco-Latin squares. There are also special applications of percent defective, based on variables and lot sampling. Their usage requires that a sound program is established and consideration be given to practical results to be obtained by means of these more advanced statistical techniques.

DEVELOPING AND USING QUALITY CONTROL CHARTS BY VARIABLES

As the preceding sections have explained, statistical quality inspection and its associated accept/reject procedure is based on a pattern of variation inherent in the process we are studying and we hope to keep under control. The pattern of change within this process is visualized through charting, a potent tool for planning and controlling quality that can effectively be used to aid in building quality into products and processes.

Control charts are based on the rule that variation will follow a stable pattern as long as the system of chance causes remains the same. Once a stable system of chance causes is established, the quality control limits for the resulting pattern of variation can be determined.

A control chart typically has two limits: upper and lower, though there are some exceptions where the lower limit is unnecessary because we deal with a truncated distribution. Such limits serve as guides for future quality information. Future data streams can be expected to fall within the same limits as past data, unless there is a change in the system of causes.

Exhibit 8.4 presents two charts $\bar{\bar{x}}$ and $\bar{R}$. The $\bar{\bar{x}}$ chart in the upper half has both *tolerance* and *quality control* limits. There are also upper and lower limits in this chart. By contrast, the $\bar{R}$ chart in the bottom of Exhibit 8.4 has no lower control limit because the minimum value a range may have is zero.

Tolerances are established by an authority: the engineering department, the central bank, or the board of directors. By contrast, quality control limits are established by the process itself, and should be based on 20 samples or more.

Causality sees to it that future data might fall outside the upper and lower control limits. When this happens, an investigation must be made to determine the cause of the change in pattern. The notion underpinning this investigation has been used previously

Exhibit 8.4 $\bar{\bar{x}}$ and $\bar{R}$ Control Charts for Mean and Range

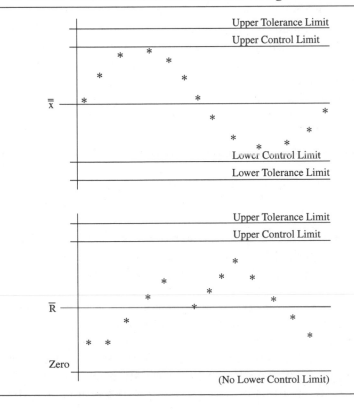

(Benefits Provided by the Operating Characteristics Curve) as an example leading to the prognostication of extreme events.

If the job stream and/or the operating environment has changed, then both the central tendency of the chart and the limits must be adjusted, otherwise they will no more correspond to reality. This statement is in the background of the feasibility of using statistical quality control charts to track outliers and extreme events.

Statistical quality control techniques have a rich inventory of tools from which to choose. Different types of control charts serve different functions. By and large, the practice of quality control charts by variables can be classified into two groups, each focusing on the type of quality control being selected, and the operating characteristics curve resulting from this choice:

- We use $\bar{\bar{x}}$ and $\bar{R}$ charts on problems where we are confronted by a measurable variable.
- We employ p and c charts, respectively, for percent defective and defects per unit.

Industries that have used statistically accurate quality control charts for more than five decades say that they have found plenty of worthwhile applications for $\bar{\bar{x}}$ and $\bar{R}$, p, and c charts throughout their organization in connection to processes and products. As I already have stated, banks only now start in this implementation domain, therefore, I will keep my examples simple.

Let's start with quality control by variables. Say that a production run, for instance foreign exchange transactions, has a given pattern of variation. To assure good quality this pattern must be maintained. The $\bar{\bar{x}}$ and $\bar{R}$ charts shown in Exhibit 8.4 reflect a pattern of variation for the variable being measured throughout the production run. *If* the process under control is exchange rates applied to these transactions and the Treasury division posts on the banks network the exchange rate of key currencies through *tolerances—then,* any deviations from the mean value, $\bar{\bar{x}}$, should fall within such tolerances, and the range of deviations should also be controlled in regard to a central tendency $\bar{R}$ and upper tolerance.

In this example on exchange rates, the production run may be a day or a month. The quality control plan may choose to group small transactions, but handle big transactions individually. The central tendency of the $/£ distribution and its variation from lot to lot will be the plot in an $\bar{\bar{x}}$ chart. The spread (range) within the lot is mapped into the $\bar{R}$ chart.

It is self-evident that the average of a sample, x, is obtained by adding the values of the variable measured in each of the individual pieces in a sample then dividing by sample size. The range, R, is obtained by subtracting the smallest value in the sample from the largest.

This charting may be used by the Treasury to control the adherence of branch offices to guidelines. It requires no extra effort because all transactions are databased. An expert system can nicely do the plotting.[4]

Alternatively, a similar method may be used to track variations in exchange rates of any two currencies. With tick-by-tick information on exchange rates available through bid-ask by the main information providers, the average may be all the ticks in, say, 5-minute intervals or in 30-minute intervals. This would make a nice pattern of intraday variation in \$/£ exchange rates—and it can lead to prognostication.

With flexible exchange rates, $\bar{x}$ and $\bar{\bar{x}}$ will change over time; $\bar{x}$ may change intraday depending on how nervous the market is. The average range, $\bar{R}$, and its upper control limit may also change, helping to identify a trend in volatility.

Let me repeat these statements in a slightly different manner. The central tendency of the chart of the means is $\bar{\bar{x}}$; the plotted values of the variable are $\bar{x}$. As shown in Exhibit 8.4, this chart features tolerances as well as upper and lower control limits. The upper and lower tolerance may reflect one of several issues, for example, the band targeted by the government or central bank or projected levels of intervention.

In principle, tolerances should be outside the control limits. This way, as long as the process is in control (keeps within the upper and lower limits), it respects the tolerances.

In the case of a currency exchange application, the $\bar{\bar{x}}$ chart shows whether the \$/£ exchange rate is running high or low or around the central tendency. Trends resulting from trading are also clearly shown. Because values of the means of the variable are depicted by successive points, when the run is completed, the chart serves as a permanent record of the variable charted.

$\bar{R}$, too, is a valuable guide to process uniformity or lack of it. It indicates how accurately a dimension in \$/£ volatility is held, and therefore it constitutes evidence as to whether a certain tolerance can be met. A good application of $\bar{R}$ is where a range of variation has been set as in the case of the European snake (in the 1970s) and in the mid-1990s (prior to January 1, 1999) in connection to the euro.

If we study the range of variation in currency exchange in a free market with flexible rates, the range may be set by the market. Alternatively with nearly fixed rates, it is set by the central bank(s) which intervenes to support a currency. Widely used in the manufacturing industry, there is a rule in statistical inference based on trends which says that *if* a process is to meet the specified tolerances, *then* the average value of the sample ranges, $\bar{R}$, must be less than the total specification tolerance divided by 2.6, when the sample size is 5.

This is an excellent rule and has to do with quality of output. High quality is characterized by small variance and therefore a small standard deviation. The range is a different way of expressing spread around the mean.

Another statistical rule relating to trends, is that if 3 points, $\bar{x}$, succeeding each other in a sequence, whether going north or going south, establish a trend. According to this rule, when this happens the likelihood is high that a fourth successive point will follow in the same direction eventually breaking the upper or lower control limits. Recall that in a SQC chart quality control limits should be based on 20 samples or more.

While quality control limits are established from *past performance*, they serve as a guide to *future performance*. Future points on the $\bar{\bar{x}}$ and $\bar{R}$ chart would continue to fall inside the control limits as long as the system of chance causes remains the same. Finally, the formulas for calculating the control limits for the $\bar{\bar{x}}$ and $\bar{R}$ chart are fairly simple. For the $\bar{\bar{x}}$ chart of the sample means:

$$\text{Upper control limits} = \bar{\bar{x}} + k_1\bar{R}$$

$$\text{Lower control limit} = \bar{\bar{x}} - k_1\bar{R}$$

$$\text{where } \bar{\bar{x}} = \frac{\text{Sum of the sample averages}}{\text{Number of samples}}$$

$$\bar{R} = \frac{\text{Sum of the sample ranges}}{\text{Number of samples}}$$

Where k_1 = a constant for each sample size. For instance, k_1 = 0.73 for a sample size of 4; 0.58 for 5; 0.48 for 6; and so on. As stated, only the upper control limit is used for sample ranges $\bar{R}$:

$$\text{Upper control limit} = \bar{R} + k_2\bar{R}$$

Where k_2 is also a constant with values depending on sample size. k_2 = 2.28 for a sample size of 4; 2.11 for 5; and 2.00 for 6. Statistical tables provide these and all other values needed in an implementation of quality control tables. There is no lack of statistical tables, but there is lack of skill for their successful implementation.

QUALITY CHARTS FOR THE NUMBER OF DEFECTS PER UNIT

The $\bar{x}$ and $\bar{R}$ charts by variables we studied are used widely in industry, and they are applicable in any system and on any variable representing a quality characteristic that can be measured on a continuous basis. By contrast, c charts for defects per unit and p charts for percent defective are based on quality control by attributes and serve in the inspection of general quality levels.

The c chart can have a wide area of application in banking because it is of value when quality is determined in terms of defects per unit of production, including accounts and office work. Technically, one defect makes an item defective whether this is financial reporting targeted by COSO or any other product or process.

The c chart is of particular value on assemblies or completed products, like accounting statements. A journal kept by computer can fall into this class. In manufacturing, the aircraft industry has used c charts to good advantage on defects per plane to control plane production quality. Financial institutions can use c charts for quality assurance of branch offices.

Exhibit 8.5 $\bar{c}$ **Chart for Number of Defects per Unit in a Week on an Hourly Basis**

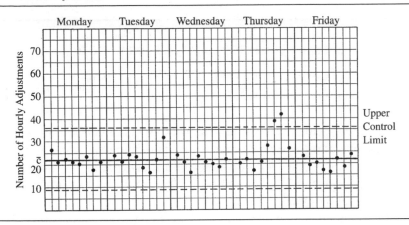

Other successful applications of c charts have been in the automobile frame industry regarding defects per hour's production. This concept should not be alien to banking. One of the reasons for its potential lies in the fact that it helps in keeping tight hourly control on the quality of office work, including accounting and risk management activities.

Exhibit 8.5 shows a c chart. Its object is to map into a graphic form the number of hourly adjustments on the production floor. Similar charts can be plotted for a range of applications in office work, including the execution of customer orders and documentary credit for export trade. The use of the c chart is appropriate if:

- The opportunities for a defect in a production unit are nearly infinite.
- The probability of a defect at any point in the unit is rather small and fairly constant.
- The area where defects can show up, that is the size of the unit, is constant.

Control limits for these charts are calculated from the formulas:

$$\text{Upper control limit} = \bar{c} + 3\sqrt{\bar{c}}$$
$$\text{Lower control limit} = \bar{c} - 3\sqrt{\bar{c}}$$

where $\bar{c}$ = Average number of defects for whatever production unit is used

In the $\bar{c}$ chart in Exhibit 8.5, the quality control limits were based on an average value taken from previous data collected at a production floor. In this particular application which tracked quality *intraday*, $\bar{c}$ was equal to 22.1 adjustments per hour. With this statistic, the resulting upper and lower limits are:

$$\text{Upper control limits} = 22.1 + 3\sqrt{22.1} = 36.2$$

$$\text{Lower control limit} = 22.1 - 3\sqrt{22.1} = 8.0$$

In principle, future points on the $\bar{c}$ chart should fall inside control limits based on past performance as long as the system of chance causes remains the same. If points fall outside, then the breaking of control limits indicates a change in the production process and an investigation should reveal the reasons for it. The consistency of inspection is another factor that can affect the chart.

Whether the application domain is banking, manufacturing, or any other, fundamental to the use of a percent defective quality control plan is the method used for classifying defects. Typically, a classification is an enumeration of possible defects of a unit, product, transaction, or account. Often this is done according to their importance.

A *critical defect* is one that can result in unsafe conditions or crucial errors of account. If accounts are massaged and there are double books—one of them for management, the other for regulators—this is a major defect even if the book for the regulators reflects true events while management misinforms itself through creative accounting.

A *major defect* is one, other than critical, that could result in failure or reduce the usability of a unit, process, or ledger. Breaking one or more of the rules established by COSO for reliable financial reporting is an example of a major defect that can have important financial and disciplinary consequences.

A *minor defect* has no immediately significant bearing on the effective use or operation of the unit, but still it should be corrected.

Note that there is movement between these three defect classes. Minor defects can graduate into major, and major into catastrophic. All of the categories represent deviations from specification of requirements, as well as events falling outside tolerances. To flush them out, the institution should sample its production process and test for defects, identifying them, classifying them, plotting them in quality control chart(s), and taking corrective action.

PLOTTING PERCENT DEFECTIVE FOR QUALITY CONTROL REASONS

While $\bar{c}$ charts track defect per unit in a quality control process, $\bar{p}$ charts address percent defective. In many financial applications, percent defective can constitute a good measure of performance. In production, for instance, a $\bar{p}$ chart measures and maps the quality of manufacturing performance. Applied in an office environment, it measures the accuracy of paperwork, such as documentary credit.

Exhibit 8.6   Operating Characteristics Curve for Percent Defective

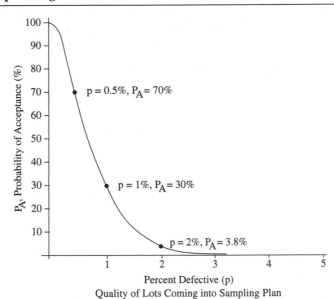

There is an operating characteristics curve associated with $\bar{p}$ charts. The example in Exhibit 8.6 resembles a Poisson distribution. The statistics behind the curve come from the computer industry. The *abscissa* is the quality of lots coming into the sampling plan, expressed in percent defective, *p*. The *ordinate* is the probability of acceptance of each lot, P_A.

The level of quality is shown clearly by this type of chart, as are any trends or changes of which management should always be aware. In the general case, the percent defective is obtained by dividing the number of defective units by the total number of units inspected, the quotient being multiplied by 100.

Percent defective charts work equally nicely at the production floor and in the office, and they have proven to be a very good tool for controlling general quality levels. A *p* chart can be effectively used on individual parts, assemblies, and accounting—as well as for the evaluation of personnel. Its flexibility makes it an ideal tool in banking and finance.

Sometimes *p* charts are kept by office function, *if* this function has important characteristics or significant costs. In other cases, *p* charts keep track of one dimension, such as the result of go/no-go testing used in control by attributes. Therefore, *p* charts can be both a complement and an alternative to the accept/sample again/reject procedures in connection to quality control by attributes. All pertinent data is noted on the chart so that the pattern of a complete written history can be obtained. Control limits for the *p* chart are computed from the formulas:

$$\text{Upper control limit} = \overline{p} + 3\sqrt{\frac{\overline{p}(1-\overline{p})}{m}}$$

$$\text{Lower control limit} = \overline{p} - 3\sqrt{\frac{\overline{p}(1-\overline{p})}{m}}$$

$$\text{where } \overline{p} = \frac{\text{Total defective}}{\text{Total production}}$$

$$m = \frac{\text{Total production}}{\text{Total units of time}}$$

New limits should be calculated as improvements are made to the office process and the percent defective changes. Incorrectly, however, many companies follow the policy that even if a quality condition worsens, the old limits are maintained—hoping that it is possible to return without effort to the previous system of chance causes. This is the wrong way to control quality.

These $\overline{p}$ charts are flexible. In each case, a chart can be plotted for whatever time unit is practical. Department or group performance is usually plotted daily. Where it is imperative to exercise close control of quality plotting, percent defective should be tracked intraday. For instance, $\overline{p}$ charts on the quality of production of individual parts or assemblies are often plotted hourly, and a similar principle is applicable in banking.

In addition, $\overline{p}$ charts can serve as early warning tools flushing out abnormal percent defective situations. Outliers indicate out-of-control conditions. The best thing management can do is to correct the causes and get back the process to its usual pattern. One of the worst things management can do is to ignore warning signals and let the process go deeper and deeper into out-of-control conditions.

The $\overline{p}$ chart in Exhibit 8.7 reflects office work. The variable being measured is a critical function characterizing a large back office operation. Information on quality became available as each lot is given a thorough test upon completion. At negligible cost, information from this check serves to guide inspection, eliminating some of costs for auditing that were necessary in the past, as well as reducing the causes for future trouble in the office work in reference.

The $\overline{p}$ chart can also be used as a gage on the consistency of inspection. Companies that employ percent defective quality control charts found them to be excellent yardsticks on progress. In many cases, $\overline{p}$ charts prove to be ideal tool for improving or maintaining a quality level because:

- They show an abnormal variation in percent defective, where it exists; therefore, depicting trends.
- They act as a strong psychological tool on personnel for maintaining an above average quality level.

Exhibit 8.7 $\bar{p}$ **Percent Defective Chart, Monthly Performance in a Large Backoffice Operation**

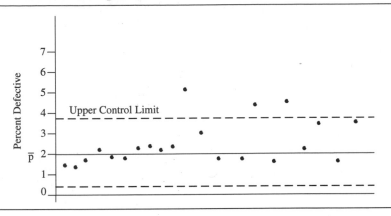

One of the major fields where institutions have been successful with the implementation of percent defective charts is accounting and auditing—hence compliance to COSO. In another case, obtained results have strengthened the company's position in a number of areas like financial planning, budgetary control, overhead analysis, and cost control. Percent defective charts also proved to be one of the best tools of statistical quality inspection.

NOTES

1. *Outstanding Investor Digest* (New York: September 24, 1998).

2. D.N. Chorafas, *The 1996 Market Risk Amendment: Understanding the Marking-to-Model and Value-at-Risk* (Burr Ridge, IL: McGraw-Hill, 1998).

3. D.N. Chorafas, "How to Understand and Use Mathematics for Derivatives," *Advanced Modeling Methods,* vol. 2 (London: Euromoney, 1995).

4. D.N. Chorafas and H. Steinmann, *Expert Systems in Banking* (London: Macmillan, 1991).

CHAPTER 9

Statements by the Financial Accounting Standards Board and Regulatory Reporting Practices

Behavioral controls discussed in Chapter 6 and the implementation of statistical quality control, which was the subject of Chapters 7 and 8, are tools for effectiveness and efficiency—the second phase of COSO's application in the banking industry. There are two reasons I gave priority to these subjects:

1. They lie at the frontiers of reliable financial reporting, and therefore are new to most readers.
2. They are powerful means for implementing the latest Statements of Financial Accounting Standards (SFAS), by the Financial Accounting Standards Board (FASB).

The Treadway Commission accomplished its work in the late 1980s. Subsequently, the implementation of its recommendation for reliable financial reporting has been promoted by the Committee of Sponsoring Organizations of the Treadway Commission. Over the years since the early 1990s, many of these recommendations have found their way into a number of SFAS by FASB.

In this chapter, we will examine those FASB statements having an impact on general accounting practices, including a comparison between SFAS 119 and SFAS 133. Chapter 10 will focus on the latest FASB statements that regulate reporting for derivatives products.

Whether made by the central bank or by other authorities, the regulatory reporting practices of financial institutions must be homogeneous and they should follow well-established directives. This is setting form and content for uniform reporting: weeding fraudulent practices out of financial statements and setting standards for reporting.

Typically, prior to publishing new standards a regulatory authority issues a discussion memorandum. This provides the basis for obtaining opinion (often contradictory) about financial accounting issues, as well as about measurement tools and procedures. The goal of a discussion memorandum is to set and test:

- Suggested objectives.
- Proposed scope.
- Recommended methodology.

Among other issues, discussion memoranda address recognition, derecognition, and evaluation of a financial instrument in regard to its gains, losses, and exposures. Initial measurements, a golden horde of subsequent reporting practices, and tools for doing a clean job are included in this reference.

Recognition is the definition of assets and liabilities to be mapped into a statement of financial position, within appropriate time brackets for regulatory reporting. *Derecognition* is the inverse process, removing an asset or liability from the statement of financial condition. Depending on the law of the land, some gains and losses may be recognized but not yet realized. They will most likely be realized in a further-out time bracket.

A steady update of definitions and regulations is necessary because the market steadily evolves, while innovative financial instruments and new types of transactions raise many questions that in accounting terms, company executives and accountants find difficult to resolve using existing standards. There are always questions regarding apparent inconsistencies and gaps in old standards. This is particularly apparent when they are used in connection to new financial instruments

For instance, should financial assets be considered sold if there is recourse or other continuing involvement with them? Should financial liabilities be considered settled when assets are dedicated to settle them? How should highly market-sensitive financial instruments be measured? Should this process be based on market value or on accruals (historical prices, see Chapter 14)? No definition and no regulation last forever. The more dynamic the market is, the faster regulatory reporting practices need to be reviewed and revamped.

REGULATIONS SHOULD PROVIDE INVESTORS WITH GREATER TRANSPARENCY

"Sunshine is the best disinfectant," Judge Louis Brandeis once said. As we have seen since Chapter 4, transparency in financial reporting and the accurate presentation of financial conditions are the best examples of transparency in banking. If the board and senior management think that a transaction can hurt the institution, they should avoid doing it rather than trying to hide it afterward.

During the hearing of October 1997 by the U.S. House Banking Committee, Arthur Levitt, the chairman of the SEC testified that SEC will enforce the FASB accounting rules for 15,000 American companies that are public. He also warned that FASB must remain independent, and that he was there to shield it from political pressure:

> It is very inappropriate for the Congress to suggest any further delays. I believe that we would be playing Russian roulette with our markets.

Cognizant people in the derivatives business would appreciate that the fight over the FASB's new accounting standards—which were published in May 1998 as Statement of

Financial Accounting Standards 133 (see also Chapter 10)—has been more than just an issue over accounting rules. Bringing to light the full derivatives exposure is similar to telling the world that the financial system is healthy, and that any repair which is necessary is brought immediately to the attention of regulators.

As explained in Chapter 4, James C. Treadway, Jr. who headed the Commission under the same name on fraudulent financial reporting was an SEC commissioner. The Securities and Exchange Commission has always been at the forefront of regulation that casts light on what might have been otherwise obscure connection and doubtful reporting practices.

Both in absolute and in relative terms, the sources of income of a bank and of any company are important information for investors. Net interest income gives an indication of how much interest risk an institution has taken. The next crucial information is how well transactions and positions have been hedged (see Chapter 10).

Net fee and commission income is relatively stable stuff, but chances are high that income from trading operations—therefore, largely from derivatives—is speculative. Exhibit 9.1 presents the income pattern that prevailed over five years in a major money center bank. The larger increase is from trading operations and should be kept in perspective by both investors and regulators.

Let me take as another example payment for order flow. On the initiative of the SEC, a regulation has been implemented that brokerages disclose to their customers their policies and practices regarding receipt of payment for order flow. This term means compensation or other consideration paid to a brokerage firm by:

- A registered stock exchange.
- An association.
- Another broker-dealer.

Exhibit 9.1   Operating Income according to the Annual Report by a Money Center Bank

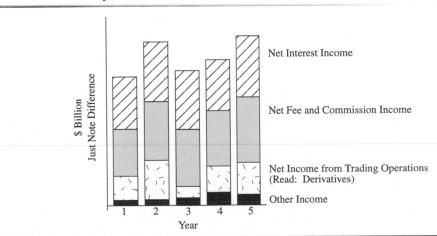

This is typically done in return for a certain favor, precisely for directing customer orders for execution. Examples of noncash compensation include reciprocal arrangements, discounts, rebates, reductions, or credits against fees that would otherwise be payable in full by the brokerage firm—as well as other similar acts.

Another initiative worth bringing under perspective is the regulation of financial sectors that have been running for some time without appropriate supervisory controls—as well as better information for investors. The SEC has worked with mutual fund companies to develop summaries for mutual fund prospectuses that lay out clearly a fund's riskiness; the SEC supervises mutual funds.

Such regulatory steps were taken at a time when neither in the United States nor anywhere else was it possible to gauge the probability that a large problem could occur because vast sections of the global financial market remained largely invisible. Reduced visibility of financial conditions because of the growing role of hedge funds and nonbank banks can permit large structural defects to develop undetected, eventually leading to a bubble.

The emergence of a market in financial derivatives during the 1980s was part of a greater change in the nature of banking and trading. It came with disintermediation, globalization, and the wider use of computers and networks, replacing elder approaches by newer ones where international debt, international equity, greater use of commercial paper, and booming over-the-counter (OTC) trades set the stage for rapid developments in financial innovation. Derivatives became the common denominator of fast-developing financial products, and with them there was a switch away from established exchanges. By the early 1990s, the OTC market, particularly in interest rate swaps and currencies, was growing at a rate far exceeding the exchange-based market. This gave rise to risks additional to market risks associated with traded instruments:

- Credit risks.
- Legal risks.
- Settlement risks.

Banking strategy was changing, too. From fundamentally domestic institutions, many banks progressively became international, actively establishing extensive networks all over the globe as well as growing by acquisitions abroad. It is therefore only reasonable that regulation, too, got internationalized:

- For credit institutions through the Basle Committee on Banking Supervision at the Bank for International Settlements (BIS).
- For brokers/dealers, as well as for a large part of financial reporting, through the International Organization of Securities Commissions (IOSCO).

One can never be too prudent in the management of assets and liabilities, particularly under leveraging. While some people assume that the chance a major economic shock would result in domino failure of major financial institutions has declined, in reality there is no other basis than pure optimism on which to make such an assertion. Building on this background, the following sections take a closer look at FASB statements. This is intended as a summary rather than an all-inclusive review.

REPORTING COMPREHENSIVE INCOME: SFAS 130, 131, AND 132

Comprehensive income is the change in equity of a firm over a given time period. This change is the result of transactions, inventoried positions, and other events initiated or triggered from owner sources, including all changes in equity over the period in reference except those resulting from investments by owners and distributions to owners.

A comprehensive income statement includes all changes in equity during the reporting period. These typically originate from transactions and other events relating to non-owner sources.

In June 1997, the Financial Accounting Standards Board issued SFAS 130, "Reporting Comprehensive Income," and SFAS 131 "Disclosures about Segments of an Enterprise and Related Information." Both statements provide for additional disclosure. Effective January 1, 1998, SFAS 130 requires companies to report comprehensive income which includes net income, foreign currency adjustments, and unrealized gains and losses on marketable securities classified as available for sale.

Effective December 1998, U.S. companies adopted SFAS 131. It calls for reporting segment information, used internally to allocate resources and assess performance. SFAS 131:

- Establishes standards for reporting information about operating segments in annual financial statements.
- Requires that certain selected information about operating segments be reported in interim financial reports.
- Outlines rules for related disclosures about products and services, as well as geographic areas.

One of the requirements of SFAS 131 is to disclose a measure of segment profit or loss (like operating income), segment assets, and reconciliation to consolidated totals. It also calls for entitywide disclosures based on management approach to segment reporting, establishing requirements necessary to report selected segment information quarterly, as well as entitywide disclosures about products, services, major customers, and countries in which the entity holds assets and reports revenue.

Operating segments are defined as components of an enterprise about which separate financial information is evaluated regularly by the chief operating officer, or decision-making team. Targeting senior management decisions is a new policy by regulators, which is instrumental in increasing the sense of accountability.

In February 1998, FASB issued Statement of Financial Accounting Standards 132, "Employers Disclosures about Pensions and Other Postretirement Benefits." FAS 132 standardizes disclosure requirements for pensions and postretirement benefits. It also demands for additional information on changes in benefit obligations and fair values of retirement plan assets (for definition of fair value see Chapter 14).

Depending on how a company has managed its pensions and postretirement benefits, SFAS 132 may or may not have a significant effect on its disclosure. The same is practically true with all financial accounting reporting standards. Those institutions have the most problems in meeting new regulations which are internally organized in a poor manner, and/or in the past have been lax with their disclosures.

The newly required regulatory reports on comprehensive income and its components, including all changes in equity during a period except those due to owner investments and distributions and covering items like foreign currency translation adjustments, and unrealized gains and losses on available-for-sale securities. They also require that companies disclose information on how management makes decisions about allocating resources and how the company measures segment performance. Both are key issues to prudential management of financial institutions.

Statements of Financial Accounting Standards 130, 131, and 132 have followed other prudential reporting regulations as for instance SFAS 128 "Earnings per Share." When it became effective in December 1997, SFAS 128 simplified the calculation of earnings per share (EPS), replacing primary EPS with basic EPS; also replacing fully diluted EPS with diluted EPS. What this means in practical terms is provided by an example from Xerox shown in Exhibit 9.2.

Basic EPS is computed by dividing income available to common stockholders by the weighted average number of common shares outstanding during the period. The computation of diluted EPS is similar to the computation of basic EPS except that it gives effect to all potentially dilutive instruments that were outstanding during the period.

Exhibit 9.2 Xerox Corporation Earnings per Share in 1996 and 1997

	1997			1996		
	Income	Shares	Per Share Amount	Income	Shares	Per Share Amount
Basic EPS			$4.31			$3.55
Income from continuing operations	$1,408*			$1,162		
Amount of shares		326,686			327,194	
Diluted EPS			$4.04			$3.32
Stock options and other incentives		3,964			5,321	
ESOP adjustment,[†] convertible debt	$ 47	29,986		$ 43	30,525	
Total income from operations	$1,455			$1,205		
Adjusted amount of shares		360,636			363,140	

*Minus accrued dividends on preferred stock.
[†]ESOP adjustment includes preferred stock dividends, ESOP expense adjustment, and related tax benefit.

Another reference that helps to explain the impact of new regulations on financial accounting procedures is SFAS 125 "Accounting for Transfers and Servicing of Financial Assets and Extinguishments of Liabilities." Issued in June 1996, this statement provides accounting and reporting standards for transfers as well as for servicing of financial assets and extinguishments of liabilities:

- It outlines consistent standards for distinguishing transfers of financial assets resulting from sales of transfers that are secured borrowings.
- It also establishes a firm accounting basis for collateral based on the notion of managerial control and accountability.

Originally it was intended that SFAS 125 become effective January 1, 1997, but in December 1996, the FASB issued SFAS 127 "Deferral of the Effective Date of Certain Provisions of FASB Statement 125." This delayed until January 1, 1998, the effective implementation date of certain provisions, but it did not alter the sense of the more rigorous standards established for reporting assets and liabilities.

To complete this list of FASB Statements of Financial Accounting Standards relevant to our discussion on the implementation of clauses which uphold the COSO principles, I should add SFAS 133, "Accounting for Derivative Instruments and Hedging Activities."

Issued in June 1998, it establishes accounting and reporting standards for derivative instruments and hedging activities, requiring that an entity recognize all derivatives as either assets or liabilities in the statement of financial position and measure those instruments at fair value. Companies must adopt SFAS 133 for their first quarterly filing of fiscal year 2000. We will look more carefully into SFAS 133 in Chapter 10.

THE EVOLVING NATURE OF FINANCIAL STATEMENTS AND REPORTING REQUIREMENTS

Because financial markets are so dynamic, new instruments are steadily born and new procedures develop. As a result, the Financial Accounting Standards Board works on updating form and content of financial statements, having concluded that more disclosure about a number of instruments, such as derivatives, is required while some of the old definitions should be revamped.

The updating of definitions and of reporting systems is very important to the proper management of business and industrial entities. Just as important is the fact that the terms and regulations are understood and appreciated by the companies themselves and by investors.

Active participants in the financial markets need detailed information about the purposes for which financial instruments are issued, bought, and held—as well as the profit and loss resulting from this strategy. They also need to understand the instruments leveraging features and exposure created by gearing. Leverage means more debt.

Neither should the connection that exists between new and old financial instruments be a matter of mystique, or an unknown. Loans are as old as civilization, but loans have also taken on leveraging effects from securitization and credit derivatives[1] to internal interest rate swaps, which:

- Weed out of the banking book interest rate risk.
- Put this risk in the trading book where it can be marked to market or to model.

The first norms published by FASB concerning the regulation of financial reporting in connection to derivatives came into effect in the early 1990s. These were Statements of Financial Accounting Standards 105 and 107. Then in October 1994, SFAS 119 was issued which improved the preceding two statements by amending them; and in June 1998 came SFAS 133 which restructured the whole reporting practice connected to derivatives (see Chapter 10).

Some of the changes brought by the new SFAS were important. Others were limited to a clarification. For instance, while the changes to FAS 105 and 107 made by FAS 119 were limited to the addition of a footnote, the substitution of the word class by category, and the insertion of two new paragraphs (concerning SFAS 107) were considerably more extensive.

One of the clarifications brought by SFAS 119 was by way of redefining the fair value of a financial instrument. Another change distinguished between financial instruments held and those issued for trading reasons—thereby introducing the concept of *management intent*. A third, focused on the accompanying notes of a financial statement. A fourth, regarded the combination or aggregation of fair value of derivatives and of non-derivative instruments.

Similarly, SFAS 133 completed and at the same time restructured FAS 119, demonstrating that changes in regulatory reporting practices are inevitable because of the pace at which financial markets evolve, magnitude of the process of innovation, and evolution of concepts underpinning financial operations. Still, the differences between SFAS 105, 107, 119, and 133 are not necessarily radical. By contrast, a truly radical difference exists between the accruals method, and the fair value solution.

This difference is fundamental and brings our discussion to a crucial issue in financial regulation: Should the measurement of assets and liabilities be based on what was received or paid for them? On the amount stated on the contract and associated conditions? On expected net future cash flows? Or on market value?

The method that originally prevailed practically in every jurisdiction, and which has a long historical precedence, has been accruals—which can be briefly described as historical evidence written in the books plus something else. The new method promoted by FASB with SFAS 105, 107, 119, and 133 is *fair value*. Accruals and fair value are radically different concepts and often contradict one another in financial reporting.

Historical cost is a static approach, which still dominates the law in continental Europe. One of the problems with accruals is that it leads to book value which, in the large majority of cases, has little or nothing to do with market value. Another problem is that it rests on a very conservative financial accounting and reporting method, known as "lower of cost or market value."

Fair value is market value. It is the market price established by a willing seller and a willing buyer under no fire-sale condition. This method, which fits well in a dynamic market, has become the standard in America (thanks to FASB) and in Britain.

Except panics and other major market upheavals, there is always fair value of an asset or a commodity. If we cannot find this market value, as in the case of custom-made bilateral agreements, we compute it through models.

The fact that fair value is a dynamic approach saw to it that many major continental European banks, from the German Deutsche Bank and Dresdner Bank to the Dutch ING, have transferred the center of their investment banking activities to London. New financial accounting and reporting regulation in France gives French multinationals the option of choosing between the so-called Anglo-Saxon model, hence fair value, or the historical French model: accruals.

DISCLOSURE RULES BY THE FINANCIAL ACCOUNTING STANDARDS BOARD

The new disclosure rules by FASB, specifically SFAS 133 (see also Chapter 10), require that an institution that writes, buys, holds, or issues derivatives or nonderivative instruments designated for hedging must disclose its objectives in connection to these instruments. This is the famous clause of management intent. It must also outline:

- The context needed to understand those goals.
- The strategies for achieving them.

The sense of the new regulation is that qualitative disclosures about an organization's objectives and strategies relative to the use of derivatives may be more meaningful if these are presented within the perspective of the company's overall risk management profile. Or, if they are coupled with a discussion on the use of other financial instruments. The description to be disclosed to the authorities must distinguish between derivatives and nonderivatives:

- Designating at fair value hedging instruments.
- Identifying those designed as cash flow hedging.
- Distinguishing those designated as hedging currency exposure of net investment in foreign operations.
- Listing all other derivative financial instruments.

The descriptive material to be submitted to supervisory authorities shall also indicate the institution's risk management policy for each type of hedge, including a characterization of the items or transactions for which risks are hedged. For derivatives not designated as hedging instruments, the description shall indicate the purpose of the derivative activity.

This is a far cry from past reporting practices. The new regulations that were established post-COSO are designed to make transparent both management intent for entering into transactions and the exposure embedded into the portfolio of the institution. These requirements could not be answered through accruals. According to the new regulation, the disclosures made by an institution should also include nonhedging derivatives.

Fair value hedges incorporate both derivative and foreign currency denominated non-derivative instruments that have been designated by the institution as fair value hedging instruments—a matter involving management intent. Reporting to the supervisory authorities includes the separate amounts of gains and losses:

- On the hedging instruments.
- On the related hedged items.

These must be recognized during the reporting period. Evidently, there will be gains or losses, with losses representing the amount of the hedges' ineffectiveness. There should as well be a description of where those gains and losses are reported in the statement of income or other statement of financial performance.

A special clause treats gains and losses recognized in earnings when a hedged firm commitment no longer qualifies as fair value hedge. This closes a major loophole with previous regulations concerning reporting practices, whose origin has been a certain inconsistency in recognizing fair value hedges.

For derivatives that have been designated (and qualified) as cash flow hedges, as well as related hedged transactions, the institution must report the separate amounts of gains and losses. Once more, the losses are due to the hedges' ineffectiveness.

Regarding the effectiveness of the hedge, there should be a description of the transactions or other events that results in the recognition in earnings of gains and losses, deferred in accumulated other comprehensive income. The new regulation also requires disclosure of the amount of deferred gains and losses that will be recognized within the next 12 months.

Statement of Financial Accounting Standards 133 also calls for a description of where gains and losses on hedging instruments recognized in earnings during the reporting period are reported in the statement of income, or other document of financial performance. Also to be reported is the amount of gains and losses recognized in earnings as a result of the discontinuance of cash flow hedges because it is probable that an originally forecasted transaction will not take place.

For hedges of net investment in one or more foreign operations, reporting is required for derivatives and foreign currency denominated nonderivative instruments that qualify as hedges of foreign currency exposure. Evidence must be provided on the amount of foreign currency transaction gain or loss on the hedging instrument.

Another element to be reported is the amount of any other changes in fair value of the hedging instrument included in earnings during the reporting period. Along with this must be a description of where those gains and losses are reported in the statement of income (profit and loss), or other statement of financial performance.

The separate amounts of gains and losses during the reporting period should also be reported for derivatives that have not been designed as hedging instruments. This must be desegregated by business activity, risk, or other class consistent with the management of that activity. Such practice essentially amounts to qualitative and quantitative disclosures.

Statement of Financial Accounting Standards 133 takes exception of not-for-profit organizations, such as defined benefit pension plans, or generally an entity that does not report earnings as a separate caption in a statement of financial performance. In this case, the gain or loss on a hedging instrument shall be recognized as a change in net assets. This must be done in the period of change. The exception is if the instrument is designated as a hedge of foreign currency exposure or a net investment in a foreign operation.

For organizations that do not report earnings, the changes in the carrying amount of the hedged item shall be recognized as a change in net assets in the period in reference. Given that for nonprofit organizations the format of statement of financial performance does not report earnings separately, such entities are not permitted hedge accounting for derivatives used to hedge forecasted transactions.

FIRM COMMITMENTS AND FORECASTED TRANSACTIONS

As a matter of general principle, the new FASB regulatory reporting requirements state that, if certain conditions are met, a financial institution may elect to designate a derivative instrument or a derivative portion of a contract in either of three ways:

1. A firm commitment, where fair value is the criterion.
2. A forecasted (hedged) transaction, with cash flow prerequisites.
3. A hedge of foreign currency exposure.

Firm commitment with a counterparty is usually a legally enforceable agreement, whose performance is probable because there is a sufficiently large disincentive for nonperformance. A firm commitment should specify all significant terms of the contract, including quantity to be exchanged, price, and timing of the transaction. A fair value hedge is a firm commitment attributable to a particular risk.

A firm commitment can be viewed as an executory contract that represents both a right and an obligation. *If* a firm commitment that is designated as a hedged item is accounted for in accordance with the FASB statement, *then* an asset or liability is recognized and reported in the statement of financial position related to the recognition of gain or loss in the firm commitment.

The concept of a *forecasted transaction* is linked to that of the cash flow of a recognized asset or liability. A cash flow hedge is attributable to a particular risk, projected to characterize a transaction. Statement of Financial Accounting Standards 133 defines a forecasted transaction as being one expected to occur, but for which there is no firm commitment. Given that such transaction has not yet occurred, and when it occurs it will be at prevailing market price, a forecasted transaction gives the bank no future benefits or assets, nor does it present obligations for future liabilities.

Because a forecasted transaction is essentially a hedged transaction expected to occur, but not characterized by a firm commitment, it does not give any present rights or obligations relating, respectively, to future benefits or liabilities. It does not oblige the institution to support future sacrifices.

The third item, *foreign currency exposure,* may be a firm commitment, or an available-for-sale debt security; both are foreign currency fair value hedges. The same is true of foreign currency-denominated forecasted transaction, representing:

- A foreign currency cash flow hedge.
- A net investment in a foreign operation.

As the order of these three criteria indicates, the most important concept advanced by Statement of Financial Accounting Standards 133 is *fair value.* This has become a very relevant measure for derivatives. The new regulation sees to it that all derivative financial instruments should be measured at fair value, and adjustments to the carrying amount of hedged items should reflect gains and losses.

To a substantial measure, this closes the loophole which so far existed regarding the ways in which organizations may designate a derivative instrument as hedging the exposure to changes in the fair value of an asset or liability, while in reality they think of that item as a trading instrument more than anything else. From now on, designated hedging instruments must be subjected to fair value hedge accounting, according to a number of criteria that define eligibility.

In terms of financial reporting responsibilities, some clauses of SFAS 133 relate to those of Statement of Financial Accounting Standards 127, "Deferral of the Effective of Certain Provisions of FASB Statement 125." SFAS 125 requires balance sheet recognition of collateral related to certain secured financing transactions entered into after December 31, 1997. The adoption of such provisions is part of the COSO framework, an initiative that creates additional captions on the consolidated balance sheet regarding:

- Securities received as collateral.
- Obligation to return securities received as collateral.

The balances recognized in these captions primarily represent securities received as collateral in term resale and repurchase agreements (repos) for which the collateral provider does not have the explicit contractual right to substitute.

The completion of a complex reporting structure for reliable financial statements and its steady update require many contributors. There are always new items to be addressed or challenges resulting from the evolution of existing regulations. While some of the rules and definitions are issued by an authority such as FASB, which derives directly from the SEC; others are promoted by professional organizations.

Take as an example the contribution of the American Institute of Certified Public Accountants (AICPA). In March 1998, AICPA's Accounting Standards Executive Committee issued Statement of Position (SOP) 98-1, "Accounting for the Costs of Computer Software Developed or Obtained for Internal Use." SOP 98-1 requires capitalization of certain internal applications software costs—rather than writing them off during the exercise year.

Finally, while FASB rules and regulations are generally well-studied and pay attention to detail, they might also contain a loophole until regulators find it out and close it. Take FASB 133 as an example (see also Chapter 10). At a time when *catastrophe derivatives* start taking off, and traders believe that they have a great future, it states that contracts that are not traded in exchanges are not subject to its requirements if they address a climatic, geological, or other physical variable.

When traders discover this loophole, they will give a great boost to weather derivatives and catastrophe derivatives, until a new regulation takes stock of the systemic risk associated to the booming trade and closes the window. Sometimes the interpretation of regulatory rules and directives is akin to a labyrinthine pattern. Creative accounting has grown out of such a maze after one or more smart entrepreneur(s) found a way to massage accounts at the frontier between legal and fraudulent reporting.

NOTE

1. D.N. Chorafas, *Credit Derivatives and the Management of Risk* (New York: New York Institute of Finance, 2000).

CHAPTER 10

FASB Statements of Financial Accounting Standards and Derivative Financial Instruments

A derivative is a financial instrument featuring two distinguishing characteristics: It has one or more underlyings (or underliers), and it features one or more notional principal amounts. This is the latest definition advanced by FASB in its Statement of Financial Accounting Standards 133 which, as we saw in Chapter 9, replaced SFAS 105, 107, and 119 as well as the previous definition of derivatives which was instrument-specific, involving a reference to options, swaps, forwards, and futures.

An *underlying* may be a commodity price, share price, interest rate, currency exchange rate, an index of prices, or some other variable. Depending on the type of transaction, an algorithm is applied to the notional amount to determine the cash flows or other exchanges required by the contract. The underlying may be the price of an asset or liability, but is not itself an asset or liability.

A *notional principal amount* (NPA), also called face amount, is a metric of currency, number of shares, or number of other units specified in the contract. It is a term borrowed from swaps indicating a reference amount; one which is not actually exchanged between counterparties but helps in estimating the cash flows (see also Chapter 2).

In a derivatives contract, the writer (seller) or buyer is not required to invest or receive the notional amount but is responsible for the aftermath of the transaction specified by the instrument. The effects of market risk will be computed through an agreed-upon algorithm: interest rate swap, forward rate agreement, knock-in/knock-out, inverse floater, and the like.

The new financial reporting standard promoted by SFAS 133 will significantly change the accounting treatment of derivative contracts used by a company and its customers. Depending on the underlying and on management intent, accounting changes would affect reported earnings, assets, liabilities, and stockholders' equity. An institution and the customers to which it provides derivative products—whether these are based on interest rates, foreign exchange, or other commodities—will have to reconsider their risk management strategies.

Among all authorities having to do with standardization and with regulation, FASB in the United States has been the first (to my knowledge) to define in a significant amount of detail reporting on derivative financial instruments whether for trading or for hedging. This has been influenced by the principles of COSO, and led to an effort among other Group of Ten countries to put order on the handling of off-balance sheet commitments in the sense of their recognition and regulatory financial reporting. In the background of the new rules lies the fact that:

- Trading in derivatives should target specific pre-announced management goals.
- Hedging should be part of the bank's strategic plan.
- There should be a regulatory assessment of hedge effectiveness.

We have spoken of this in Chapter 9, where the statement was made that according to the SFAS 133, reporting to supervisory authorities has to distinguish, in a factual and documented manner, between three classes of hedging targets: fair value hedges, cash flow hedges, and foreign currency hedges. In this chapter, we will look more carefully into what is implied in regulatory reporting by SFAS 133, after a quick review of the politics behind new regulation.

U.S. CONGRESSIONAL HEARING ON DERIVATIVES REGULATION, OCTOBER 1997

Because legislation and regulation often go hand-in-hand, let me start with a legislating reference. On October 1, 1997, there was a hearing by the House Banking Committee, Subcommittee on Capital Markets, Securities and Government-Sponsored Enterprises, which focused on the implementation of proposed new rules, formulated by FASB.

The objective of this regulation was to assure transparency in derivatives trades as well as in exposure resulting from portfolio positions in derivatives. Effective January 1, 1999, the new rules required that all publicly traded corporations, including banks, report their derivatives holdings on their balance sheets at fair market value (see also Chapter 9).

FASB Chairman Edmund Jenkins testified that the primary focus of his standards board is to put into effect rules that would require all corporations, whether financial or industrial, to report their derivatives holdings on their balance sheet by marking them to their current market price. "If ever a case can be made for reporting something in more detail, it is for derivatives," Jenkins suggested.

In the background of this statement lies the fact that without appropriate regulatory reporting practices, which are precise and explicit, different companies may report very similar activities differently. Jenkins pointed out that even an individual company may report similar activities in different, incompatible ways. Prior to the new regulations, gains and losses on derivatives have not been explicitly disclosed, and for an investor or a creditor, their effect on earnings was difficult, if not impossible, to determine.

The thesis of FASB is sound. Reporting gains or losses from derivatives on balance sheets can change radically the earnings picture. This is the net outcome of huge losses bankers, treasurers, and other investors have accumulated with derivatives—which become transparent only when they are written into the entity's balance sheet rather than continuing to be carried off-balance sheet.

Just prior to these U.S. Congress hearings, on September 30, 1997, *The Wall Street Journal* had reported that during the third quarter of 1997, Salomon Brothers lost at least $200 million in derivatives trades. At Wall Street, the actual money lost was said to be much higher. Salomon has not been one of the top eight U.S. financial institutions active in derivatives, and therefore $200 million in derivatives losses is a significant number.

A year later, derivatives losses run into billions with the Russian meltdown and the near-bankruptcy of Long-Term Capital Management (LTCM).

What was an exception in large-scale losses in 1997 became commonplace in 1998. In fact, derivatives exposure developed into a way of bypassing the 1988 Capital Accord. Released on November 30, 1998, a BIS report offers illuminating statistics on the risks taken with derivatives by the world's 67 bigger banks and 11 major brokers:

- These 78 entities held more than $103.5 trillion in notional principal—a 25 percent yearly increase.
- Assuming Paretto's law, the total NPA on December 31, 1997, was $129.4 trillion.
- Using 25 percent growth for 1998, this amount becomes $161.7 trillion, on December 31, 1998.

This hypothesis is sustained through mid-term benchmarks for Chase Manhattan and J.P. Morgan by BIS. Not only the major credit institutions and investment banks have a huge derivatives exposure, but also derivatives holdings of nonbanks are very large and growing rapidly.

In a large number of cases, management is not really in charge of derivatives exposure. The Barings bankruptcy provides an example. In February 1995, the Bank of England brought Barings to bankruptcy after a derivatives speculation which by all evidence:

- Involved *$27 billion* in derivatives contracts, expressed in NPA, out of its Singapore office.
- Ended in a $1.5 billion loss, wiping out its $900 million in capital.

At the origin of this bankruptcy was said to be the double books kept at the bank's Singapore office of which top management in London was supposedly unaware. This permitted the speculators to purchase in a few week's time 20,000 *index* contracts for proprietary trading without revealing their positions. This error was compound when the Singapore office sold puts and calls to cover margin calls. Two weeks of derivatives trades destroyed two centuries of banking tradition at Barings.

After the Barings bankruptcy, a senior Barclays executive was quoted by *Business Week* as saying: It cannot stop someone from going berserk. But you can have a system to catch it in 24 hours. Part of the problem is the fact that in spite of huge sums of money spent on information technology, the software and computer technology most banks use are medieval.

How close losses in derivatives can come to tearing apart the world's financial fabric is exemplified by the downfall of Long Term Capital Management, in September 1998. Hedge funds are known for the high leverage of their assets. When in 1994 Steinhart's hedge fund lost three-quarters of its capital, it was said that the leverage factor was 10-to-1—a huge number at the time. Four years down the line:

- LTCM managed a 50-to-1 gearing, and cornered itself into being unable to face its obligations.
- When the market turned against its gambles, it lost 90 percent of its capital of $4 billion and still had a huge amount in liabilities.

There is always the irrational, if not plain dishonest, practice of many treasurers of financial, industrial, and other corporations who do not report certain categories of derivatives at all. They hide them off-balance sheet because of the amount of exposure they involve.

FASB also exposed at the U.S. House hearings that several companies have adopted the curious way of reporting derivatives losses as increases in valuation of their assets, stating that: "The information about derivatives and hedging reported in financial statements today is incomplete, inconsistent, and just plain wrong."[1]

FASB Chairman Edmund Jenkins responded to a call for nontransparency in derivatives trades by saying that "gains or losses on derivatives that qualify for hedge accounting should have little or no effect on a company's earnings because they will be offset by comparable losses or gains on the thing that is being hedged—and the result is little or no volatility in earnings."

By contrast, if the hedge is not matched by, and does not move in the opposite direction from the underlying instrument in a compensating way, then said Jenkins: "Maybe the hedge operation was not an effective hedge." This essentially means that the hypothetical hedge was in reality a speculative investment which has turned sour.

During his testimony, Edmund Jenkins revealed some creative accounting practices and stated that these will be eliminated with on-balance sheet reporting of derivatives trades. This position is sound. The problem is that because leveraging has turned banking into a casino society, revealing the size of derivatives losses can lead many heavily exposed institutions to bankruptcy or, in a milder case, to a run on their assets.

Bankruptcy risk sees to it that contrary to the SEC, the Federal Reserve was not happy with the new regulations. Testifying on behalf of the Fed, Federal Reserve Board Governor Susan Phillips said during the same U.S. Congressional hearings that: "The desirability of meaningful disclosure is not the issue. . . . These problems can be minimized by placing market values in meaningful supplemental disclosure rather than by forcing their use in the primary financial statements."

This would have meant continuing reporting derivatives off-balance sheet, a case highly unfavorable to both lenders and investors, and with likely ominous effects on systemic risk. What the Fed and the banks feared from on-balance sheet reporting of derivatives gains and losses was that it uncovers a torrent of red ink connected to derivatives. Securities regulators do not want to continue the hide-and-seek game.

In a way that retains the COSO principles, the change in financial reporting in regard to derivative instruments comes with Statement of Financial Accounting Standards 133. As a reminder, SFAS 133, "Accounting for Derivatives Instruments and Hedging Activities" was published in June 1998. It requires companies to recognize all derivatives and specify which transactions qualify for hedge accounting.

THE EVOLUTION OF FINANCIAL ACCOUNTING STANDARDS THAT TARGET DERIVATIVES

As we saw in Chapter 9, starting in the early 1990s FASB issued four Statements of Financial Accounting Standards that regulate reporting on derivatives financial instruments: SFAS 105, 107, 119, and 133. It is rewarding to look at their differences to appreciate the gradual change in the thinking of regulators and in the rules they want to see enforced. Particularly interesting is the comparison of SFAS 119 and SFAS 133.

These four SFAS aim to standardize accounting procedures for derivative instruments, as well as the derivative portion of certain other contracts that have similar characteristics. They do so by requiring that in the statement of financial position a company recognizes those instruments as assets or liabilities.

This being done, assets and liabilities should be measured at fair value. The importance of this measure is dramatized by the fact that banks, particularly big banks, tend to be overexposed in derivatives as shown in Exhibit 10.1. Notice that this approach to transparency is close to the one adopted by the Swiss National Bank for regulatory reporting purposes, which has been effective since 1996 (see Chapter 13).

Exhibit 10.1   Derivatives Exposure of Four U.S. Banks in Notional Principal Compared to Gross Domestic Product

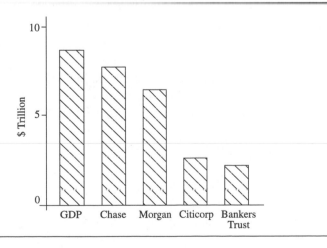

The most important change in this evolution of four successive financial accounting reporting standards, for derivative instruments came with SFAS 119. The new rules addressing derivatives and similar instruments permit the holder to participate in gains and losses without delivering the underlying.

SFAS 119, which was made mandatory at the end of 1994, required disclosures about derivative financial instruments in regard to derivatives that were not subject to Statement 105 because they did not result in off-balance sheet risk. The disclosures which became mandatory concerned the following:

- Amounts.
- Nature.
- Terms.

SFAS 119 also called for a distinction to be made between financial instruments held or issued for trading purposes and those for hedging, which was more generally defined as "purposes other than trading." This is an important change in regulatory reporting standards, introducing the concept of management intent that was further normalized by SFAS 133.

In regard to derivative instruments for trading, SFAS 119 required disclosure of average fair value and of net trading gains or losses. Banks and other entities that hold or issue derivative financial instruments for nontrading reasons, should therefore disclose their purposes. Banks and treasuries that hold or issue derivative financial instruments and account for them as hedges of anticipated transactions, must disclose:

- These anticipated transactions.
- The class of derivatives used for the hedge.
- Amounts of hedging gains or losses being deferred.

This means gains and losses recognized but not yet realized. Public entities must also disclose the transactions or other events that result in recognition of the deferred gains or losses in earnings. Another important characteristic of Statement 119 has been that it encouraged, but did not explicitly require, quantitative information about market risks of assets and liabilities, including derivatives.

Such financial reporting requirements are consistent with the way the bank manages or adjusts its risks. The presentation must be made in a way that is useful for comparing the results of applying the bank's strategies regarding holding, buying, or writing derivatives. Another milestone in regulatory reporting has been that in terms of changes from previous FASB Statements 105 and 107, SFAS 119 called for disaggregation of financial instruments with off-balance sheet risk by the following:

- Class.
- Business activity.
- Exposure.

This must be done in a way consistent with the management of those instruments. SFAS 119 amended SFAS 107 by requiring that fair value information is presented without combining, aggregating, or netting the fair value of derivatives with the fair value of nonderivative financial instruments. It also specified that such information is presented together with the related carrying amounts. This can be done in:

- The body of the financial statement.
- A single footnote.
- A summary table of comprehensive income, addressing recognized gains and losses.

SFAS 119 also specified that such supplementary reporting should make clear whether the referenced amounts represent assets or liabilities. This, too, has been an important definition because it eliminated the freedoms creative accounting sometimes takes in misrepresenting the assets of the institution. The common ground underpinning American, British, Swiss, and other regulators, which came into effect in the mid-1990s, is that more and more accurate disclosure is necessary about derivatives (see Chapter 13). The reason for the change is that derivatives have become quite an important source of exposure in finance, business and industry—and this continues to grow. Therefore, investors, creditors, and regulators need accurate information about the purposes for which derivative financial instruments are held or issued.

Risk management cannot be effectively exercised without significantly improving current reporting practices. This summarizes the reasons for new, more rigorous standards for regulatory reporting of derivatives exposure, as well as for the steady evolution of regulatory reporting requirements, as evidenced by the fact that in a few years SFAS 119 was replaced by SFAS 133.

The standards advanced by SFAS 133 apply to all entities and to all types of derivatives. Its financial reporting rule represents a comprehensive framework that standardizes derivatives accounting. The new statement was supposed to be effective for all fiscal quarters beginning after June 15, 1999, but FASB voted to postpone its implementation for 12 months until June 15, 2000.

The pressure exercised on FASB for a one-year postponement has been propelled by the fact that the Statement Financial Accounting Standard 133 requires a company to mark all derivatives to market, with a clearly defined (hence severely restricted) scope for hedge accounting. The dreaded SFAS 133 does not permit hedging on a portfolio basis.

This delay does not affect the likelihood that the ramifications of FAS 133 will extend far beyond the U.S. market. According to a report by Bank of America, SFAS 133 is expected to be the forerunner of a standard approach to accounting for derivatives.[2] The chief financial officers of non-U.S. companies will be well advised to watch closely the experience of U.S. based companies with FAS 133.

All derivatives must be carried on the balance sheet at fair value, with practically no exceptions other than of management intent (see also Chapter 9). Changes in fair value of derivatives must be recognized in income when they occur. Management intent however, makes a difference—if management intends to hold derivatives as longer term hedges.

If a derivative qualifies as a hedge, a company may elect to use accounting to eliminate or reduce the income statement (P&L) volatility that would arise from reporting changes in its fair value reflected in income. In other words, the type of accounting to be applied varies, depending on the nature of the exposure being hedged.

Income statement volatility is avoided by recording changes in fair value of the derivatives directly to shareholders' equity, thereby creating *equity volatility*. But changes in fair value of the derivative continue to be reported in earnings as they occur, though the impact is counterbalanced by the entity adjusting the carrying value of the asset or liability that is being hedged.

In conclusion, SFAS 133 promotes rigorous disclosure requirements. No grandfathering is allowed. All existing derivatives must be recognized on the balance sheet at fair value. The transition rules focus on what to do with previously unrecognized changes of both derivatives and hedge items.

STATEMENT OF FINANCIAL ACCOUNTING STANDARDS 133 AND HEDGING ACTIVITIES

The foremost contribution of SFAS 133 to reliable financial reporting is its definition that at the inception of the hedge there must be formal documentation of the hedging relationship and the institution's risk management objectives for undertaking the hedge. This puts the spotlight on management intent. Regulatory reporting now includes identification of:

- The hedging instrument.
- The related hedged item.
- The nature of the risk being hedged.
- The hedging instrument's effectiveness in offsetting exposure.

The regulators also want to see a reasonable basis for judging how the institution plans to assess the hedging instrument's effectiveness. This leads to the identification of the entity's risk management strategy for a particular hedging relationship—if any such strategy is in place.

At the inception of hedge and on an ongoing basis, the hedging relationship being worked out is expected to be effective, achieving offsetting changes in fair value attributable to the hedged risk. Such policy must be consistent with the originally documented risk management strategy of the bank. In a way compliant to COSO guidelines, SFAS 133 requires an assessment of effectiveness whenever financial statements or earnings are reported, at least every three months. Gains and losses on a derivative instrument designated and qualifying as fair value hedging must be recognized in the earnings.

As we have seen in Chapter 9, foreign currency fair value hedges are another major class to be reported. SFAS 133 regulations specify that a derivative instrument, or a foreign currency denominated nonderivative financial product, can be designated as hedging the foreign currency exposure to changes in the fair value of a firm commitment, or an identified portion of such commitment.

SFAS 133 states that any use of a nonderivative financial instrument as a means to hedge a foreign currency firm commitment must be consistent with the organization's originally documented risk management strategy. This reduces the liberty to define postmortem some instruments as hedges—which so far has been current practice.

For a foreign currency denominated nonderivative hedging instrument, the foreseeing currency transaction gain or loss on the nonderivative hedging instrument shall be recognized currently in earnings along with the change in the carrying amount of the hedged firm commitment. A derivatives transaction designated as hedging the exposure to changes in fair value of for-sale debt security, can qualify for hedge accounting if:

- It is attributable to changes in foreign currency exchange rates.
- All the fair value hedge criteria defined by the regulation are met.

SFAS 133 describes with equal detail cash flow hedges, specifying that exposure could be related to an existing, recognized asset or liability. For instance, future interest payments on floating rate debt. A cash flow hedge may also be associated to a forecasted transaction, such as a purchase or sale of assets.

The concept to retain from these references is that hedging instruments and hedged items, or transactions, qualify for cash flow hedge accounting on the condition that a number of eligibility criteria are honored. The most important is that at the inception of the hedge there exists formal documentation of the hedging relationship and the institute's risk management strategy for undertaking the hedge. Such documentation should include:

- An identification of the hedge instrument.
- The forecasted hedged transaction.
- The nature of the risk being hedged.
- The hedging instrument's effectiveness in hedging cash flows attributable to the targeted risk.

There must also be a reasonable basis for judging how the institution plans to assess the hedging instrument's effectiveness (see the following section). Both at inception of the hedge and on an ongoing basis, the hedging relationship should be planned to be effective in achieving offsetting risk management tactics.

This is not written in general, abstract terms, but it is focused on a particular hedging relationship during the period that the hedge is designated. Here again, an assessment of effectiveness is required whenever financial statements are made and earnings are reported, at a frequency of at least every three months.

An equally important reference is the one bringing together cash flows and foreign currency transactions. A clause in SFAS 133 addresses derivative instruments designated as hedging the institution's foreign currency exposure to volatility in cash flows. Such cash flows are associated with either:

- A foreign currency denominated forecasted transaction with a counterparty, or
- A foreign currency denominated forecasted intercompany transaction like sale to a foreign subsidiary.

Other criteria to be met include the institution being a party to the transaction; the transaction being denominated in a currency other than the entity's functional currency, and so on. A qualifying foreign currency cash flow hedge shall be accounted for as specified in the FASB regulations for cash flow hedges. Contrary to what concerns fair value, a nonderivative financial instrument may not be designated as a hedging instrument in a foreign currency cash flow hedge.

A special case is that of hedges of foreign currency exposure of a net investment in foreign operations. An organization may designate a derivative instrument as hedging the foreign currency exposure. The gain or loss from the foreign currency transaction on a hedging instrument will be reported in the same way as a transaction adjustment. If there is a difference between gain or loss on the hedging instrument and the amount is reported as a translation adjustment, this difference must be reported in earnings.

THE ASSESSMENT OF HEDGE EFFECTIVENESS

As part of the designation of a hedging relationship, Statement of Financial Accounting Standards 133 requires that a financial institution or other organization define how it will assess a hedge's effectiveness in achieving offsetting changes in fair value or cash flows attributable to the risk being hedged.

Another clause of SFAS 133 specifies that an organization use the accounting method that it chooses consistently throughout the hedge period. For instance, it employs the same method to assess at inception of the hedge and on an ongoing basis whether it expects the hedging relationship to be highly effective in achieving offset; and to determine the ineffective aspect of the hedge.

An important reference to this new regulatory requirement is that the FASB Statement does not attempt to specify a single best method to assess whether a hedge is expected to be effective, measuring the changes in fair values or cash flows used in that assessment or determining hedge ineffectiveness. Instead, it leaves to financial institutions the choice of method which should be in accord with the way the organization specifies its risk management strategy.

In defining how hedge effectiveness will be assessed, an entity must identify whether or not all of the gains, losses, or cash flows, on a hedging instrument will be included in that assessment. However, if assessment of effectiveness is done in a different manner for similar types of hedges, this difference should be justified by the reporting entity.

As expected, in some cases, hedge effectiveness will be easy to assess, or ineffectiveness will be fairly simple to determine. In most cases, however, either job will be rather difficult requiring a sophisticated approach to the measurement of effectiveness or ineffectiveness.

A prerequisite to the measurement of effectiveness is that the critical terms of a hedging instrument and of the entire hedged asset (or liability) are clearly stated. This being done, the institution can more easily evaluate whether changes in fair value or cash flows are or are not attributable to the risk being hedged. Management could also judge whether the hedge can completely offset the risk at inception, and on an ongoing basis.

Essential terms that would need to be the same for a hedge of a financial instrument with an interest rate swap are notional principal amount, maturity, repricing dates, cash settlement date, interest payment, and underlying interest rate basis. When those critical terms of the hedged item or transaction are the same, it could be reasonably concluded that there is an effective aspect of the hedge.

SFAS 133 permits a special handling of a component of the hedging instrument's gain or loss, or cash flows, related to the associated time value. This component can be excluded from the assessment of hedge effectiveness under four different conditions that relate to the question "when" a contract should be excluded from the assessment of hedge effectiveness:

1. When the effectiveness of a hedge with an option contract is assessed as based on changes in the option's intrinsic value.
2. When the effectiveness of a hedge with an option contract is assessed as reflecting changes in the option's minimum value.
3. When the effectiveness of a hedge with a forward contract is assessed as reflecting changes in spot foreign currency exchange rates, and
4. When the effectiveness of a hedge with a forward or futures contract is assessed as based on changes in the spot rate for a commodity.

In each of these conditions, the resulting profit and loss should be reported directly in earnings. No other components of gain or loss, or cash flows, in connection to hedging operations should be excluded from the assessment of hedge effectiveness. These rules are crisp and promote prudential accounting. Therefore, they should be welcome by all parties.

WHAT SHOULD BE THE RISK PREMIUM WITH CREDIT DERIVATIVES?

SFAS 133 underlines the need for disclosing the reporting entity's risk strategy. This is a significant change in regulatory thinking.

Quantitative disclosure of the risks taken with derivative financial instruments is now considered by regulators to be useful and at the same time unlikely to be misunderstood or out of context. Hence the recent drive for disclosing more details about current positions using models, and for experimenting with the most likely effects of recognized gains and losses on equity.

Supervisory authorities have capitalized on the fact that during the last seven years derivatives have been the subject of major studies by different government agencies as well as independent research organizations. All these studies cited the need for significant improvements in risk management and in regulatory reporting.

One of the problems with rules of regulations is that institutions and their rocket scientists are ahead of the curve in new product development which poses new reporting needs. Therefore, calculating the capital at risk day-to-day and at the end of the reporting period is a good practice, but it is insufficient without the addition of management intent and risk strategy.

For example, let's look at the reporting requirements posed by credit derivatives—a relatively new instrument. This is written in a dual sense: for internal management accounting purposes, to guide the hand of the board and of senior management, and for prudential financial reporting to regulators.

For starters, banks tend to extend the notion of risk premiums to longer term loans by using the concept of an expected net present value (ENPV). Specifically, they exploit the difference between the amount the lender realizes by holding the loan for its cash flows (LCF) and the amount the lender would get if he sells the loan at present value (LPV):

$$\Delta L = LCF - LPV$$

Where ΔL is the difference on that loan. Present value is taken as fair value (see Chapter 9) and fair value could be interpreted as market value if the expected net present value (NPV) is calculated with regard to the open market credit spreads. One way of looking at the lender's sale of the loan is as an essentially internal transaction.

This has the effect of transferring credit risk directly to the lender's shareholders. Alternatively, the lender can sell part of his portfolio to the market through credit derivatives.

To appreciate the flow of cash and assumed risk, we can think of lenders as maintaining separate entrepreneurial and capital accounts.[3] The exchange of cash flows between lender and borrower is managed through the entrepreneurial account. But default losses are underwritten by the capital account.

The transfer of credit risk from the entrepreneurial account to the capital account is effected through an internal return swap. If arbitrage pricing is used, this swap has a fair price which is the market price: LPV. The net cash flow into the entrepreneurial account under the swap is this fair price. The expected cash flow into the capital account which results from acquiring and holding the swap is:

$$\Delta L = LCF - LPV$$

This difference between loan cash flow and loan present value can be seen as being equal to the risk premium. In other terms, in expected present value terms, the risk premium derived from a loan represents the net flow of cash into the lender's capital account in return for the credit risk which is in that account.

These references regard internal transactions, executed in a way similar to internal interest rate swaps for the exchange of floating interest rates with fixed interest rates. Both are done for management accounting reasons. Credit derivatives are still to a large degree unregulated. Hence, with some exceptions, there are no precise regulatory requirements concerning them at this particular moment, but they are coming. Most likely, they will be included in the next Statement of Financial Accounting Standards targeting derivatives positions.

In fact, the problem is bigger than one single instrument, involving structured financial products and credit derivatives at large. One of the major issues confronting regulators in connection to their supervision of banks and of the risks taken by institutional investors, is that individual transactions are increasingly collateralized. What this means is that most of good assets of the bank come out of its reach because of collateralization. Therefore, the other asset holders might find they are secured against practically nothing.

To get themselves protected, counterparties now ask for first class collateral. This is true all the way from prime assets to nonfinancial, commercial credit. Regulators are sanguine about their concern on the effects of an extensive collateralization. Because of cherry picking by lenders and counterparties, the best assets are those that go first. Eventually this can make up a bubble that will burst and a financial institution might be worth 10 cents to the dollar.

BENEFICIAL ASPECT OF FASB'S NEW REGULATIONS IN TERMS OF RISK CONTROL

The 1933 and 1934 acts which created the Securities and Exchange Commission in the United States gave the SEC the responsibility to promulgate and enforce accounting standards for the companies that have publicly listed stock and trade on a stock exchange that is regulated. Today there are 15,000 companies that need to go forward with new standards, practically as fast as these are being published. One should fully appreciate that through these changes in regulatory accounting rules, FASB is not attempting to shut down the derivatives market. Its goal is to bring derivatives gains and losses into the light of day.

This can only hurt the high rollers in the derivatives business who tend to exploit a paradox to its limits. Derivative financial instruments have an important role to play in the modern economy, but when they become subject to overgearing, they create a global casino economy, eventually destroying the world's financial fabric. How far exposure goes on a per capita basis is shown in Exhibit 10.2. Why calculate per capita the derivatives exposure? The answer to this query is that overexposure in derivatives particularly characterizes the big banks, and the big banks are seen by regulators as too big to fail.

Exhibit 10.2 The Heavy per Capital Burden of Some Countries Because of Derivatives Overexposure by Banks

	1995 Notional Amount of Derivatives Holdings (Billions $)	1995 Derivatives Holdings per Capita (Thousands $)	1999 Derivatives Holdings per Capita (Thousands $)	1999 Real Money per Capita ($)
Switzerland	6.321	877.7	1.755	70.200
France	9.374	161.7	323	12.920
Sweden	1.278	145.6	291	11.640
United Kingdom	7.367	126.5	253	10.120
Canada	3.321	112.7	225	9.000
Netherlands	1.596	102.9	206	8.240
Japan	11.532	92.2	184	7.360
United States	23.129	87.9	176	7.040
Belgium	689	68.1	136	5.440
Germany	4.258	52.2	104	4.160

As the Continental Illinois Bank in the United States and Credit Lyonnais in France have demonstrated—among so many other examples—it is the taxpayer who finally pays the bill. The government and the central bank find themselves obliged to act to avoid a systemic crisis.

The source of the per capita statistics shown in Exhibit 10.2 is "Public Disclosure of the Trading and Derivatives Activities of Banks and Securities Firms," a joint report by the Basle Committee on Banking Supervision and the Technical Committee of the International Organization of Securities Commissions (IOSCO). The statistics released date back to 1995, therefore, they should be at least doubled to represent 1999 realities, as derivatives trades increase 25 percent to 30 percent per year. Then, they should be divided by 25 to convert notional principal amounts to real money on a per capita basis.

In a derivatives panic, the heaviest taxed will be the Swiss citizen; to the per capita tune of $70.200—or SF 105.300 at current exchange rates.

The lightest burden befalls the German citizen, only to the tune of $4.160 per capita— or DM 7.613. Indeed, the German per capita burden is only 7 percent that of the Swiss, while the French, Swedish, and British citizen (in that order) follow the Swiss in terms of per capita burden in case central banks must do a massive rescue following a derivatives panic.

Does this risk of a derivatives meltdown look far fetched? Not really. When the Indonesian economy collapsed, Peregrine, the premier investment bank of Hong Kong, went down with it because of a huge derivatives exposure with counterparty risk hanging solely from the oral guarantees of one of Suharto's daughters. Right after, with the meltdown of South Korea, the counterparties to derivatives contracts to Korean banks were left high and dry. The same scenario repeated itself with the collapse of the Russian economy.

The best example of the world coming close to systemic risk was the near bankruptcy of Long Term Capital Management (LTCM) at Wall Street in September 1998. If the New York Federal Reserve had not intervened immediately to act as broker in saving the institution, system risk would have been the full $200 billion.

When looking at derivatives gains and losses in the four corners of the global financial system, supervisors face a great challenge. International cooperation is today more fundamental than ever, as contagion between different national markets in the globalized economy is a most likely event.

The good news is that while our financial system is in the midst of rapid transformation, regulatory action is not far behind the new twists. The industrial revolution began in the nineteenth century. The late twentieth and early twenty-first century will see the beginning of the financial revolution that poses a horde of new problems—and of business challenges. SFAS 133 and COSO should be examined under this light.

NOTES

1. *EIR* (October 17, 1997).
2. *Futures and OTC World* (June 1999).
3. D.N. Chorafas, "Credit Risk Management," *Analyzing, Rating, and Pricing the Probability of Default,* vol. 1 (London: Euromoney, 2000).

PART THREE

The Counterparties of COSO: A New Capital Adequacy Framework and Capital at Risk

CHAPTER 11

A New Capital Adequacy Framework by the Basle Committee on Banking Supervision

On June 3, 1999, the Basle Committee on Banking Supervision published "A New Capital Adequacy Framework." While still a Discussion Paper, this document is more sophisticated than the 1988 Capital Accord and to a significant degree modifies the latter's clauses. It will be remembered that the 1988 Accord has been reflected into the European Union's Capital Adequacy Directive (CAD). The rules embedded into the June 1999 document are issued for comment by March 31, 2000.

In principle, proposed rules and regulations regarding capital adequacy focus on internationally active banks. However, the underlying principles are suitable for application to institutions of varying levels of business activity and complexity. This is what CAD has done.

To appreciate the goals of the new capital adequacy framework by the Basle Committee, and the extent of its coverage, it is wise to keep in mind that the original 1988 Capital Accord primarily concerned minimum capital standards to cover credit risk. If and when capital charges were supposed to cover other types of risk, these were effectively assumed to be proportional to credit risk.

The Basle Committee recognized the need to address market risk. After three years of incubation, it published the 1996 Market Risk Amendment that developed explicit capital charges for market risk, but also introduced concepts totally new to the majority of banks like modeling, confidence intervals, and value at risk.

In 1999, the new framework formally takes account of a wider range of actual and potential exposures faced by the banking industry. The proposed rules show that the Basle Committee remains committed to the concept of a level playing field for credit institutions operating in international markets. At the same time, it tries to cope with differences in national accounting, legal, tax, and banking structures that tend to create heterogeneity between national markets influencing a bank's global behavior. The three main pillars on which the new frame of reference is based are:

1. Minimum capital requirements under "standard" and "advanced" regulatory solutions.
2. Review of capital adequacy by the national supervisory authorities.
3. Market discipline to encourage reliable disclosure standards.

Market discipline follows to a very substantial extent the COSO guidelines. No. 2 and No. 3 are the way through which the rules of COSO filter down the organization. A fourth pillar, which is in the making, concerns *operational risk*. By all evidence, this will be elaborated to a much further detail by the Basle Committee in the coming years.

But the fifth pillar of the new capital adequacy regulations is already in place: It is the use of ratings by reputable independent agencies such as Standard & Poor's (S&P), Moody's Investors Service, Fitch IBCA, and A.M. Best for the evaluation of credit risk.[1] As it has been the case with models with the 1996 Market Risk Amendment, this is a "first" in the banking industry regarding its formal acceptance by regulators. The same is true of the sixth pillar: The recognition of credit derivatives as legitimate instruments for the management of credit risk volatility.

The New Capital Adequacy Framework also pays significant attention to characteristic requirement of international institutions, in connection to both banking book and trading book. It addresses the extent of risk reduction made feasible through the use of rating of counterparties and instruments not only by independent agencies, but also by means of *internal ratings*. The use of internal ratings-based (IRB) capital adequacy is the seventh pillar of the framework and it might lead to precommitment (see Chapter 12). If so, this will be a major innovation in capital adequacy regulations.

THE REVISED NOTION OF MINIMUM CAPITAL REQUIREMENTS

One of the distinguishing characteristics of the New Capital Adequacy Framework is the effort to make it flexible and able to evolve with the changes taking place in the financial market. As is to be expected, the proposed framework reflects supervisory objectives including avoidance of systemic risk; promotion of safety and soundness in the financial system; an enhancement of competitive equality; reliable financial reporting (see Chapters 4 and 5 on COSO) and a comprehensive approach to addressing risks.

The original 1988 Capital Accord also evolved over time. For instance, in 1998 the Basle Committee reviewed the subject of composition of Tier-1 capital, by answering the query whether innovative capital instruments should be assigned to the prudential concept of *core capital*:

• Based on Citigroups annual report of 1998, Exhibit 11.1 distinguishes between Tier-1 and Tier-2 capital.
• Also based on annual reports, the Union Bank of Switzerland shows the proportion of Tier-1 capital in the capital base (Exhibit 11.2).

Other initiatives should retain the reader's attention. In October 1998, during the meeting of the International Conference of Banking Supervisors (ICBS) in Sydney, the

Exhibit 11.1   Citigroup's Tier-1 and Tier-2 Capital under Regulatory Guidelines*
(in US$ Millions at Year-End)

	1998	1997
Tier-1 Capital		
Common stockholders' equity	$ 40,395	$ 38,493
Perpetual preferred stock	2,313	3,353
Mandatory redeemable securities of		
subsidiary trusts	4,320	2,995
Minority interest	1,602	1,395
Less: Net unrealized gains on securities		
available for sale	(1,359)	(1,692)
Intangible assets:		
Goodwill	(3,764)	(3,697)
Other intangible assets	(1,620)	(1,202)
50% investment in certain subsidiaries	(110)	(129)
Total Tier-1 Capital	$ 41,777	$ 39,521
Tier-2 Capital		
Allowance for credit losses	$ 6,024	$ 5,910
Qualifying debt	7,296	6,977
Unrealized marketable equity securities gains	21	—
Less: 50% investment in certain subsidiaries	(110)	(129)
Total Tier-2 Capital	$ 13,231	$ 12,758
Total capital (Tier-1 and Tier-2)	$ 55,008	$ 52,279
Net risk-adjusted assets	$481,208	$472,095

* As shown in Annual Report of 1998.

Basle Committee agreed on a set of guidelines subject to which innovative instruments, including contributions to the capital by silent partners, may be assigned to core capital. Under these guidelines, up to 16 percent of core capital may consist of innovative components.

A comprehensive approach to capital requirements usually evolves around the constituent parts of capital. The Basle Committee's definition of elements of capital was originally set out in the 1988 Accord, and it was further clarified in the press release of October 27, 1998, on "Instruments Eligible for Inclusion in Tier-1 Capital." There is no proposal at this stage to make further amendments to the definition of capital, other than stating that minimum capital requirements will continue to consist of:

- Established regulatory capital guidelines.
- Metrics for measuring risk exposure.
- Rules specifying the level of capital in relation to assumed risks.

Because homogeneity in the way capital reserves are computed, maintained, and reported is most crucial, the Basle Committee, International Monetary Fund (IMF), and

Exhibit 11.2 Union Bank of Switzerland: Basle Committee Capital Adequacy Ratio at Group Level

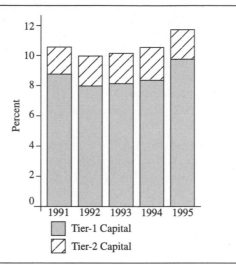

World Bank have repeatedly urged common principles in banking supervision to be applied at the global level. A basic concept is one of achieving agreement on the definition, implementation of, and compliance of *core principles.*

To reach this objective, the Basle Committee set up a Liaison Group consisting of banking supervisors from the Group of Ten (G-10) and other countries, to which IMF and the World Bank are participating as observers. The first mission of this Liaison Group was to carry out a global survey on compliance with core principles, in some 150 countries participating to the International Conference of Banking Supervisors in Sydney (October 1998).

As the results of this study indicated, some countries are not in compliance with the rules. Therefore, the Liaison Group submitted a proposal for a more detailed method with criteria enabling an accurate definition of compliance with core principles. No doubt such findings have filtered through the New Capital Adequacy Framework, even if the latter concerns only countries of the G-10.

In connection with regulatory capital and measures of risk exposure, the Basle Committee underlines the importance of sound accounting (see Chapters 2 and 3) and valuation procedures (see Chapter 14) able to produce realistic and prudent measures of assets and liabilities as well as to calculate recognized and realized profits and losses. All these elements impact on the determination of capital reserves. In a way that fully fits the COSO principles, the Committee also underlines that weak or inadequate accounting policies, and financial reporting practices have the effect of undermining prudential capital requirements and their usefulness. Faulty accounting causes overstated and unreliable capital ratios and wrong estimates of financial staying power. Reliable financial reporting must therefore rest on a solid accounting basis.

In developing a revised framework for capital adequacy, the Basle Committee emphasizes the importance of *minimum regulatory capital requirements,* considering this its first pillar. This approach is seen in conjunction with a prudential supervisory review amplified by the need for greater *market discipline.* As stated earlier, these are the pillars on which is built a structure much more sophisticated than the 1988 Capital Accord, which is able to address different levels of senior management literacy in technology.

The current Accord will serve as a standardized approach for capital requirements, probably at the majority of banks. The model-based part of the new regulation will appeal to high-technology banks able to comply with its requirements.

High-technology financial institutions that employ rocket scientists[2] will benefit from an internal-ratings-based system that might form the basis for setting capital charges through quantitative and qualitative standards subject to supervisory approval. This will work on a country-by-country basis at the discretion of national supervisors. In consultation with the banking industry, the Basle Committee intends to examine IRB in its effort to develop an alternative approach to a flat rate of capital adequacy.

The underlying concept is that internal rating, which might eventually lead to precommitment, will be an important step in aligning capital charges with underlying exposure. However, the die is not cast and the Basle Committee will closely monitor developments in portfolio credit risk modeling for possible use of algorithms and heuristics in regulatory capital definitions.

The Group of Ten central bankers and regulators are also examining a number of important credit risk mitigation techniques for the purpose of more accurate computation of capital needs. New instruments have also attracted the regulators' attention. The Committee is seeking comment on ways and means for devising a rigorous approach for:

- Credit derivatives.
- On-balance sheet netting.
- The evaluation of collateral.
- Covenants and guarantees.

As explained in the Framework document, the more sophisticated part of the rules that will govern capital requirements serves to clarify and broaden the scope of application of analytical computations addressing minimum prudential levels. Risk weights will be applied to different types of exposures helping in obtaining greater accuracy.

For instance, in regard to sovereigns, the Basle Committee proposes replacing the existing approach by a system that would use external credit assessments for determining risk weights. Directly or indirectly, a similar concept will apply in varying degrees to the weighting of exposures to correspondent banks, securities firms, high leverage institutions (HLIs, which practically means hedge funds), and corporate clients.

The background notion is that with appropriate diversification and choice of business partners, it might be possible to reduce risk weights for high quality credits while, at the same time, introducing a higher-than-100 percent risk weight for low quality exposures. Thus closely approximates the concept of reduced, normal, and tightened inspection. Another risk weighting scheme is projected to address asset securitization. The discussion paper also talks about the application of a 20 percent credit conversion factor for certain types of short-term commitments.

Another major improvement to current regulatory practices is that new capital rules will go beyond explicit capital charges for market risk in the trading book. They will cover interest rate risk in the banking book (see Chapter 15) as well as operational risk. The Basle Committee proposes to develop a capital charge for interest rate risk in the banking book for those credit institutions where interest rate risk is significantly above average. It also projects capital charges for operational risk and some other risk factors.

A MORE RIGOROUS SUPERVISORY REVIEW OF CAPITAL ADEQUACY

The definition of a framework regarding supervisory review of capital adequacy is important because, as with the 1996 Market Risk Amendment, national regulators retain significant freedom of action in terms of the implementation of capital accords. The Basle Committee seeks to assure that a credit institution's capital position is consistent with its overall risk profile and management strategy. This approach is intended to encourage early supervisory intervention.

The basic thinking underlying an agreement that is binding to the G-10 central banks and other regulatory bodies is that supervisors should have the ability to require credit institutions to hold capital in excess of minimum regulatory capital ratios. Concomitant to this is the drive to convince the senior management of commercial banks about the need for:

- Developing a rigorous internal capital assessment process that is both qualitative and quantitative—and one that can be successfully tested.
- Setting targets for capital commensurate with the bank's particular risk profile, market operations, and adequacy of internal controls.

The second item reflects guidelines by COSO. The Basle Committee expects that this internal process will be subject to supervisory review and intervention, where and when such action proves to be appropriate. Emulating COSO's standards, the Basle regulators want to see that a bank would publicly disclose qualitative and quantitative information about its exposure in a way characterized by:

- *Transparency* regarding the risk profile inherent in on-balance sheet and off-balance sheet, which allows judgment about the stability of an institution's financial position.
- *Reliable disclosure* of a bank's capital position, risk exposure, and other elements illustrating whether an institution is able to remain solvent under stress.

The New Capital Adequacy Framework emphasizes the need for information on the sensitivity of a bank's earnings to market changes. Therefore, it specifies that an institution should present sufficient data to help regulators understand both the nature and magnitude of risks. Position data is an example of quantitative information, while management intent and corporate strategies constitute qualitative information.

The discussion paper also asks for comparative information relative to previous years to provide regulators and other users of financial statements with a perspective on *trends* in the institution's underlying exposure. A bank is asked to disclose its risk-based capital ratios calculated in accordance with the methodology prescribed in the 1998 Capital Accord and any other regulatory capital standards that it must meet. The goal is to assure enough information for assessment of whether available capital is sufficient to meet the following:

- Credit risk.
- Market risk.
- Other types of risk.

Confirming the policy that has been developed by many central banks regarding the examination of internal controls, the New Capital Adequacy Framework specifies that a bank should make qualitative disclosures about the internal processes it uses for evaluating its exposure and its own capital adequacy. The underlying concept is that these disclosures will assist market participants in judging:

- How an institution's management of its capital adequacy relates to its other risk management processes.
- How well the credit institution will be able to withstand future volatility and liquidity challenges in financial markets.

This leads to the issue of *capital structure.* The new regulation specifies that a bank should disclose information about its capital structure, including the components of capital and associated terms, as well as key features of capital instruments. This is particularly required in connection with innovative, complex, and hybrid capital instruments (read: derivatives).

A credit institution should also disclose information about its reserves for credit losses, and other exposures leading to red ink. Such data must provide a clear picture of the bank's capacity to absorb losses, including any conditions that may merit special attention. The requirements add up to an analysis of strength of financial staying power, including:

- Maturity of positions.
- Level of seniority.
- Step-up provisions.
- Interest or dividend deferrals.
- Terms of derivatives embedded in hybrid capital instruments.

Regulatory rules and directives with specific reference to disclosure requirements have been included, regarding Special Purpose Vehicles (SPVs) which are set up and capitalized by several institutions as a way of improving their rating.[3] SPVs have been crucial to counterparties whose policy is to deal only with high-rated business partners. Now, with the emphasis placed by the Basle Committee on external ratings, their importance increases.

The New Capital Adequacy Framework iterates that in terms of capital structure, a bank should disclose the components of its capital based on the 1998 Accord, including the amounts of Tier-1, Tier-2, and Tier-3 capital (the latter if applicable). We have seen an example with Tier-1 and Tier-2 capital earlier. This disclosure is strengthened by the requirement for information on the bank's accounting policies, including those regarding income recognition, valuation of assets and liabilities, and provisioning.

Another clause included in the Discussion Paper in connection to supervisory review, concerns capital above regulatory minima. This clause classifies capital requirements established by the 1998 Accord as *minima,* and credit institutions are expected to hold capital in excess of that level as appropriate for their exposure.

A significant number of factors enter into this equation: The commercial bank's management experience, risk appetite, quality of its key personnel, nature of the markets in which it operates, dependability and volatility of its earnings, track record in managing exposure, quality of capital and access to new capital. Each one of these factors varies from one institution to the next.

Other factors influencing the add-on over minima are operational risks, diversification of bank's activities, concentration of exposures, assets, liabilities, and liquidity profile. Equally important is the complexity of the credit institution's legal support services as well as its organizational structure. The adequacy of risk management systems and internal controls plays a key role, and so does the degree of supervision by other regulatory authorities.

While the New Capital Adequacy Framework is still a discussion document, the fact that so many elements are included is most significant because it identifies a trend in bank supervision. The list of factors just mentioned implies that a credit institution should allow for appropriate margins above the minimum regulatory capital requirements. These margins will differ across credit institutions.

As part of the process for evaluating capital adequacy, the board and senior management should be able to identify, evaluate, and experiment with risks across all business lines in which the bank is active. An institution must position itself in a way permitting it to determine whether its capital levels are indeed appropriate:

- Differentiating risk exposure among various channels.
- Providing a complete overview of banking book risk profiles.
- Identifying concentrations of credit risk.
- Being sensitive to trends in the portfolio.

For instance, are there more lower quality loans as a percentage of total loans than targeted by the board's strategy? Have investments grown more risky over time? Are credit risk and market risk limits violated? Is there a process of internal controls able to assure objectivity and consistency in senior management evaluations? Is regulatory financial reporting done in full compliance to rules and standards? Most of these queries are similar to those asked in regard to compliance with the rules established by COSO.

THE NEED FOR APPLYING A MARKET DISCIPLINE

Some experts think that the rules of the New Capital Adequacy Framework that are closest to COSO concern *market discipline*. Peer evaluation and a more general definition of watchdogs, including counterparties, are seen as a good way to encourage higher disclosure standards and to promote the role of market players in inducing credit institutions to hold adequate capital, commensurate with the risks they take.

The Basle Committee intends to issue further guidance on public disclosure, but also to look at market discipline as having the potential to reinforce capital regulation as well as other supervisory duties and procedures. The goal is to put in place strong incentives on institutions to conduct their business in a safe and efficient manner, including the establishment of appropriate cushions against potential future losses arising from trading, investments, loans, and other exposures.

There is no doubt that supervisors have a strong interest in facilitating effective market discipline as a way to strengthen the banking system and its safety nets. Issued in September 1998, the Basle Committee's "Enhancing Bank Transparency" explains how a bank perceived by the market as safe and well-managed is likely to obtain more favorable terms and conditions in its relations with depositors, creditors, investors, correspondent banks, and other counterparties.

Everyone of these players will require higher risk premiums and additional collateral or other safety measures if the credit institution with which it deals presents more risk. An example is *Japan Premium* instituted by the financial market in the mid- to late 1990s as soon as counterparties detected the existence of inordinate risks associated with Japanese institutions.

No doubt, because of its size and sophistication, the global financial market is like a giant in the land of the liliputians. Peers are the other "giants." But we should not forget the existence of conflicts of interest. Because peers tend to trade with peers, they know they are all exposed and therefore self-explanatory measures may not function so well— in spite of what one might think that this is a foregone conclusion.

Let's look at a recent example: In September 1998, the threat of one hedge fund— Long-Term Capital Management (LTCM)—to trigger a meltdown of the global financial market forced a direct intervention by the Federal Reserve of New York. The peers, and even the proprietors, did not act as watchdogs through their own initiative.

It was the regulators who persuaded a group of 14 LTCM shareholders and creditor institutions to step in with $3.5 billion in new cash, and it was this intervention by the Fed as broker, which prevented liquidation of LTCM's highly geared derivatives positions in every major world market.

How much money was at stake? Early estimates suggested the LTCM exposure amounted to $100 billion. By late November 1998, this had grown to $200 billion—a gearing of 50:1. But by May 1999, some estimates brought this amount to the astronomical level of $1 trillion. No matter if it were $100 billion, $200 billion, or $1 trillion, the peers, and the market, had not disciplined LTCM.

There was a lack of prudence by major players in the world's financial system in extending a practically unlimited amount of credit to one single institution, which was known to be highly leveraged. Most surprising, until the September 23, 1998, meeting at the New York Federal Reserve, none of the LTCM's 14 creditors were aware of how much money the other 13 had loaned to LTCM.

This is what happens with lack of transparency in off-balance sheet deals and credit line masquerading as *margin accounts.* To avoid a repetition of this potentially catastrophic incident, the SEC is now issuing new rules requiring any publicly traded company to reveal all significant lending exposure to hedge funds. This will help in market discipline.

Regulators of credit institutions and securities firms would demand new reserve provisions against losses at banks and brokers lending to hedge funds. This is an attempt to close the so-called "Basle Loophole," of secret bank loans to hedge funds disguised as margin accounts. There is also a Basle Loophole that concerns:

- Financial derivatives.
- Interest rate swaps (IRS).
- Forward rate agreements (FRA).
- Equity index trades, and more exotic instruments.

Also, with the 1988 Accord, no risk contingencies were required for certain off-balance sheet lending by a bank to finance derivative positions of hedge funds and other high leverage institutions (HLI). Such credits could be more or less hidden from regulators by burying them in a vague declaration of liabilities—in spite of the fact that credit risk, reputational risk, and legal risk may be hidden in this transaction. To close this loophole, proposed legislation would also require that hedge funds file financial information every quarter indicating degree of gross risk, most likely without including specifics on the fund's trading positions.

Congress might also pass a law on contract netting, settling a contested gray area of derivatives exposures, in the event that one party to a contract fails. Offshore bank secrecy havens are also being pressured by the Group of Ten to require more compliance with international regulatory standards in their supervision of resident hedge funds and other institutions.

Speaking at the May 3, 1999, financial conference in Manila, Japanese Finance Minister Kiichi Miyazawa noted that government authorities in several Western nations "feel that hedge funds have to do very much with the occurrence" of the 1997–1998 crisis in East Asia. "So," Miyazawa says, "we are now thinking about what hedge funds can do in the future."[4] Many other government officials and regulators feel similarly. Market discipline starts at credit institutions and takes under its wings the HLIs.

There will be many surprises when greater transparency is achieved. Transparency in financial reporting today is very uneven, not only in the Third World but also among G-10 countries. The frightening statistics shown in Exhibit 1.6 and repeated here as

Exhibit 11.3 Demodulated Derivatives Exposure Compared to Equity and Assets of Major Credit Institutions as of March 31, 1999 (in U.S.$ Billions)

	Equity	Assets	NPA in Derivatives	Demodulated Derivatives Exposure*	Ratio to Equity	Ratio to Assets
JP Morgan	11.3	261	8.861	295.4	× 16.1	1.132
Bankers Trust	4.7	133	2.563	85.4	× 18.2	0.642
Chase Manhattan	23.8	366	10.353	345.1	× 14.5	0.943
Citigroup	42.7	669	7.987	266.2	× 6.2	0.398
BankAmerica	45.9	618	4.438	147.9	× 3.2	0.239
Banc One	20.6	262	1.472	49.1	× 2.4	0.187

*By a factor of 30.

Exhibit 11.3 concentrate on American banks because data cannot be easily obtained from European and Japanese banks who specialize in keeping high exposure figures close to their chest, while local legislation and national regulators permit them to do so.[5]

The inordinate amount of exposure taken by big institutions is the reason why I call these statistics frightening. At the top of the list, the Morgan Bank has an exposure in derivatives amounting to 1610 percent of its capital. Derivatives exposure at Bankers Trust (now part of Deutsche Bank) is even higher, 1820 percent of its capital. But J.P. Morgan also has the distinction of having exposed in derivatives alone more than 100 percent of its assets. Chase Manhattan comes second with nearly 100 percent of its assets on the block.

The Basle Committee acknowledges that the goal of a global market discipline may in a way be negatively affected because of differences in legal systems in various countries, with the resulting difficulties in implementing this third pillar of market discipline. It also recognizes that differences in a credit institution's reliance on financial markets can see to it that the potential of market discipline varies across countries.

A bank may not be subject to market discipline from fully insured depositors who have nothing at risk, hence no motive to impose discipline. While it is true that public opinion may exercise pressure, by all likelihood this will be felt in an indirect way via legislation. A proposal made by the faculty of Columbia University in the direction of market discipline is that global institutions buy equity in each other, thereby having a say through the lever of management control.

An integral part of market discipline is the use of ratings by reputable independent agencies in connection with the exposure taken with counterparties and instruments. How this may work for different classes of counterparties will be explained later. We should take notice that this is the first time regulators officially discuss that the evaluation of credit institutions by third parties is a means for fine-tuning capital requirements.

The Basle Committee further suggests that effective market discipline requires reliable and timely information, enabling counterparties to make well-founded risk assessments. Credit institutions should disclose all key features of the exposure that may give rise to losses, and of their financial staying power in positioning themselves against such losses. The keywords, suggested in the Discussion Paper are those qualifying eligible external credit assessment:

- Objectivity.
- Transparency.
- Credibility.
- Staying power.

National supervisory authorities will be responsible for recognition of institutions based on such criteria. Market participants need similar kinds of reliable information to judge a bank's ability to remain solvent. Such dependable and detailed information should, at a minimum, be provided in annual financial reports, including qualitative and quantitative details on the institution's business activities, risk profile, risk control systems, financial condition, and performance.

Correctly, the Basle Committee does not attempt to set disclosure standards across countries. This is the business of national supervisors who have the power to implement disclosure requirements directly through binding regulations that respect the cultural differences and business practices of each country, but at the same time provide a homogeneous basis of risk evaluation and a playing field where institutions can compete on equal terms.

THE FORMAL REFERENCE MADE TO OPERATIONAL RISK

The New Capital Adequacy Framework acknowledges the importance for institutions of risks other than credit and market risk, and it suggests that a rigorous control environment is essential to prudent management of these other risks. The goal is that of limiting compound exposure, leading to the notion that additional steps to those taken with credit risk and market risk are necessary to assure sound management.

For the first time in documents issued by the Basle Committee a clear reference is made to *operational risks* and the need for capital to readily face it. This is followed by the statement that the Committee is soliciting comments on ways and means to gauge operational risk, including a range of approaches that will enable it to achieve the aim of an objective evaluation and measurement of such risk(s).

The notion of operational risks did not appear overnight. During the last two years, one of the worst guarded secrets in the financial industry has been that among the most advanced institutions analytical studies are under way aimed at developing ways to manage a broad category of such risks. But even Tier-1 banks have only recently begun to develop a framework for explicitly measuring and monitoring operational risk.

The first question one has to address is: What is operational risk really representing? Practically all banks see some form of linkage between credit, market, and operational risk. An operational problem, for instance in settlements, can create market risk. But operations is no monolithic event happening in just the payment channel. Based on my research, operational risk has these constituent parts:

- Board risk.
- Management skill risk.
- Professional skill risk.
- Transaction risk.
- Fiduciary/Trust risk.
- Payment risk.
- Settlement risk.
- Back office risk.
- Security risk.
- Technology risk.

Each of these parts of operational exposure can be detailed with grater precision. For instance, technology risk can be analyzed into risk of falling behind, risk of professional obsolescence in skills, risk of slow time-to-market, vendor failure risk, network risk, database risk, software risk, and so on.

No two parties currently agree on the exact definition of operational risk. Coopers and Lybrand (now PriceWaterhouseCoopers) studied operational risk based on a self-assessment questionnaire. The questions posed to participants to this research ranged from strategic planning to settlement risk—a broader definition than the one used here. A near consensus has been that operational risk stems from *uncertainty* due to:

- Management directives are comprehensive and clearly stated.
- Employees are performing their duties as instructed.
- They exercise their authority in a manner consistent with enterprise value.

During the 1980s and 1990s, we have witnessed several spectacular manifestations of operations risk in the financial services industry, including the events that led to the demise of Drysdale, Barings, NatWest Markets, and Kidder Peabody. Such events contributed in some cases to mergers of impacted firms, in others to outright bankruptcy, and in still others to a large-scale reorientation of corporate efforts.

Events connected to operational risk are distressing to the financial institution under their spell, but they also present an opportunity for others in the industry to learn how to improve their own internal control and risk management practices. A rigorous internal control appears to be the best answer to operational risk, keeping a clear separation between front desk and back office.

The Basle Committee has identified a number of options, ranging from simple benchmark to modeling techniques, among likely approaches for assessing capital against *operational risk*.[6] A relatively simple benchmark might be based on an aggregate measure of business activity such as gross revenue, fee income, operating costs, managed assets, total assets adjusted for off-balance sheet exposures, or a combination of these references reflected into the balance sheet by means of an anchoring reference. One of the challenges is to incorporate a system of merits and demerits—acting as incentives to better operational risk control.

Neither is operational risk the only issue requiring thorough study. Other critical factors are reputational risk and legal risk—both sufficiently important to devote necessary human and financial resources to quantify their level and incorporate them into an assessment of overall capital adequacy by institution. Examples on how costly legal risk can be are the settlements by:

- Merrill Lynch to Orange County and the City of San Jose.
- Bankers Trust to Gibson Greetings and Procter and Gamble.

We should welcome the change in rules and directives for prudential regulation. The widening range of regulatory attention in terms of capital requirements is a natural sequel to the globalization of banking. The growing importance of risk categories that in the past were not taken as outstanding has led the Basle Committee to conclude that such exposures are too vital not to be treated within the capital adequacy framework. Therefore, the Committee proposes to develop an explicit capital charge for other risks than those relating to market factors and counterparties, and is exploring ways in which this could be done in a practical manner and in a way sensitive to the changes taking place in banking and finance.

While the focus of these references is on international banks, the guiding principles embodied in the control of operational, reputational, and legal risks are generally suitable for any bank in any jurisdiction. Rather than distinguishing between global and national banks, account should be taken of individual circumstances—from the legal framework, to microeconomic and marcoeconomic factors. Regulators will need to consider whether essential preconditions are met, starting with sound accounting principles and practices as well as reliable financial reporting. COSO provides an example on sound practices. Circumstances of individual banks such as business strategy, management culture, risk appetite, level of technology, size of equity and assets, diversification, and risk management systems are most relevant to how and when operational risks make themselves felt. Indirectly, the New Capital Adequacy Framework advises that supervisors in countries that are subject to sizable changes in economic conditions and banking practice should consider imposing higher capital requirements on their banks to take account of operational and legal risks.

As this chapter has documented, even credit risk must be rethought in terms of computational requirements (therefore technology risk) and the existence of factual, documented references beyond the three pillars examined earlier in this chapter. The use of external rating by reputable independent agencies will bear significant weight in credit risk evaluation.

This new-found emphasis on outsourcing credit risk management expertise is a departure from past policies where the only outside source of credit standing was the organization that succeeded the Marshall Plan. For more than a decade, money center banks based in countries of the Organization for Economic Cooperation and Development (OECD) have had to abide by the 1988 Capital Adequacy Accord of the Basle Committee on Banking Supervision, but at the same time OECD members enjoyed a de facto higher credit standing.

The Basle Committee sees the potential for focused work in identifying in more detail specific factors that should be considered in assessing a bank's overall risk profile, adequacy of capital, and extent to which it should hold capital above minima. Considering approaches more directly relating a bank's capital requirement to its operational risks is an issue still in its beginning. Clearer perspectives are expected to develop through internal study and feedback received by the consultative process the Discussion Paper has launched.

USING RATINGS BY INDEPENDENT AGENCIES TO GAUGE EXPOSURE IN THE BANKING BOOK

The New Capital Adequacy Framework proposes a new standardized approach for risk weighting of assets and liabilities in the banking book, placing greater reliance on external credit assessments than that available with the 1988 Capital Accord and the 1996 Market Risk Amendment. However, there is a precedent. The Market Risk Amendment did confirm the use of credit assessments by independent rating agencies in regard to certain trading book items. The Basle Committee brings this concept into the banking book but also states that there are some concerns about:

- Incentives for proceeding along the path of a rating procedure by third parties.
- Possible effects of an extensive use of external assessment on the independent rating agencies themselves.

As a result, the Committee proposes that national supervisors should not allow banks to place in an automatic way assets in preferential risk weighting categories, based on external credit risk rating. Institutions should do so when they themselves and their supervisors are satisfied with the quality, skill, and methodology of the assessment source.

The Committee also wants to see that credit institutions adopt a consistent approach in using third-party assessments and do not try to capitalize on differences existing among such assessments; the so-called cherry picking. Current guidelines distinguish between categories of claims on:

- Sovereigns.
- Subnationals, such as noncentral government public sector entities.
- Credit institutions.
- Securities firms.
- Corporates.
- Property loans.
- Higher risk institutions.
- Off-balance sheet items.
- Asset securitization.
- Other claims.

Regarding sovereign borrowing, the 1998 Capital Accord has already applied different risk weights to claims of commercial banks on sovereign and central bank obligations. Such weights depend on whether or not the claim is on a member of the Organization of European Cooperation and Development. This concept extends to claims on banks that are weighted differently depending on whether the issuer is incorporated in a country that is a member of the OECD.

In the past, such differentiation led to some problems exemplified by the case of Mexico, which nearly defaulted right after it joined OECD. For the purposes of the 1988 Capital Accord, the OECD group comprises all members of the OECD or countries that have concluded special lending arrangements with the IMF, specifically, a country that is associated with IMF's General Arrangements to Borrow (GAB), and has not rescheduled its external sovereign debt within the previous five years.

At the time this approach was taken, the notion was present that some countries might not qualify for inclusion on the so-defined preferential group, on grounds related to default likelihood. There has been as well the opposite risk: Potentially low credit risk countries outside the OECD would be paying a higher interest rate.

In spite of such shortcomings, in the late 1980s the OECD/non-OECD criterion was retained as a workable proxy for identifying sovereigns that should be eligible for better risk-weighted treatment—and this led to several contrarian opinions. As a result, in the ensuing years the Basle Committee discussed ways to address this problem. Other items, too, were brought up for reevaluation, such as the impact of derivatives on credit risk.

Most people who run a credit evaluation process today understand that risk criteria have to be objective and that establishing and maintaining them requires skill. If the OECD/non-OECD dichotomy is not that well documented, and ends by being questionable because of the risks it involves, then outsourcing the credit rating job to professional independent agencies might be a good alternative.

Outsourcing part of the responsibility of grading credit risk suggests itself because of the complexity of the problem. Talented people are at a premium, public databases hold a wealth of information, and dependable ratings could be available on short notice.

The biggest and best known independent rating agencies: Standard & Poor's (S&P), an independent business unit of McGraw-Hill; and Moody's Investors Service, an independent business unit of Dunn and Bradstreet; the Anglo-American Fitch IBCA; and U.S.-based A.M. Best (which specializes in ratings in the insurance industry), are regulated by the SEC which is known to be a tough supervisor.[7] While smaller rating agencies do exist in other countries, such as Japan, they tend to be local and therefore do not enter into our discussion about global rating.

The Basle Committee has used S&P's rating scales to convey the rating message, but (correctly) the New Capital Adequacy Framework goes to some lengths to explain this is only an example. One could equally use the rating structure of Moody's or Fitch IBCA, or some other agency. The Committee also makes reference to an internal ratings-based (see Chapter 12) solution to help in calculating capital requirements. It would not be sufficient for a bank to include banking book claims that are unrated but only deemed to be of comparable quality. The Committee proposes to use the general approach adopted for trading book reasons to establish a similar solution for the banking book.

Credit institutions should appreciate the novelty of the rating issue, its bifurcation between independent agencies and internal credit risk models, and the fact that a number of assessments will be required before their use is permitted as the basis for capital charges. Two assessments by eligible independent rating agencies would be needed, except where no eligible institution has given a lower assessment. Then, one assessment will be enough.

What is in essence proposed by the Basle Committee is the use of ratings by independent agencies to replace the current approach for claims of sovereigns and central banks with a system that permits risk weights applied to such claims to be benchmarked in the traditional way:

- The assessment to be used should generally be in respect of the sovereign's long-term foreign currency obligations.
- Claims of sovereigns and central banks of higher rating could be eligible for a zero risk weight.

This does not necessarily mean that the new method being proposed has no shortcomings. For instance, the Basle Committee says that for sovereigns rating agencies currently have a rather limited track record with regard to nonprime borrowers. Also, it is not always sure that such ratings always take full account of strengths and weaknesses of the financial infrastructure in a particular country. The Committee therefore proposes to make use, as well, of other entities performing assessments, such as export insurance agencies in the Group of Ten.

RESERVE REQUIREMENTS FOR EXPOSURE TO SOVEREIGNS, SUBNATIONALS, AND BANKS

The New Capital Adequacy Framework recognizes that different external credit assessment institutions use heterogeneous credit analysis methodologies and ratings terminology, but seems confident that cross-checking between methods would help to increase the level of ratings dependability. Until a global rating system stabilizes, the Basle Committee proposes that:

- The zero-weighted category is limited to sovereigns with higher credit quality, for example, with a minimum of AA−.
- Claims on countries rated A+ to A− would be eligible for a 20 percent risk weight.
- Claims rated BBB+ to BBB− would be eligible for a 50 percent risk weight.
- Claims rated BB+ to B− would be risk weighted at 100 percent, as would those on countries without a rating.
- Claims on countries rated below B− would be weighted at 150 percent.

Exhibit 11.4 summarizes reserve requirements for lending to sovereigns, banks, and corporates, based on ratings by independent agencies. (The two options available for banks as well as the row securitized instruments are discussed next.) The last two bullets

Exhibit 11.4 Reserve Requirements for Loans to Sovereigns, Banks, Corporate Clients and Securitized Instruments Based on Ratings by Independent Agencies*

Rated by	High Quality	Average Quality		Low Quality		Unrated
Standard & Poor's and Fitch IBCA	AAA to AA−	A+ to A−	BBB+ to BBB−	BB+ to B−	Below B−	
Moody's Investors Service	Aaa to Aa3	A1 to A3	Baa1 to Baa3	Ba1 to B3	Below B3	—
Export Insurance Agencies	1				7	—

Claims on		High Quality (%)	Average Quality According to Rating		Low Quality According to Rating		Unrated (%)
			A (%)	BBB (%)	BB,B (%)	Less Than B (%)	
Sovereigns		0	20	50	100	150	100
Banks[†]	Option 1	20	50	100	100	150	100
	Option 2	20	50[‡]	50[‡]	100[‡]	150	50[‡]
Corporates		20	100	100	100	150	100
Securitized Instruments		20	50	100	150	Deducted from Capital	

*For other claims, 100% weighting would remain the standard risk accounting approach.
[†]With Option 1, risk-weight is based on risk-weight of the sovereign in which the bank is incorporated. With Option 2 risk-weight is based on assessment of individual credit institution.
[‡]Claims, on banks, of original maturity less than six months would receive one category more favorable risk-weight than is usual on bank's claims.

leave a loophole since countries would rather not be rated than risking getting a B−. It is better not to be rated, if one qualifies for B− or worse.

A more flexible treatment is advanced for exposures taken by credit institutions to their own sovereign or central bank, if these are denominated in domestic currency and funded in that currency. National supervisors must decide if a lower risk weight can be provided for such exposures, but it is proper to remember that independent agencies tend to rate the domestic debt higher than the external debt.

The Basle Committee does not believe banks should rely on an external assessment of a sovereign borrower, where the sovereign does not provide sufficient information about its financial and economic status. To be eligible for a risk weight below 100 percent, the country would have to subscribe to the IMF's Special Data Dissemination Standards (SDDS) publicly available economic and financial statistics. Supplemental disclosure requirements are also under study.

The New Capital Adequacy Framework suggests that claims on public sector entities should generally be treated as claims on banks of that country, though national supervisory authorities have the right to treat claims on domestic public sector entities in the same way as claims on the sovereign. When this choice is made, other supervisory authorities may allow claims by their banks on such entities also to receive such weighting.

The 1988 Capital Accord provides some special treatment for claims on banks incorporated in OECD countries. To these are added short-term claims on banks incorporated in non-OECD countries. The Framework suggests that both may be risk-weighted at 20 percent.

By contrast, long-term claims on banks incorporated in non-OECD countries are risk-weighted at 100 percent. Because the methodology for risk-weighting claims on sovereigns is about to shift to an approach based on credit assessments by independent rating agencies, the Basle Committee has drafted two main options.

1. A revision of the 1988 Capital Accord so that claims on credit institutions would be risk-weighted on the basis applied to claims on the country in which the bank is incorporated.

   In this case, the weight used for the bank would be one category less favorable than that used for the sovereign. There will also be a cap of a 100-percent weight, except for claims on banks of the lowest rated countries, where the risk weight on the institution would have a cap of 150 percent.

2. The use of ratings assigned directly to banks by an independent rating agency, when these are available (which, usually, is the case for major institutions).

   It is projected that in this case most claims on banks, including those unrated, would receive a 50 percent weighting. However, claims of high quality (AAA to AA–) would receive a 20 percent weight, while claims on banks with a rating of BB+ to B– would receive a 150 percent risk weighting.

A special case is that of short-term claims on banks; those of an original maturity of less than six months. In cases other than that of lowest rated institutions, these would receive a weighting that is one category more favorable than the usual risk weight on the bank's claims. Risk always tends to increase when the maturity is further out in the future.

Claims on securities firms subject to supervisory and regulatory arrangements that include risk-based capital requirements, would generally be weighted in the same way as claims on banks. Such claims may only receive a risk weighting of less than 100 percent if that broker's supervisor has endorsed and is in the process of implementing the 30 *Objectives and Principles of Securities Regulation* set out by the International Organization of Securities Commissions (IOSCO).

RESERVE REQUIREMENTS, CORPORATE CLIENTS, AND SECURITIZED INSTRUMENTS

The New Capital Adequacy Framework pays much more detailed attention to claims on corporates than has been the case with the 1988 Capital Accord, emphasizing different credit qualities of claims. The proposal is that the standard weighting of claims on corporates remains at 100 percent, but in an ingenious implementation of reduced and tightened inspection (see Chapters 7 and 8):

- A weighting of 20 percent is given to claims on corporates of higher quality, with a minimum rating of AA−.
- A weighting of 150 percent is given to claims on corporates which are of very low quality, below B−.

No claim on a corporate could be given a risk weight preferential to the risk weighting assigned to a claim on sovereign debt of the corporate's country of incorporation. This is a wise clause that would avoid the loopholes created by crony capitalism. The Basle Committee is proposing a preferential risk weight only for very high quality credits, but takes note of the fact that coverage of firms receiving external assessments among the Group of Ten countries is currently uneven.

In connection with loans secured by property, the New Capital Adequacy Framework suggests that lending fully secured by mortgages on residential property that is (or will be) occupied by the borrower, or that is rented, should continue to be weighted at 50 percent. However, the Discussion Paper holds to the view that mortgages on commercial real estate do not justify less than 100 percent risk-weighting because in many countries commercial property lending has been under stress.

Historically, commercial property lending had been less risky in some countries than in others. But in every country regulators can point to specific, more risky or less risky elements in property lending. Differences between countries are bound to exist but this should not make it impossible to establish a global playing field.

In a globalized financial market, no country should be given the privilege of allowing some of its banks to put aside an amount of capital that most other regulators think inappropriately small in connection to commercial mortgages. Neither should mortgage banks get much cheaper funding than do their rivals, or issue a form of subordinated debt to bolster core capital at the expense of fair play.

Correctly, the Basle Committee pays particular attention to the case of highly leveraged institutions (HLI). This led to clauses addressing higher risk categories and the commitment to make the New Capital Adequacy Framework very sensitive to credit risk. The Committee is proposing to reduce the risk weights of certain high quality assets *if* there is positive default history and low price volatility. To the contrary, it intends to risk-weight certain assets at more than 100 percent in the case of negative default history and high price volatility, establishing a 150 percent risk weighting category to include:

- Instruments from sovereigns, banks, and corporates rated below B−.
- Securitizations that are rated BB+ to BB−, which essentially means junk bonds.

Another consideration is that of introducing additional higher risk weights for more risky assets. A comment is sought on how a 150-percent category should be defined. The goal is to assess a broader range exposure where volatility of losses arising from credit risk is, on average, significantly higher than that of claims in lower weighted classes.

In connection with off-balance sheet items, with the exception of commitments, the Basle Committee is not proposing a radical change to existing conversion factors for derivatives. Under the 1998 Capital Accord, commitments with original short-term maturity, or those which can be unconditionally canceled at any time, do not have capital requirements—while for commitments with original maturity over one year, a credit conversion factor of 50 percent is applied to determine capital charge.

But there will be some amendments. A problem with the aforementioned approach is that to considerable extent it has been circumvented by banks that structure commitments with a term of 365 days or less, and roll them over. Given that even short-term commitments entail risk, the New Capital Adequacy Framework proposes a credit conversion factor of 20 percent, which would principally apply to business commitments that are unconditionally cancelable. This and similar examples focus attention on the impact of *maturity*. The Basle Committee states that:

- The maturity of a claim is a factor in determining the overall risk presented to the institution, therefore, it must be part of computation of exposure.
- When credit quality of two borrowers is equivalent, the exposure to the borrower with the longer term claim would tend to be riskier than that to the shorter term borrower.

There is a reverse problem in pursuing greater precision by differentiating among maturities of claims through capital charge: A high-quality borrower is generally less risky than a short-term claim, poor-quality borrower, even if there is a difference in maturity. The New Capital Adequacy Framework is not closing the issue of factoring maturity more explicitly into credit risk assessment.

In regard to asset securitization and most particularly credit derivatives, the Basle Committee recognizes that it can serve as a valid way for diversifying credit risks of an institution, marketing them to other banks and nonbank investors. However, regulators have become increasingly concerned with the way some institutions use structured financing to avoid maintaining capital commensurate with current risk exposures.

The Committee also comments that there is a case for correcting a certain lack of consistency in the 1988 Capital Accord, in the sense that the same type and amount of risk might result in different capital requirements depending on the transactions done by the institution. Because of this, a credit institution may be able to achieve an overall risk-weighted capital ratio that is nominally high, but hides capital weakness in regard to embedded risks.

Hence, the Basle Committee suggests a revision to the 1988 Capital Accord that makes use of ratings by independent agencies in setting capital requirements for asset securitization. The proposal primarily concerns transactions that result in a special purpose vehicle issuing paper secured on a pool of assets.

The Committee further observes that this proposal reflects current realities because securitization is a global market that includes an important number of international banks and other major players. Asset-backed securities issued in that market typically have a credit rating, which means that external assessments have already been embedded into current culture.

The New Capital Adequacy Framework advances the following threshold in connection to securitized instruments: AAA to AA− would use a risk weight at 20 percent; A+ to A−, at 50 percent; BBB+ to BBB−, at 100 percent; BB+ to BB−, at 150 percent; and rated B+, below this or unrated would be deducted from capital. Finally, in regard to other claims, the current 100 percent weighting would remain the standard risk accounting approach. This system of weights, which resembles that of sovereigns, is important on its own merits and as a key ingredient to internal rating-based solutions discussed in Chapter 12.

NOTES

1. D.N. Chorafas, "Credit Risk Management," *Analyzing, Rating, and Pricing the Probability of Default,* vol. 1 (London: Euromoney, 2000).
2. D.N. Chorafas, *Rocket Scientists in Banking* (London: Lafferty Publications, 1995).
3. D.N. Chorafas, *Credit Derivatives and the Management of Risk* (New York: New York Institute of Finance, 2000).
4. *EIR* (May 14, 1999).
5. For discussion on demodulation of notional principal to the level of credit equivalent see D.N. Chorafas, "Credit Risk Managment," *The Lessons of VAR Failures and Imprudent Exposure,* vol. 2 (London: Euromoney, 2000).
6. D.N. Chorafas, *Managing Operational Risk-Risk Reduction Strategies for Banks Post-Basle* (London: Lattenty Publications, 2000).
7. D.N. Chorafas, "Credit Risk Management," *Analyzing, Rating, and Pricing the Probability of Default,* vol. 1 (London: Euromoney, 2000).

CHAPTER 12

An Inside View of a Bank's Capital Requirements

Only during the last few years have top-tier banks started focusing in a dynamic manner on the integration of on-balance sheet and off-balance sheet (OBS) assets and liabilities, as well as on accounting for OBS exposure by means of adjusting capital requirements. This strategy brought to the foreground the need to rethink the classical definition of a bank's capital. The New Capital Adequacy Framework is the regulators' response to this requirement.

Because an inordinate amount of exposure has been associated to derivative financial instruments, some Group of Ten regulators moved ahead of their colleagues requiring the integration of on-balance sheet and off-balance sheet exposure as part of regulatory financial reporting by credit institutions. Like every other country, Switzerland has its own rules on how derivatives should be accounted for. Positive and negative replacement values are provided by the reporting institution in connection with derivatives positions. Recognized but not realized derivatives gains are reported as "other assets," and derivatives losses as "other liabilities."

By mapping both other assets and other liabilities into the balance sheet, Swiss regulators see to it that the banks' on-balance sheet and off-balance sheet exposures are effectively integrated. Exhibits 12.1 and 12.2 show the pattern of this reporting over a 5-year period. The statistics come from annual statements of a Swiss money center bank. Exact numbers are not important. What is interesting is the method and the pattern. This bank is losing money with derivatives.

Key to the definition of gains and losses that are recognized but not yet realized, is the fact that some OBS trades can be either assets or liabilities depending on which way the market goes. This approach goes beyond the classical balance sheet structure. A practical example is interest rate swaps. An IRS is typically constructed with a zero market value. But right after the deal has been made, it may become an asset *or* a liability for the holder depending on market risk. For a bank entering into an interest rate swap:

- The trade will be an *asset* if the market moves in the direction it thought it will.
- But this same trade will be a *liability,* if the market moves in the opposite direction.

Exhibit 12.1   Assets in the Balance Sheet and Off-Balance Sheet of a Major Financial Institution

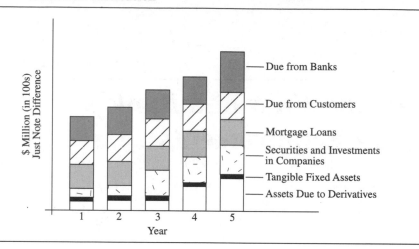

Exactly the same statement but with opposite balances is valid for the counterparty and therefore for estimates of credit risk. On this notion rests the process of *internal ratings*. For our bank, when this trade is an asset, it will carry mainly credit risk. When a liability, it will be characterized by market risk.

Notice that with high frequency financial data (HFFD), this change from asset to liability and vice versa, will happen intraday. Therefore, at the technology side, tracking it will require online accounting methods, models able to map market values in real-time,

Exhibit 12.2   Liabilities in the Balance Sheet and Off-Balance Sheet of a Major Financial Institution (up to $300 Billion)

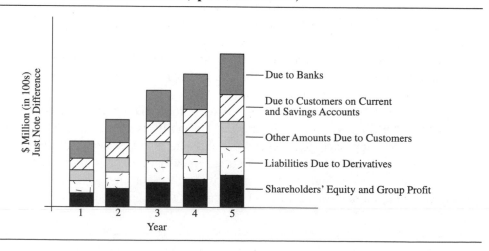

and means for immediate visualization—increasing by so much the sophistication of needed internal management accounting requirements.

It is wise to keep these references under perspective when, in this chapter, we discuss about internal ratings for counterparty risk, associated credit risk modeling solutions, and evolution toward more sophisticated bookkeeping methods. A sound policy requires that management redefines the notion of capital, of gains and of losses. The only rigorous way for doing so is to start with equity and look into the different classes of reserves necessary to see the bank through tough times. This is the sense of establishing a *financial staying power*.

BASIC NOTIONS UNDERLYING INTERNAL RATINGS

COSO advanced sound rules both for reliable financial reporting and for senior management's commitment to capital needed to face adversity. As discussed in Chapter 11, in June 1999, the Basle Committee on Banking Supervision issued a Discussion Paper that makes the computation of capital requirements a dynamic process, leaving significant flexibility to those financial institutions that have the culture and technology needed to compute their capital requirements with a certain accuracy.

To appreciate the impact of this evolution, we should look at its origins. With the publication of the 1996 Market Risk Amendment, regulators have approved the use of eigenmodels (internal models) for the calculation of exposure due to transactions and positions in the banking book.[1] The New Capital Adequacy Framework extends the use of eigenmodels to an *internal rating-based* (IRB) approach to computation of needed capital.

The Basle Committee believes that for sophisticated banks an internal rating-based solution could form the basis for estimating capital charges. Therefore, in consultation with the banking industry, the Committee would examine basic issues related to eigenmodels for setting capital requirements, seeking to develop a normalized approach. In the background of this solution lies the fact that at some of the more technologically advanced banks that make use of internal ratings:

- Simulation is providing assistance that is not available with approaches resting on classical credit assessments.
- Credit risk models have been designed and used to capture exposure from banking book and trading book.

Simulation is a working analogy. When similar systems and processes are found to exist, then measurements made in one of them help in estimation and computation of requirement pertaining to the other. This is the objective of modeling and of algorithms and heuristics we use to map a real-life situation into the computer.

In their professional life, most people use analogical thinking of this sort, but few appreciate they are doing so. What this process involves is abstraction and idealization. As Exhibit 12.3 suggests, whether for credit risk or market risk purposes, what we do is essentially to idealize and simplify, so that it is possible to model a real-world situation.

Exhibit 12.3   Solution to Real World Problems Can Be Helped through Simulation

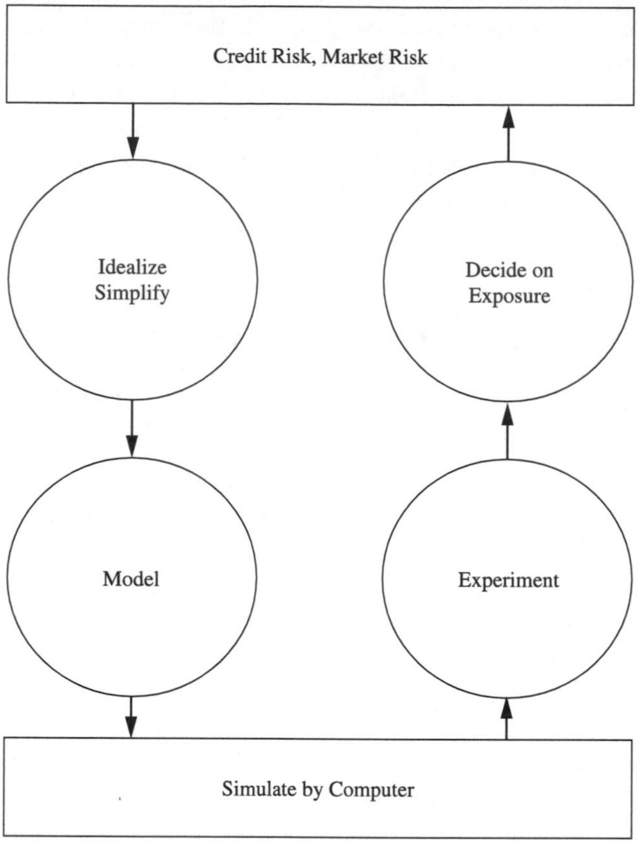

This we do through algorithms. While the two words are often used indiscriminately, there is a difference between a *model* and an *algorithm:*

- The *model* describes a physical or financial system or process, and the way it operates.
- The *algorithm* maps the processes governing the behavior of the model into a computable sequence of events and corrective action.

Real-world exposure is the name of the game in the implementation of IRB. The Basle Committee realizes that there exist both advantages and drawbacks connected to the use of internal ratings for capital adequacy. Greater detail on individual credit exposure is one of the modeling advantages. Among technologically advanced institutions, such detail is increasingly incorporated into various functions, including:

- Operational applications, like determining loan approval requirements counterparty by counterparty.
- Most effective risk management, from analysis of pricing to internal control and corrective action.

Mathematically, it is feasible that eigenmodels for internal ratings will be able to incorporate supplementary customer information through detailed monitoring of customer accounts and specific knowledge of all guarantees and value of collateral. This, however, requires a greater counterparty sensitivity as well as rich databases and a great deal of database mining.

An internal ratings based method may also cover a broader range of borrowers than those covered by independent agencies, providing assessments of the credit quality of individuals as well as of analytical factors. The institution can cover in its credit risk studies different sized companies through credit scoring and detailed consideration of individual firms. Based on database mining, this will provide a better alternative to the standardized approach of a flat rate of capital requirements.

Exhibit 12.4 suggests that a credit institution has three alternatives from which to choose in fulfilling capital requirements. It can stick to the 1988 Accord which established the standard method, develop proprietary models for capital evaluation, or buy software to be publicly offered for credit rating reasons. As with market risk, however, a bank must be extremely careful to change its culture—otherwise it will misuse its software.

The Basle Committee hopes that through modeling banks will be encouraged to further develop and enhance internal credit risk assessment techniques. An IRB solution shares certain similarities with existing credit risk models in terms of reliance on the institution's internal credit evaluation procedures. It may as well provide incentives for banks to further refine their credit risk management methodology.

While there is always the possibility of model risk, in several cases the use made of eigenmodels in the management of exposure provides a basis for fairly rigorous estimates. The process is rewarding but it will not be easy. Among the challenges are:

- The lack of complete and fully updated databases.
- Scant acquaintance with the concept of modeling itself.
- The need for rigorous procedures for model validation.

Exhibit 12.4   A Commercial Bank Has Three Alternatives from Which to Choose for Capital Needs

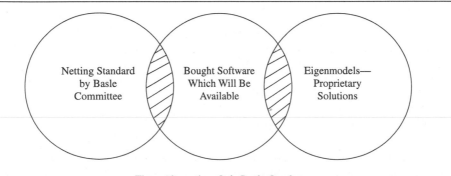

These Alternatives Only Partly Overlap

The Basle Committee appreciates that credit risk models are not yet at the stage where they can play an explicit role in setting regulatory capital requirements, but proposes to verify how this could become possible after further development and testing. It also intends to monitor closely progress on use of eigenmodels and credit risk mitigation techniques such as *credit derivatives,*[2] which enable banks to improve their control methods.

Part of the challenges lying ahead are the treatment of credit risk protection schemes such as maturity mismatches, asset mismatches, potential future exposure on hedges, variations in value of collateral, guarantees, and on balance-sheet netting. In the past, these have resulted in different policies by national regulators, in regard to the acceptance of credit risk mitigation techniques.

Policy issues do affect credit risk modeling solutions. For instance, maturity of a claim is a factor in determining the overall credit risk it presents to the institution. While at present the New Capital Adequacy Framework is not proposing to take maturity of claims into account for capital adequacy purposes, except in a very limited case, the Basle Committee seeks ways to:

- Distinguish more accurately the credit quality of exposures.
- Consider means for factoring maturity into the assessment of credit risk.

The goal that transpires from this effort is that of developing an approach to regulatory capital that increasingly assures that capital requirements reflect a credit institution's specific risk profile. As part of the IRB effort, the Basle Committee will be analyzing internal rating systems of financial institutions as well as evaluating qualitative and quantitative standards for use by supervisors in recognizing, validating, and monitoring internal rating systems of banks under their authority. Into this responsibility is integrated the evaluation of methodologies for linking capital requirements to internal ratings. Among the approaches being considered is the mapping of internal rating categories to risk weights established by the Basle Committee (see Chapter 11), use of an expanded system of risk weights, or a capital charge that explicitly reflects internal ratings.

The Basle Committee expects that at the least after the systems approach stabilizes an internal rating-based solution will provide an acceptable trade-off between conceptual soundness and operational feasibility—while assuring dependability of results. It is also expected that the method will make feasible accurate and consistent capital charges under IRB, both among different computational approaches and in regard to the standardized capital adequacy solution.

COULD INTERNAL RATINGS LEAD TO A BETTER CAPITAL BASE?

The New Capital Adequacy Framework explicitly states the Basle Committee's awareness that the 1988 Accord does not fully capture the extent of risk-reduction that can be achieved by credit risk mitigation techniques. For instance, under the current *substitution approach,* the risk weight of collateral or guarantor is simply substituted for that of the original underlying obligor. Yet, a credit institution would only suffer losses if *both* the loan and its guarantor default. In other terms, the size of capital requirement should, up to a point, depend on correlation between default probabilities of original obligor, and the guarantor.

If the guarantor's default were certain to be followed by the borrower's default, then the current substitution approach would be right. If, however, the probabilities of default do not correlate, then a smaller capital charge than currently exists could be justified. Because the guarantor's action acts as a *reinsurance,* a more accurate algorithm would likely reinforce incentives to manage risk.

There are mathematical challenges connected to a more accurate approach, which considers reinsurance effects. For example, the double default described is not symmetric, because failure of the guarantor would re-expose the bank to the original obligor and, so, to the risk of a future default. One of the mathematical challenges lies in the fact that the often talked about use of covariance is still at an early stage in its application in finance.

Other approaches are more classical even if they use novel instruments. The opposite is also true. Credit derivatives is an example with a dual effect: credit risk mitigation and the ability to go short on credit. Credit risk mitigation techniques may provide a valid solution to the management of poorer quality exposures.

Outliers and extreme events pose another challenge. This is important inasmuch as most analytic studies are based on the assumption of a normal distribution of events. The approach considered by the Basle Committee in identifying outliers includes evaluation of qualitative factors, which will be linked to the supervisory review process of capital framework.

The Committee as well looks forward to a bank's compliance with sound interest rate risk management practices, such as those included in *Principles for the Management of Interest Rate Risk.*[3] This document has recognized the significance of interest rate risk within the banking book, depending on a bank's risk profile, and market conditions.

Accordingly, the New Capital Adequacy Framework proposes to develop a capital charge for interest rate risk in the banking book for credit institutions whose interest rate risks are significantly above average—which therefore are "outliers." Current policy allows for discretion by national supervisors regarding the definition of outliers and the methodology of calculating interest rate risk in the banking book.

The Basle Committee recognizes that several banks, particularly the larger ones, rely on sound measurement techniques for interest rate risk as an integral part of controlling exposure in both the trading and banking books. But it also notes that such processes involve some controversial issues related to the quantification of the duration for core deposits and other subjects that still constitute procedural challenges.

There are also several important differences between interest rate risks in banking book and trading book, which need to be addressed. In principle, interest rate risk is contained in the 1996 Market Risk Amendment: standardized approach and eigenmodels, might be extended to the treatment of interest rate risk in the banking book. Therefore, the Basle Committee undertook a study of incentives for banks of explicit interest rate risk charges in the banking and trading books.

The New Capital Adequacy Framework also notes that there are other challenges to the 1988 Accord stemming from differences between minimum capital requirements for trading book and banking book. Credit risk is set in different contexts in the two books as a result of several factors, including:

- Variations in accounting standards.
- Prevailing valuation methods.
- Assumed holding period horizons.
- The implementation of risk weightings.

Because of different ways of looking at these factors, capital requirements for credit risk tend to be lower in the trading book. This provides an incentive for banks to undertake regulatory capital arbitrage between the two books. In fact, every one of the aforementioned factors impacts on the accuracy of modeling solutions. Given the initiative to amend capital requirements in the banking book, the Basle Committee will review the treatment of trading book positions to assure consistency between the two books, and reduce the incentive for regulatory capital arbitrage.

Supervisors also consider imposing additional capital requirements for banks that are exposed to large foreign exchange settlement risk.[4] Furthermore, given big and increasing market volumes, the regulatory treatment of reverse repo transactions in the trading book has become an issue of special concern. To address the potential counterparty risk of repo transactions, the Basle Committee proposes to specify adequate capital requirements able of reflecting:

- Price volatility of underlying securities.
- Frequency with which positions are marked to market.

Another concern is current heterogeneity in directives for handling residual risks. Particular problems arise where the hedge is imperfect. Inasmuch as imperfect hedges can reduce credit risk, they might be desirable. At the same time, it is necessary to deal in a consistent manner with residual risks which take a number of forms:

- *Maturity mismatch,* where the hedging instrument expires before the underlying asset.
- *Asset mismatch* arising when an asset is hedged by a credit derivative with different risk characteristics.

These examples help in documenting that the challenge with simulation is only in part mathematically centered on algorithms. Because we try to model real-world situations, we must be clear about what these situations are. This involves both policy and procedural issues whose effective resolution becomes a prerequisite to successful IRB.

The Basle Committee expects that the second and third pillars of the New Capital Adequacy Framework—namely supervisory review of capital adequacy and market discipline (see Chapter 11)—will play a key role in an internal rating based solution. The supervisory review process is also likely to impact ways and means for determining accuracy and comparability of internal rating systems across banking institutions. Part of the foundation of the projected system enhances market discipline in its broader sense.

Some supervisory issues, too, need to be resolved. Prior approval by national regulatory authorities would be necessary before credit institutions are allowed to use internal ratings systems for setting minimum capital requirements. Therefore, a crucial subject in considering IRB is how supervisors should assess the overall adequacy of a bank's rating system. To address this issue, the Basle Committee will:

- Review the factors that influence eigenmodels and internal rating solutions.
- Evaluate methodologies that can be used by banks to translate internal ratings into a common benchmark.
- Elaborate qualitative and quantitative criteria that may be used by supervisors in assessing and validating eigenmodels.

This task will be a complex one. To consider the design of a bank's rating system for use in setting regulatory capital requirements, supervisors would need to determine many critical issues: From assumptions and hypotheses being made, to algorithms and heuristics being used, validity of the bank's database, whether the number of gradations is appropriate to distinguish meaningfully among the range of risks faced by the institution, and so on.

Other factors that seem to attract the attention of supervisors relate to the rating scale in use for management purposes, and its ability to link to a measurable loss concept. Regulators need to decide whether all appropriate risk factors are incorporated into the criteria for assigning exposures to rating categories, as well as if the criteria themselves are sufficiently explicit, accurate, and unambiguous. Only after these prerequisites are fulfilled can one talk of implementing internal rating based solutions in a meaningful sense.

EQUITY OF AN INSTITUTION AND ECONOMIC CAPITAL

How is a credit institution expected to satisfy its capital requirements? An obvious (but only partial) answer is through stockholders' equity. This is the capital that constituted the net worth of the company in the first place. However, as we saw in Chapter 11, in today's highly leveraged economy, equity capital is a chimera. Here is an example on how much of the equity is exposed to derivatives risk, in notional principal amounts:

- Bankers Trust has 54.600 percent of its equity.
- J.P. Morgan has 48.300 percent of its equity.
- Chase Manhattan has 43.500 percent of its equity.

Even demodulating by 30 to obtain a very conservative estimate of credit equivalence, Bankers Trust has 1.820 percent of its equity on the block with derivatives deals alone, J.P. Morgan 1.610 percent, and Chase 1.450 percent. Other money center banks are not much better. BankAmerica for example has 320 percent of its equity in derivatives in de-modulated notional principal.[5]

Part of the satisfaction of capital requirements will come from extraordinary reserves through retained earnings. Another part will come from assets. However, assets like loans are at risk. That's why the Basle Committee implies ratios which go from 20 percent to 150 percent of committed amounts (see Chapter 11). Aside from that, the assets too are leveraged through derivative deals. The ratio of demodulated notional principal to assets is:

- 1.13 for J.P. Morgan.
- 0.94 for Chase Manhattan.
- 0.642 for Bankers Trust.

We spoke of this in Chapter 11, when reference was made to the fact that with derivative instruments some credit institutions have on the block a little more or a little less than all of their assets. This is more perilous than it seems because liabilities correspond to these assets. By and large, this money does not belong to the bank, but to its depositors and other business partners.

This is tantamount to saying that we have to look at equity and reserves to see the basic strength of the institution. In a public company, the term *equity* has classically been used to mean stockholders' equity. More recently, however, this term has become relatively elastic. Under the heading *total equity* companies lump together share capital, open reserves, and provisions with a reserve character. Then there is the notion of economic equity, or *economic capital,* which we discuss later.

The definition of equity is important because financial analysts, and the markets at large, look at return on equity (ROE) as a crucial indicator of how well management performs. Not all markets have the same expectations. During the last few years, ROE in the American market has been more than twice ROE in the European Union; and in the EU, companies perform slightly better than in Japan.

It is normal to care about the remuneration of equity, because this is always capital at risk. Bondholders have a prior call on corporate assets in the event of liquidation, while stockholders are the last in the line. On the other hand, stockholders share in the increase of earnings; bondholders do not. Reserves usually come from retained earnings.

Provisions with a reserve character made by a credit institution are essentially extraordinary reserves which, quite frequently, are not disclosed. This is the policy followed in central Europe, but it is illegal or at least inadmissible in other countries. The New York Stock Exchange (NYSE) does not register companies that hold secret reserves and the Internal Revenue Service looks at such reserves as tax evasion. No law however says that a bank cannot distinguish between entrepreneurial capital, and economic capital.

The lowest allowable level of *entrepreneurial capital* is capital required by regulators. For instance, after the 1988 Capital Accord by the Basle Committee on Banking Supervision, international institutions must have a capital base equal to 8 percent or more of their balance sheet commitments in Tier-1 and Tier-2 capital (see Chapter 11). By contrast, for banks limited to national activities, this level is 4 percent.

Not all institutions have been able to meet such capital requirement with liquid resources. Many found themselves obliged to sell assets. Neither is it true that once reached, the 8 percent (or 4 percent) level is stable. Severe losses may reduce this amount. When in 1998 the Tokyo Stock Exchange index fell below 14,000, many of the big Japanese banks could no longer match the 8 percent level and some found it difficult to meet the 4 percent.

Economic capital, or capital at risk (see also Chapter 13), is equal to or less than entrepreneurial capital. It is the amount of money senior management allocates to the different operations channels, associated to specific limits. In setting limits, some institutions further divide the economic capital into two categories:

1.   One addressing classical entrepreneurial risk such as loans.
2.   The other covering deals in new instruments and products such as derivatives.

As we will see in Chapter 13, because it is in the frontline of business activity, capital-at-risk is volatile. It is there to produce gains but also to cover losses resulting from loans, leveraged trading transactions, and other channels. Gearing has the potential of higher return but also carries a significantly bigger amount of exposure. In other terms, economic capital is set aside to cover deliberate risks.

Economic capital is essentially a pool. Apart from the initial contribution of equity and reserves, this pool benefits from a catchment area covering different fees, trading profits, interests, repayments as well as premiums in the form of reinsurance. For instance, an extra premium rate may be connected to the counterparty, the same way the Risk Adjusted Return on Capital (RAROC) works.[6]

While the idea of differentiating between entrepreneurial capital and economic capital is basically sound, its implementation would make so much more sense if systems for allocating it, supervising it, and reporting on plan versus actual, worked in real-time. This requires highly technological solutions and a great amount of organizational readiness.

Only real-time reporting can bring to senior management's attention deviations in plan versus actual. Such feedback should lead to immediate corrective action, whether the deviation concerns established limits or unplanned commitments.

Technological requirements aside, real-time reporting will become a reality only when the balance sheet structure differentiates between, and reports on, the details hidden under assets and liabilities—and whether these are short-, medium-, or long-term. Another requirement for effective risk control is to integrate into one document on-balance sheet and off-balance sheet accounting. This, too, must be done in real-time.

Since the early 1980s, there have been significant developments in the production and presentation of balance sheets (see also Chapter 13). Balance sheets used to be prepared per quarter plus one month delay in compiling; then it became once per quarter, but within a week; twice per quarter; once per month; once per week, once per day.

Today Tier-1 banks have available virtual balance sheets every 30 minutes, through real-time update of and access to databases anywhere in the world.

The next goal is the production of balance sheets every 5 minutes for all assets and liabilities, at an acceptable level of accuracy and detail.

A modern bank needs an integrative procedure addressing on-balance sheet and off-balance sheet items at any time, at every corner of the globe it operates. Models associated to this implementation should make possible a flexible re-allocation of assets and liabilities as well as the effective control of risk.

Because the regulators need to know fair value to better assess a company's financial strength, SFAS 115, by FASB, allows management discretion in classifying assets so that changes in market value can be reflected in earnings. By contrast, liabilities are usually not dealt with in a crisp manner—and without a methodology for their fair valuation, it is not clear what a financial statement may mean.

Part of the difficulty of addressing the challenges of valuing the liabilities side is that while the market for liabilities exists, so far it has been very narrow. There are only a few transactions a year and most are confused by assets that tend to travel with the liabilities. Financial analysts therefore suggest using fair value in a way consistent with the market value of heavily traded assets of similar characteristics. This changes the classical form of financial reporting as established by Luca Paciolo in his seminal work in 1495, leading to more sophisticated bookkeeping methods.

AN EVOLUTION TOWARD MORE SOPHISTICATED BOOKKEEPING METHODS

Old approaches to the evaluation and presentation of assets and liabilities in the balance sheet are a case of diminished geriatric returns. Therefore, Tier-1 banks and the more enlightened regulators look favorably on the evolution of more sophisticated bookkeeping methods. One of the advantages of flexible allocation for on-balance sheet and off-balance sheet assets and liabilities is that it can permit a more dynamic definition of capital requirements than it is otherwise possible. Whether marked-to-market or marked-to-model, assets can be risk-weighted on the basis of:

- Counterparty rating for credit risk (see Chapter 11).
- Fair value estimates that permit embedding the valuation market risk.

Market risk is reflected in fair value by instrument. Replacement value quantifies the risk associated to the counterparty. The integration of market risk and credit risk by major counterparty can give a more realistic appreciation of exposure than current value-at-risk (VAR) models which have several limitations.

A contrarian opinion to this statement is that the calculation and integration of credit risk and market risk by counterparty can become complex because different sources of risk accounting are not independent from one another. Covariance becomes important if we wish to estimate the probability of bankruptcy, but, as we saw earlier in this chapter, the study of covariance in banking is still in its beginning. Other factors entering a more refined calculation are:

- The duration or maturity of a transaction in a given financial instrument.
- A well-documented and dynamic grading scheme reflecting counterparty risk, and
- The level of confidence α we choose in estimating capital at risk.

Bankruptcy studies usually involve default probabilities and are based on a Bernouli distribution.[7] A precise study of the likelihood of bankruptcy and of remaining value will take into consideration not only contractual time per instrument and commitment but also the additional three lags:

1. Reporting lag.
2. Decision lag of supervisors.
3. Liquidation lag.

The choice of the confidence interval will lead into a family of curves, with the greater level of significance having associated to it the greater risk factor. To dramatize this statement, Exhibit 12.5 presents an example with market risk levels as a function of maturity years versus volatility and confidence intervals. Notice how fast the market risk factor increases as the level of confidence goes from 90 percent to 99 percent.

Both senior management and the bank's professionals need to change significantly their culture to make meaningful decisions based on levels of confidence. It is therefore not surprising that only the most technologically advanced institutions, have so far implemented analytical solutions along this frame of reference. Yet, an analytical approach makes sense because it helps to convert every position to *cash* based on certain assumptions.

If we convert all assets and liabilities to cash on the basis of fair value accounting, we can create a vector of expected values which, within certain risk limits, represents the capital available at liquidation time. One of the prerequisites in this valuation is to distinguish between short-term and long-term—and stick to our definitions, because definitions used by different companies are not necessarily comparable, and some banks even change their definitions midstream.

Conditioned by market behavior, a flexible allocation of assets and liabilities in the balance sheet can substitute for netting requirements, as defined by the Basle Committee's standard method. Dividing all off-balance sheet instruments in their trading book

Exhibit 12.5   Market Risk Factor with a Historical Volatility of about 17 Percent at Three Levels of Confidence Intervals

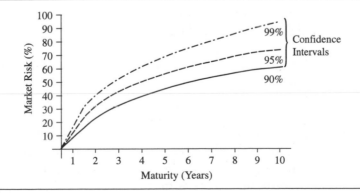

and banking book into derivatives that can be netted and those that can not, some banks have tested the volume and value of leveraged financial products against their on-balance sheet net worth. In one specific case:

- In notional principal amount, the market value of these derivatives was stated to be $2.5 trillion.
- After netting, the remaining value was $30 billion, in notional principal—or about 10 percent of the bank's balance sheet.[8]

This netting result is an underestimate, based on awfully optimistic hypotheses. Netting is a process involving uncertainties because the creditors will always ask for their money while the debtors' obligations are subject to credit risk and other exposures. In market risk terms, as the Metallgesellschaft's and many other experiences demonstrate, hedging is by no means an exact science.

Netting is imprecise because it rests on too many assumptions about similarities and equivalencies in terms of A&L in trading book and banking book. Furthermore, most importantly, netting has not been tested in court. Many cognizant bankers and financial analysts believe that even if it proved to be legally acceptable within a single country, netting will not hold in cross-jurisdiction terms.

Adding to my reserves about netting is the fact that it is not a procedure that can be applied to intraday financial reporting—yet this is the way to competitiveness in a marketplace more demanding than ever. Much more sophisticated models are necessary and these have to be developed in full appreciation of stress connected to the bank's capital because of its daily operations and longer term commitments, and on the notion of capital at risk (see Chapter 13) within the broader perspective of global management of exposure.

Another basic objection I have to netting is that only items that are not correlated can be offset with one another. It can happen that there exist noncorrelated items, but they are rare birds in banking and finance. As we will see in the following section, one of the pillars of classical accounting is that assets and liabilities should not be offset. Assets and liabilities tend to correlate with one another—if nowhere else, in the balance sheet, which is the foundation of reliable accounting.

RETHINKING THE RECOGNITION OF ASSETS AND LIABILITIES IN THE BALANCE SHEET

Assets confer upon their holder controllable economic benefits. *Liabilities* are obligations for probable future sacrifices of an economic nature. In a transaction, each party contracts the assets or liabilities of the counterparty in exchange for his own assets or liabilities. When the financial transaction that takes place concerns an item that meets the established definition of an asset or liability, the operation connected to this transaction must be recognized in the balance sheet. There are however some conditions to be observed in this process. Some of these conditions are described by laws and regulations, others have been established by the bylaws of the firm.

The first condition is that there is sufficient evidence of the existence of the item, including evidence that a future cash flow will occur where appropriate. This leads to the second condition: the transaction can be measured with sufficient dependability in terms of amount of money it involves—therefore of the amount of capital it commits or consumes.

Events subject to this recognition in the balance sheet are also subject to continued recognition. The same is true about exposure to the risks inherent in the benefits resulting from the transaction. In practically all jurisdictions, the law says that the asset or liability must continue to be recognized even if no profit or loss is realized in a given period.

Definition, recognition, measurement, and disclosure issues are the pillars on which rests a framework containing general accounting rules which are applicable to financial instruments. The New Capital Adequacy Framework by the Basle Committee is no exception to this statement. For the majority of transactions in financial instruments, *recognition* poses no difficulties and the same can be said of *derecognition* as the financial asset is, for instance, settled by payment of cash, or disposed of through sale.

Difficulties arise with derecognition in regard to transactions such as the factoring or sale of debts with recourse and securitization. The Financial Accounting Standards Board and other authorities have clarified the do's and don'ts with derecognition. With securitization, for example, a residual interest or obligation related to the financial instrument is retained whether this is an asset or a liability.

The definition of *asset* requires that access to future economic benefits is controlled by the reporting institution. Access to economic benefits normally rests on legal rights, even if legally enforceable rights are not essential to secure such benefits. Future financial benefits inherent in an asset are never completely certain in amount or timing. There is always the possibility that actual benefits will be less or more than those expected.

The concepts presented in the preceding paragraphs are not alien to accountants, bankers, and treasurers. Uncertainty regarding eventual benefits as well as expected and unexpected losses and their timing is the very sense of risk. Risk is encompassing both an upside element of potential gain and a downside possibility such as exposure to loss and/or the creation of a new liability.

The definition of *liability* includes the obligation to transfer economic benefits to another party or parties. In this connection, while most obligations are legally enforceable, a legal obligation is not a necessary condition for a liability. An institution may be commercially obliged to adopt a certain course of action perceived to be in its long-term best interests, even if no third party can legally enforce such course.

The notion of *obligation* implies that the entity is not free to avoid an outflow of resources—whether money or other assets. For instance, there can be circumstances in which the institution is unable to avoid an outflow of money, whether for legal or commercial reasons, because of the liabilities that it has assumed.

This brings our discussion back to netting. One of the important rules in classical accounting and associated reporting practices is that assets and liabilities should not be offset. For instance, debit and credit balances can be aggregated into a single net item *only* where they do not constitute separate assets and liabilities.

But while the basics of accounting are the same in practically all countries, the implementation of accounting rules and reporting practices is not uniform. Several efforts are under way for the standardization and for coordination of accounting rules, but these efforts themselves are not necessary coordinated as Chapters 2 and 3 will document.

In a world of globalization and deregulation, the lack of homogeneity in accounting rules, systems, and practices is most regrettable. Not only is it better that the basis be universal, but it is also necessary that the procedures are forward looking because decisions made in a dynamic market cannot be based only on past values.

A basic business principle is that future value is a function of risk(s) being taken. This fact of financial life is not answered by current accounting procedures and internal management accounting systems.

Furthermore, many financial institutions are interested in measuring risk but fail to appreciate that they must first measure capital. Many of the issues involved in measuring capital have not yet been resolved, but what is available can provide the basis for new departures if the bank is willing and able to be state-of-art.

Better global solutions do not come easily because they require a consensus, and they also need strong safeguards for reliable financial reporting. This is one of the key contributions made by COSO. At the same time, financial reporting practices do evolve over time. Examples are:

- The concept of a going concern and associated probability of default.
- A more generic way of looking at obligations, in the short-, medium-, and longer term.
- Accounting for off-balance sheet items in a dependable manner.
- Integrating A&L on-balance sheet and off-balance sheet.

The qualitative and quantitative assessments of counterparty creditworthiness; measurement and evaluation of on- and off-balance sheet exposures; and analytical study of events and transactions leading to potential future exposure are integral parts of a process tuned to the fulfillment of accounting requirements. Interdisciplinary and interregulatory approaches are welcome.

In March 1999, the Securities and Exchange Commission, Federal Reserve, Office of the Comptroller of the Currency, Federal Deposit Insurance Corporation, and Office of Thrifts Supervision saw fit to issue a joint letter to financial institutions urging enhanced disclosure and increased credit-loss provisions. That should be seen as a sign of change regarding the attention supervisory authorities are now paying to the polyvalence of risks facing credit institutions as well as to the need for interregulatory approaches.

THE AUDITING OF RISKS, INTRADAY VALUES, AND MANAGEMENT CONTROL

With all commitments being included, a market-sensitive daily estimate of available capital can be instrumental in assuring the monitoring of trading, lending, and asset management activities. It can also assist in establishing appropriate organizational measures necessary to keep business risks under control.

Transactions at prices or rates out of line with market conditions, though nothing new, are alarm signals. They invariably play a major role in spectacular cases in which banks run into difficulties that shake the market.

Transactions out of line with market conditions and fraudulent financial reporting correlate. Such transactions can be used to arbitrarily shift losses or profits to other accounting periods or between counterparties as well as to falsify financial statements. COSO is very explicit on the need to avoid such incidents.

Conflicts of interest are another example. Most banks are well aware of the significance of a clear functional and organizational separation of trading activities from back office processing, accounting, and monitoring. Somehow, senior management often fails to effectively implement this separation of duties and responsibilities. The principle of a segregation of functions has to be assured by:

- Top management decisions.
- Appropriate procedures.
- Rigorous safeguards.

This reference to procedures and safeguards is valid all the way to computer-based trading systems and their software. Also, attention must be paid to the fact that the distinction between data processing and bookkeeping is not so clear-cut. Existing incompatibilities and differences end by becoming accounting loopholes.

Both management intent and management accountability come into play. Every executive must assure that the commitments he or she makes are rational, comprehensive, and fall within the limits assigned by the board. To help in the implementation of a procedure which is both rigorous and controllable, Chapters 7 and 8 detailed benefits derived from the use of statistical quality control charts.

Auditing responsibilities are executed best when a significant part of the analytical work is done online through database mining. Audit reports must be interactively available to all members of management and quality defects remedied systematically and promptly. That's the sense of timely corrective action which also is a cultural change because in most cases shortcomings identified by internal auditors are not remedied speedily. Therefore, internal control requirements must prescribe that defects not immediately remedied, and recommendations not yet implemented are brought to the notice of all managers without delay. "Delay" means anything beyond a prescribed short time frame for corrective action which should be an integral part of the bank's bylaws. Beyond this, the tasks of internal auditors must be specified in the bank's rules. Effective internal auditing is one of the key instruments for detecting and remedying undesirable developments in a financial institution.

Internal auditors should be required to examine, among other issues, the limit system, functional separation of duties, degree to which product prices represent market realities, and level of sophistication of information technology. They should also ascertain what's the nature of corrective action and if it is exercised with little time-lag, before deficiencies that have emerged cause greater damage.

Because business operates at compressed time scales, delays which in the past were considered to be "normal" are today an aberration. Because of globalization, rapid product development, and a relatively high amount of volatility, some top-tier financial institutions are now valuing assets and liabilities daily. Through this approach, financial statements are improved; they become more transparent for both investors and regulators, and their reliability improves.

This change is inevitable. As market values affect balance sheets, some kinds of abuses of A&L values have come into the spotlight. For instance, certain institutions tend to sell assets that have market values above book, while retaining assets where the market value is below book. This is one of the problems confronting regulators, lenders, investors, and other market players—particularly so because the current accounting system does not provide necessary information for intraday evaluation of A&L, in addition to the problem of finding the correct market value.

Within the guidelines established by COSO for reliable financial reporting, it is part of top management's responsibility to assure that a fail-proof process is in place for measuring, analyzing, and monitoring assets, liabilities, and risks; there is a daily evaluation of exposure; and there exists performance control. As a matter of principle, the board and senior management should:

- Get involved in the design and implementation of technological solutions, accounting controls, and reporting practices.
- Steadily review the functioning of the institution's risk monitoring system, in terms of accuracy and timeliness.

These requirements place heavy demands on banks, particularly those that have been for a long stretch of time managed intuitively. For instance, while some financial institutions already have effective risk measurement and limits systems, the majority are not yet in a position to put into place a real-time, uniform integrated solution for the entire institution.

Boards that are keen to get results see to it that the task of real-time capturing, measurement, and reporting on limits observance and assumed risk, for all transactions, is entrusted to a member of senior management who has no direct responsibility for day-to-day trading activities. Boards must also establish policies able to ensure that:

- All senior executives are informed at least daily on risk and performance in their individual trading area in an institutionwide sense.
- A system is put in place to draw senior management's attention to overshootings of limits, unusual deals, and other unwarranted events.

As Chapters 7 and 8 demonstrated, statistical quality control charts and advanced financial technology can be instrumental in keeping management informed of all risky transactions, helping to prevent abuses and cover-ups of financial difficulties, and assuring that both expected and unexpected risks are followed up steadily.

As we saw through exposure statistics, by far the greater damage can come from huge losses in derivative financial instruments contracted over the counter in secretive ways, and from unsecured loans to undercapitalized companies and high-leveraged institutions that take positions in derivatives. In connection with the late September 1998 fiasco with Long Term Capital Management, the big banks who had lent cash to LTCM seem to have had little idea what the firm was up to. Neither did they care as long as the paper profits kept rolling in. Similarly, one wonders how much BankAmerica knew when it sharply increased its exposure to risk assets in D.E. Shaw's portfolio of equity derivatives, and the toxic waste this portfolio contained.

At the end of the day, management pays dearly for these failures. The shareholders are not the only ones being hurt. Following the huge losses at LTCM, at the United Bank of Switzerland—one of its major investors—the Chairman of the Board, the General Manager of Trading, Chief Credit Officer, and Chief Risk Management Officer resigned. To reduce a small part of their huge losses, big banks have been reducing their payroll. UBS eliminated 1,800 jobs. ING Barings announced that it will terminate 1,200 of its 10,000 staff. What is new with these setbacks is that even the Chief Executive Officer's job is no longer secure.

NOTES

1. D.N. Chorafas, *The 1996 Market Risk Amendment. Understanding the Marking-to-Model and Value-at-Risk* (Burr Ridge, IL: McGraw-Hill, 1998).

2. D.N. Chorafas, *Credit Derivatives and the Management of Risk* (New York: New York Institute of Finance, 2000).

3. Basle Committee on Banking Supervision, Basle, September, 1997.

4. The Basle Committee will soon be issuing a consultative paper on *Supervisory Guidance for Managing Settlement Risk in Foreign Exchange Transactions.*

5. D.N. Chorafas, "Credit Risk Management," *The Lessons of VAR Failures and Imprudent Exposure,* vol. 2 (London: Euromoney, 2000).

6. D.N. Chorafas, *Credit Derivatives and the Management of Risk* (New York: New York Institute of Finance, 2000).

7. D.N. Chorafas, *Understanding Volatility and Liquidity in the Financial Markets* (London: Euromoney, 1998).

8. In this real-life example, the numbers are fictitious but the proportions are right.

CHAPTER 13

Capital at Risk

The basic problems faced by financial institutions in controlling their exposure have never changed in a radical fashion, though the means at management's disposal continued to evolve over time. For many banks, the goal has been that of keeping risk shy, and this is also the aim of regulators. One alternative the board has is to try to over-regulate exposure by missing some good profit opportunities. Conversely, it may allow free reign to the traders and loans officers hoping that nothing wrong will happen.

Risk is subject to Murphy's law: If something can go wrong, it will. By opening the gates of risk taking, euphemistically called hedging, while at the same time failing to put in place the appropriate internal control policies and instruments, the board and senior management find themselves in an awkward position. They can no longer control in an effective way:

- The quality of counterparties, with the result a crop of bad loans, poor investments, as well as credit risks with derivatives.
- It is not possible to control the use of highly leveraged derivative instruments, whose market risk can ultimately wreck the bank.

There is a better alternative than either over-regulating or providing an invitation to disaster. This lies in the ability to define the *capital at risk* (CAR) the bank is willing to invest in its channels of operations. As we saw in Chapter 12, most commercial banks and supervisory authorities consider entrepreneurial capital synonymous with regulatory capital, while the internal allocation of *economic capital* is typically done for trading reasons as well as for loans, investments, and other business activities.

Some people believe that economic capital is the resource needed to cushion unexpected losses. This is not a mainstream definition. Economic capital is allocated to a channel to capitalize on business opportunities presented by the resources of that channel. As such, it will be at the frontline of both expected and unexpected gains and losses.

For any practical purpose, capital at risk is economic capital. Close to 60 percent of respondents to a questionnaire claimed that return on[1] economic capital is already used by their banks as a performance guide. This begs the question as to how the formula is calculated. Of those who use a return on economic capital model, 85 percent claim that the calculation includes both market risk and credit risk.

Leaving aside the argument that eventually the revision of the 1988 Capital Accord (see Chapter 11) may eliminate the difference between regulatory capital and economic capital, in this chapter we will concentrate on the concept of capital at risk and how this can be used to improve performance while keeping exposure under control.

Basically, all economic capital is at risk no matter which is the line of business of a company. But some of this money is much more at risk than the rest because management takes more chances in certain channels than in others.

In the present chapter, we will see for which money in the economic capital chapter the likelihood of loss is higher, and why it is so. Also, how the internal management accounting system should work for an accurate reporting of the overall risk situation in compliance to COSO directives.

Another goal of this chapter is to present a method for determining the capital at risk to be set aside, explaining how to distribute it according to individual risk categories. Also, how to look for the worst case factor for each risk category, and how to convert risk capital into overall limits per risk class by means of a worst-case scenario.

NOTIONS UNDERLYING SOPHISTICATED APPLICATIONS OF CAPITAL AT RISK

While risk is as old as banking itself, *capital at risk* is a relatively new notion in finance, which is particularly appreciated by the leading money center banks because it helps in connection with the study and implementation of prudential limits as well as in the estimation of risk and return. But not all institutions define capital at risk the same way.

Some institutions consider capital at risk as synonymous to economic capital, while others restrict the term to the more exposed part of economic capital. Also, some of the banks using this concept consider CAR as their buffer against losses that may eat into regulatory capital, while a growing number of banks start looking at capital at risk as money held against positions in loans, investments, and derivatives trading. The challenge therefore is to:

- Estimate credit risk and market risk associated to a transaction.
- Evaluate exposure embedded in positions held in the portfolio.
- Allocate capital at risk to transactions and positions in a proactive manner.

Proactive means that such allocation must be made dynamically and be updated as market values change, making use of prognostication. Several financial institutions have successfully applied the concept of capital at risk, in connection to market risk, using the value at risk (VAR) model. But CAR and VAR should not be confused with one another:

- Based on past experience and on simulation, CAR is calculated a priori, when business plans are made, both for the trading book and for banking book (see Chapter 16).

- By contrast, VAR is computed on the basis of worst case market risk exposures in the trading book, at a certain level of confidence. This is done after commitments have been made.

CAR and VAR have in common a shortcoming: The present method of their calculation does not cover extreme events and spikes. As in the case of VAR, many banks compute CAR at the 95 percent or 99 percent level of confidence. A few compute it at four levels—from 90 percent to 99.9 percent.

During the First International Conference on Risk Management in Banking,[2] Dr. Werner Hermann of the Swiss National Bank explained how this approach helps to integrate all levels of capital at risk into a single framework. Dr. Hermann's method is superior to other alternatives employed in the banking industry. As shown in Exhibit 13.1, the suggested approach displays all assets and liabilities at their present value, but sustains the concept of prudence through confidence intervals appreciate associated capital used as reserve.

This approach could be made more sophisticated by introducing other variables like the time horizon of lenders, investors, and traders. While there is a practical problem in estimating confidence intervals connected to different time horizons, fuzzy engineering might help.[3] What I have just described is not a system approved by regulators but a *valid concept* that still requires considerable research prior to being implemented.

In the asset side of the balance sheet in Exhibit 13.1 is the classical division into current, medium-term, and long-term assets (like land, buildings, and so on). Among them, they make up the 100 percent of *assets*. At the *liabilities* side are current liabilities, medium-term liabilities, and long-term liabilities. What the Hermann algorithm suggests is that current and medium-term liabilities make 50 percent. The other 50 percent is longer term liabilities, namely shareholder capital, open reserves, and extraordinary reserves.

The allocation of capital at risk at the 90 percent level of confidence, will leave 10 percent of all cases outside its limits. These will be covered by capital at risk at the 99.9 percent level of confidence, while many of the outliers are taken care of by "safe" capital at the >99.9 percent which acts as a buffer. Statistically speaking, for only 1 per

Exhibit 13.1 A Retructured Balance Sheet Using Capital at Risk with Confidence Intervals

Current, medium- and long-term assets (at fair value)	100	Liabilities*	50
		Capital at 90%	20
		Capital at 90%–99%	10
		Capital at 99%–99.9%	5
		Safe capital (> 99.9%)	15
			100

* Current and medium term.

thousand of all cases this buffer may not be sufficient. The challenge with this distribution is to cover at the same time:

- The probability of events stratified by the level of capital allocation, therefore of exposure.
- The synergy of credit risk, market risk, and operational risk at each channel and stratum of business activities.

Dr. Hermann's method is flexible, and a bank can reallocate the percentages associated to the different capital strata in Exhibit 13.1. Extreme events may go beyond the typical statistical outliers, also in excess of the 5 standard deviations many banks use for stress testing. Some market reactions are two-digit standard deviation events. The crash in October 1987 was a 14s case.

Let me repeat this concept: Capital at risk at the >99.9 percent level of confidence is taken as insurance against extreme events in losses. When computed in a pragmatic manner, this level of capital cushion should be related to the business being done, the board's risk appetite, the exposure which is assumed, the accuracy of internal controls and risk management system which are in place, and other factors. The goal is to significantly enhance the bank's ability of sustaining a major loss associated to a specific counterparty, instrument, and/or market.

A credit institution using the notion in Exhibit 13.1 will see to it that capital ratios at the 90 percent to >99.9 percent levels of confidence will be computed on the basis of risks associated to the business it is doing. Exposure should always be associated to profit generators. Banks with the following distribution of income:

- 45 percent private banking,
- 18 percent investment and trading,
- 17 percent consumer banking,
- 7 percent corporate banking,
- 7 percent institutional asset management, or
- 6 percent other channels

have a totally different risk profile than one with the following distribution:

- 10 percent private banking,
- 40 percent investment and trading,
- 10 percent consumer banking,
- 25 percent corporate banking,
- 10 percent institutional asset management, or
- 5 percent other channels.

Within each major class of risk and return there will be subdivisions that help in defining the amount of exposure taken by the institution. For instance, investments and trading would involve exposure in interest rate risk, currency exchange risk, and equities. As Exhibit 13.2 demonstrates, to each class is associated a different high/low capital at risk level depending on market conditions, but also on the generic gains and losses characteristics of this class.

EARNINGS AT RISK AS ALTERNATIVE TO AND COMPLEMENT OF CAPITAL AT RISK

Another concept leading toward fulfilling the same objectives with the allocation of capital at risk was advanced during the First International Conference on Risk Management in Banking by Brandon Davies of Barclays Bank. This is the *Earnings at Risk* (EAR) solution. Earnings at risk is the product of two factors:

1. The standard deviation of a position's income.
2. A multiplier reflecting the confidence level of the computation.

If we assume that the income stream from our positions is normally distributed, then computing the expected value (mean) and expressing our measure of risk in standard deviations, we can estimate the earnings at risk.

As with VAR, EAR is represented through a truncated distribution. But rather than being truncated in the right side, it is truncated in the left.

The theoretical distribution of expected earnings and the algorithm of EAR are shown in Exhibit 13.3. At 99 percent level of confidence a worst case scenario in regard

Exhibit 13.2   High/Low Capital at Risk with Different Instruments, as Presented by a Major Financial Institution

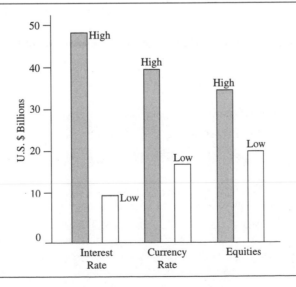

Exhibit 13.3   The Calculation of Earnings at Risk Based on the Assumption of a Normal Distribution

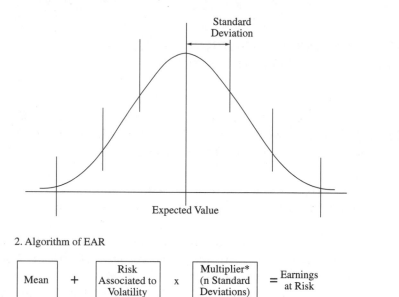

1. Normal Distribution of Expected Earnings

2. Algorithm of EAR

$$\boxed{\text{Mean}} \quad + \quad \boxed{\begin{array}{c}\text{Risk}\\\text{Associated to}\\\text{Volatility}\end{array}} \quad \text{x} \quad \boxed{\begin{array}{c}\text{Multiplier*}\\\text{(n Standard}\\\text{Deviations)}\end{array}} \quad = \begin{array}{c}\text{Earnings}\\\text{at Risk}\end{array}$$

* The multiplier reflects the confidence level.

to earnings at risk will be mean minus 2.32 standard deviations ($\bar{x} - 2.32s$). Different levels of confidence can be considered in a way similar to those of the Hermann model, though the 99 percent level is the most popular.

EAR is connected to capital at risk because it tells what would be the worst case in terms of return on capital we put at risk. Because there are compensating factors, at the bottom line, risk associated with the bank's portfolio level will tend to be less than the sum of the risk's constituent parts. This means that aggregation of risk becomes a critical issue requiring research on:

- How to sum up credit risks.
- How to aggregate across different market risk types.
- How to integrate credit risks and market risks.

Every one of these steps is important. To various degrees, each of them involves the definition, identification, summation, and integration of risks. In doing this work, we should keep in mind that while the exposure figure will most likely be less than the arithmetic sum of all individual risks, since these risks will not all materialize at the same time and up to a point they may offset one another, their synergy might as well have the opposite effect. Namely, making the sum bigger than the arithmetic addition of risks embedded in the component parts of exposure.

There is a long standing principle in system engineering that the aggregate may be greater than, equal to, or less than the arithmetic sum of its parts. Great bankers have intuitively used this principle in their decisions, but only recently it is being expressed algorithmically in financial models.

The model of earnings at risk can be improved by considering other factors that impact on earnings, such as the effect of country risk and currency risk on income sources as well as the effects of diversification. Every bank has a geographic distribution of income, whether this is regional, national, or global. Said an article in *Business Week*[4] about the United Bank of Switzerland:

- 50 percent of its business comes from Switzerland.
- 25 percent from the European Union.
- 10 percent from the United States.
- 15 percent from other countries including Japan.

While 50 percent of the income sources are from one country, the overall geographic diversification is good. Country risk is present at much less than 50 percent of business, and it corresponds to the "other countries" class minus Japan. On the other hand, currency risk is relatively high. Because Switzerland is not part of the European Union, volatility in foreign exchange rates will put earnings at risk.

This concept of earnings at risk can be extended to account for new channels of competition, for instance electronic banking and electronic commerce. American experts advise that *Internet-intrinsic* business models are needed to capture the estimated $300 billion opportunity in E-commerce in the United States, and $500 billion global potential. Internet-intrinsic business requires high technology. Short of it, the bank will be missing that market.

Strategic planners should never underestimate the Internet business. Evaluators like earnings at risk have the potential to become its valid metrics. At the end of June 1999 (when this text was written) Ecommerce/Ebanking in the United States passed for the first time the 1 percent of gross domestic product. The estimated $300 billion will be in excess of 3 percent. But there are prerequisites for earnings in that market. Building up business confidence on the Internet requires:

- Rapid customer need identification.
- Merchant-specific information.
- Counterparty verification.
- Product evaluation and brokering.
- Negotiation and confirmation.
- Payment and delivery.
- After sales product service.

The fulfillment of such prerequisites can help the emergence of *new* dynamic markets, supply chains, and distribution channels, while failure to do so has an aftermath on profits. As Charles Schwab, the brokerage house which leads in Ebanking, has demonstrated, in an Internet-intrinsic business model all of these steps are based on leadership in high technology.

Customer motivation can be propelled through product information available online. Because a fully networked environment is fiercely competitive, merchant-specific information is necessary to determine who to buy from. This also includes evaluation of merchant alternatives through buyer-based criteria like type, price, warranty, delivery time, merchant reputation, brand name, and so on.

Counterparty verification is the weak link in the chain. Network security is still wanting and this can lead to fraud. Product evaluation and brokering includes retrieval of information to help determine exactly what to buy, for instance, evaluation of alternatives through buyer criteria applicable to a set of products screened by means of merchant brokering.

Negotiation is a crucial component of Ecommerce and Ebanking. In an agent-assisted negotiation, intelligent software finds the clauses and prepares contracts on behalf of the parties these agents represent. In many cases, computational agents are better at making deals in complex settings without involving heavy human cost. Payment agreements may vary in duration and complexity depending on the market and the product. The negotiation of price and payment aspects of the deal are crucial to buying and selling.

Every transaction can be a generator of exposure. Because the environment in which we trade changes so fast, to be worth their salt new methods for the evaluation of risk and return must be open to the use of the latest technological solutions that affect sales, earnings, and capitalization. We must also be aware of the limitations that exist in the methods and algorithms we are using.

Finally, readers knowledgeable in mathematical statistics will appreciate that models addressing capital at risk, earnings at risk, and value at risk have in common an approximation to real-life conditions, whether we target credit risk, market risk, operational risk or other types of exposure. Our model will be more accurate if we do not fail to account for all relevant factors. Exhibit 13.4 brings the reader's attention to a range of crucial variables entering the aggregation of risks, including the following:

- Default.
- Technology.
- Payments.
- Settlements.

A properly tuned internal accounting system should be able to handle risk premiums based on the determination of risk(s) per counterparty for all business processes. This involves credit rating and country categories as well as the establishment of premiums rates for classes which rather recently entered into the exposure equation. It also requires that the proper attention is paid to model risk.

Exhibit 13.4   An Aggregation Function of Risk Must Consider All Risk Factors

Aggregation of Risk and Return

LITERACY IN HIGH TECHNOLOGY AND CAPITAL AT RISK

Capital at risk beyond the 99.9 percent level of confidence has been defined as being essentially a cushion against losses relating to extreme events in interest rate, currency exchange rate, equity index, or other volatilities—as well as to counterparty risk. The calculation of stratified capital at risk should be seen as an integral part of forward looking financial accounting procedures, and an important element of internal management accounting. The first basic requirement is the one defined by COSO:

Transparency in reporting, coupled with accuracy and timeliness of information.

In terms of transparency in reporting, the bank needs an accounting methodology able to reflect the level of computer literacy of people who receive the financial reports. For instance, knowledgeable executives should be interested to know the probability distribution of capital expressed by the variance characterizing the factors Exhibit 13.4 has identified, bringing their attention to existing correlations and covariance, and proceeding with experimentation connected to the likelihood of future events.

The second basic principle of prudential risk management is prognostication. The emphasis on future events is crucial because even if we know today's values, these change over time. Prognostication is important in providing lead time to study the information and react to events in a proactive manner.

The third basic principle of prudential risk management regards the implementation of an analytical structure able to satisfy the needs of the board and of senior management regarding the evaluation of risk and return. This must be done for any channel, any transaction, with any counterparty, anywhere in the world.

One of the problems with this strategy of three principles is that board members, the chief executive officer, and his immediate assistants are not necessarily literate in regard to high technology. Therefore, they find it difficult to experiment with the risks and opportunities presented by counterparties and the financial instruments in which their bank deals.

The good news is that at least the concept of a normal distribution starts being appreciated by the upper management layers in banking, because it becomes evident that to manage an institution effectively it is necessary to understand the probability distribution of capital. However, finding the stochastic behavior of a complex portfolio of assets and liabilities is no easy task. This effort is further compound by the problems posed by future transactions that alter the composition of the portfolio.

One of the objectives in the proactive investigation of effects of future transactions relates to our ability to estimate capital at risk *before* events take place, based on counterparty and instrument profiles mined from our database—therefore historical experience. A comprehensive frame of visualization of experimental results is presented in Exhibit 13.5.

One of the prerequisites for literacy in high technology is that senior management appreciates not only the need for rigorous mathematical analysis in banking, but also for experimentation. A project in which I recently participated investigated both analytic and stochastic means of financial system simulation, coming to the conclusion that in most cases a classical analytical approach is both too tedious and too complex to be of practical use with derivative instruments.

During this same project, stochastic methods to financial simulation through Monte Carlo were found to be the most promising in terms of prudential control over exposure.

Exhibit 13.5   A Finer Definition of Capital at Risk Must Be Done in a 3-Dimensional Space

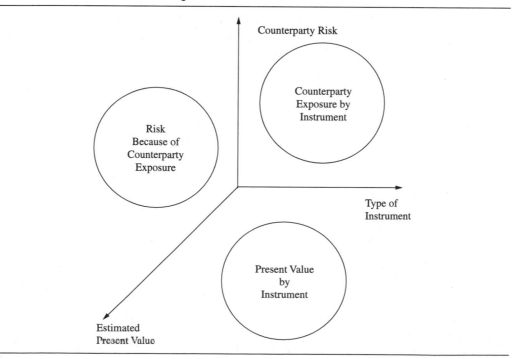

Subsequently, attention was paid on developing techniques for determining the number of Monte Carlo trials necessary to predict a financial system's performance. This was done both for initial conditions and as a function of time, and it addressed different levels of confidence in the calculation of detailed and compound exposure.

A process was elaborated permitting random selection from various channels whose distribution of risk and return may be handled through Monte Carlo simulation. The experimentation also included probabilistically defined measures of initial conditions and time-dependent performance under different market scenarios.

Projects undertaken along the aforementioned lines find their justification in the fact that behind the questions that have classically faced the senior management of a bank stand some interesting mathematical problems. Derivative financial instruments and globalized banking operations can be examined as irregularly connected 3-dimensional networks of:

- Amount of exposure.
- Time distribution.
- Frequency of different events.

Risk and return originates from one or more events whose nature and time of occurrence are stochastic. It terminates at one or more final stages, some of which may be abrupt. For instance, an event that upset the model and its carefully worked out relationships is that banks in Wall Street are now lending on margin to speculators so that the latter can maintain their positions.

This exposes the bank to a double risk, by compounding credit and market exposure. It also invalidates past default probabilities, by altering risk profiles and extending the time to default.

COSO is not talking about mathematical experimentation as a means for improving transparency, but Tier-1 banks have put it in their list of priorities. Seen from an analytical perspective, counterparty business behavior is such that a chain of succeeding events does not necessarily lead back into itself. Furthermore, the duration of intermediate events is not a known constant but is characterized by a probability distribution.

Given different risk and return distributions pertaining to lending, investments, derivatives activities, and other business channels, what is the likelihood of an "X" level of exposure during the time of occurrence of intermediate events? Of the final event? Far from posing an abstract question, this has intrinsic interest because the frequency of intermediate situations with a high-exposure quotient increases in the context of global finance.

After the organizational perspective has been set and the analytical job of qualification and quantification of risk has been done, accurate experimental methods are necessary to map market behavior and resulting exposure into the computer. The reason why stochastic processes are sought is that they provide realistic algorithms that can be profitably employed for the analysis of complex conditions as well as for risk control purposes. But if all levels of management, including the board and senior management, do not understand this methodology, the return on investment will be minimal.

CAPITAL AT RISK, IRREVOCABLE COMMITMENTS, AND CURRENT EXPOSURE

"One of the major difficulties with risk control in financial institutions," said one of the senior risk management officer who participated in my research, "is that this is a reactive job. Even if we see that an inordinate risk is taken, it is hard to prohibit certain trades to engage in perilous trades. Essentially what we do in risk control is to count the results post-mortem."

Other risk management officers expressed the opinion that a major contribution that could be done through modeling is to improve transparency at the level which starts with the board's authorization for credit risk and market risk commitments. But they also added that unless senior management appreciates the quantitative level of exposure taken by the institution, much of what is computed will have only an academic value.

Still another opinion which I registered in my research is that king-size failures are usually made by those people who regard even the errors being committed as holy and above criticism. Can the allocation of capital at risk, and the sense that it constitutes an exposure, help in facing in a more realistic manner *our* bank's commitments?

The sense of a *commitment* is that an institution takes on itself the aftermath of a future transaction that will normally result in acquiring a credit exposure at some future date. The capital at risk may relate to an asset or a guarantee. A similar statement is valid regarding market risk. A commitment is usually binding to both parties, and there may exist a predetermined date on which it must be exercised. But the commitment can also be binding only to one of the two parties, while the counterparty retains the right to choose whether or when to ask the committed party to honor its obligation. Options are an example.

There are also looser commitments where a bank has agreed on a line of credit or an overdraft facility, hence putting capital at risk, but has the right to withdraw the facility under certain circumstances. For instance, the trigger may be a deterioration in credit quality of the potential borrower. This is a soft, or revocable, commitment.

Irrevocable commitments are those that are binding on the bank in all circumstances, and from which a bank could not withdraw without penalty. This distinction between hard and soft commitments may be difficult to operate in some circumstances, but it is a very useful one in regard to planning and controlling capital at risk.

Trading leads to irrevocable commitments, whether *our bank* buys or sells through the exchanges or makes bilateral over-the-counter agreements. Loans commitments can be more flexible, depending on their covenants. Capital is at risk, but a certain clause might allow disengagement. To trace the boundary between revocable and irrevocable commitments, some banks divide the latter into two classes, each with firmly defined characteristics: Those with certain exercise or draw-down, but not necessarily a certain date for it.

For instance, it is not known in advance when the commitment will be exercised or whether it will definitely be taken up in full. However, if and when it is exercised, the bank is exposed to full credit risk. This may not be true in connection to the second class.

Commitment with uncertain draw-down, where it is unclear whether and to what extent credit exposure will materialize. The commitment is still at the discretion of the other party but there is a probability on whether or not it will be exercised; neither is the timing of any draw-down certain. Questions might as well exist regarding the most likely quality of the asset at the time of draw-down. All these factors need to be considered in evaluating credit risk exchange—and therefore capital at risk.

A factual and documented method of allocating capital at risk, and in promoting the ability to experiment and optimize the allocation of funds, can assist board members and senior management in their understanding of the implications resulting from past, present, and future commitments. Behind this statement is the fact that CAR implies the assignment of capital resources by product line all the way down to desk and trader.

This solution has the advantage of integrating well with limits placed by top management. At the foundation of both limits and capital at risk is current and future exposure. Current exposure is the net replacement value for a financial instrument contracted with a given counterparty. Since the early 1990s, financial institutions have been moving from the so-called percentage rule toward a more analytical basis in connection to replacement cost. This employs valuation or pricing formulas, which have been common in trading, and estimates worst-case change in value till maturity of the contract.

In many cases, the model involves a log-normal distribution function, as well as the computation of confidence intervals over time. Credit equivalent is calculated based on the maximum of an envelope of possible replacement values during the lifetime of the instrument(s). Interest rate swaps, floors, swaptions, global equity, and commodity derivatives are among the instruments subjected to this procedure.

Stochastic computational methods can be complemented through historic default probabilities in conjunction with a credit score assigned to the counterparty to provide an estimate of current credit capital at risk. If the bank chooses to go into detail in its CAR estimation and associated control of exposure, then CAR should be allocated by the following:

- Counterparty.
- Instrument.
- Specific transaction.

Enriched by database mining and risk analysis, models can be instrumental in capital allocation. They can also assist in estimating potential losses by means of unbundling, measuring and evaluating a range of risks, as well as through optimization studies. The capital allocation model can assist in identifying the extent to which the bank's activities are diversified, as well as how the institution is doing on a risk-adjusted basis.

Capitalizing on experience gained during the last 10 years with models like Risk Adjusted Return on Capital (RAROC), top tier credit institutions are now subjecting their channels of operations to thousands of potential market moves. This provides senior management with better insight in allocating a capital charge that would sufficiently cover 99 percent of all losses generated by business activities.

Through sophisticated modeling, experimentation, and database mining, a bank can cushion itself to a greater or lesser extent against severe shocks due to credit risk and market risk. Experimentation may also concern internal events such as the composition of the institution's trading book, banking book, and portfolio. Sophisticated risk management algorithms can provide ideal platforms from which to launch a whole range of risk control services including treasury hedging, currency, and interest rate risk exposure, leading to risk-adjusted performance measurements.

PRUDENTIAL LIMITS, VOLATILITY, AND CAPITAL AT RISK

The basic concept behind limits is to make sure that traders, loans officers and other front desk professionals don't bet the bank when they are transacting business. For this reason, the board and senior management should be keen to see in place a system that establishes an upper exposure limit for: Counterparty risk, interest rate risk, currency exchange risk, equity derivatives risk, index risk, and other business risks the bank is taking.

The large majority of financial institutions have such a system in operation, but few have gone a step further to study and establish limits on trading based on projected volatility. Flexible limits adjusted for volatility can tell when trading is prudent and when it is exposed to fluctuations which exceed the risk threshold implicitly or explicitly set through board policies.

The notions of a stochastic behavior of exposure, discussed in Chapters 7 and 8 through statistical quality control charts, as well as the capital at risk the bank puts on the block because of irrevocable commitments, converge when we establish credit risk and market risk limits. Regulators are now interested on whether or not financial institutions:

- Establish limits.
- Follow up on them.

"We started in the late 1980s asking questions about funding, liquidity, and credit controls," said a senior executive of the SEC during our meeting in New York. "We now ask about the limits structure and how they control it." This is consistent with the fact that limits are instruments of management planning and control.

The regulatory focus on limits started after the Drexel crisis, as central banks and other supervisory agencies became aware that the liquidity problems of the institutions under their jurisdiction were compound by bad treasury management. Ten years down the line, liquidity shocks in international finance fully justified the regulators' care regarding funding and limits.

The statement about the contribution of limits to prudential management is valid both with companies and with nations. Russia, Indonesia, and Korea lived with too many short-term obligations that they could not any more face when the East Asia crisis started. In all three countries, the concept of limits on funding has been non-existent both on a national and on a corporate level.

Usually it is the best managed banks who see to it that their professionals and their executives are subject to guidelines and limits on exposures. Even if the regulators establish no specific limits, the board and senior management are expected to diversify their risk—and do so in a prudent way. The concepts of capital at risk and earnings at risk can help in this effort. This is true both in terms of:

- Counterparty exposure taken with loans.
- The nature and scale of off-balance sheet activities.

Because derivatives exchange market risk for credit risk, off-balance sheet exposures should be included in a systemic manner in the bank's internal counterparty limits. A cautious approach is recommended since the objective is to contain the impact that the failure of a single customer or correspondent bank might have on *our* bank's solvency.

I have already made reference to the fact that a number of institutions have moved, or are currently moving, away from the percentage rule of exposure into an analytical basis of replacement value of transactions with counterparties, and Chapter 14 will elaborate further on this issue. With derivative financial instruments, *credit equivalent* calculations can be significantly assisted at transaction time through the demodulation of notional principle amount.

The best approach to business life, and the only one for a trader and for a risk manager, is to ask what can go wrong. As the mathematician Carl Jacobi advised: "Invert, always invert." This is what we do with demodulation of notional principal, downsizing the assumed credit risk and market risk to a level supported by historical evidence as being representative of real life exposure.

Today, several banks demodulate the notional principal of a transaction by 20 and write the resulting credit equivalent amount against credit limits. They may also demodulate positions in their portfolio by a factor varying between 20 and 35 (depending on the instrument, market conditions, and other factors) to establish loans equivalent market risk.

There are also other policies suggesting themselves in the realm of as prudent management. Both contingent liabilities and commitments, whether revocable or not, should be included within counterparty limits. A valid approach would see to it that for foreign exchange, interest rate and stock index transactions, an estimate for the replacement cost of an exposure is always in the foreground. A sound way of establishing credit limits is based on a combination of marking-to-market exposures plus a margin for volatility.

Furthermore, while it is difficult to take account in a systematic way of counterparty exposures in securities underwriting, senior management should decide on a maximum figure beyond which the institution will not commit itself in the context of large exposures. Other financial instruments that potentially subject a company to concentrations of credit risk, and therefore impact on capital at risk, are investments and trade receivables.

A sound management practice tries to place trades and investments with high-credit quality counterparties, but a rigorous risk control policy will put limits to the amount of credit exposure to any one counterparty—even the best.

A rational way to compute limits is to base them on an analysis of our counterparty's relative credit standing. As we saw in Chapter 11 in connection to the New Capital Adequacy Framework by the Basle Committee, rating by independent agencies helps, but institutions should also use internally developed criteria. The setting of limits must always keep in perspective the environment within which a company operates. This is true in industry as it is in banking.

For instance, in 1997 Intel's five largest customers accounted for 39 percent of its net revenues, and as that year came to a close amounts due from these customers represented approximately 34 percent of net accounts receivable. Given this concentration, Intel established a policy of:

- Performing ongoing credit evaluations of its customers' financial condition.
- Requiring collateral as deemed necessary on a case-by-case basis.

As this example and many others document, it is wise to adopt credit policies and standards which are both able to accommodate industry growth and to control inherent risk. Typically, credit risks are moderated by the diversity of a company's customers and its geographic sales area—but these are not reasons to do away with limits. Neither should one forget that mergers and acquisitions tend to reduce the number of key players, therefore leading to re-concentration.

Credit limits complement rather than substitute minimum acceptable ratings for counterparties. Another lesson Tier-1 banks have learned through experience is that credit limits should be market-weighted. Because this increases the reported level of exposure as the maturity of the transaction increases, it constitutes a good evaluator of capital at risk at the medium to longer term.

THE NEED FOR A STEADY EVOLUTION OF THE REPORTING STRUCTURE

A good way of evaluating the vocation of a bank is by the capital at risk it allocates to a certain industry. The example presented in Exhibit 13.6 is real estate loans among top U.S. banks. J.P. Morgan allocates less than 5 percent of total loans to real estate, while at BankAmerica that ratio is more than 20 percent. Chase and Citibank fall between these two ratios.

In a comparable manner, a sound approach to the evaluation of the risk culture of an institution is how often and by which means top management gets informed on exposure. At Deutsche Bank, the 8 members of the board of managing directors receive reports on exposure once per week. This information is mainly presented in graphical form. But at the next level, the 40 senior executives who are leading the business divisions, get the report on exposure at the end of today.

Exhibit 13.6   Capital at Risk in Real Estate Is Not Allocated at the Same Proportion by All Banks

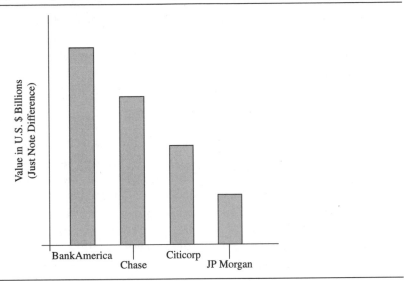

Intraday reporting is the practice with line managers. Some of these reports present to their reader the delta and gamma risk.[5] Value at risk information is provided regularly with the objective to increase management sensitivity to assumed exposure. The senior management's position is that:

- Desk managers should know immediately market exposure.
- Business line managers should receive it daily, in a comprehensive form.
- While division heads and board members get it on request and by major event.

The argument I most often hear when suggesting a reporting practice like the one just being described or, even better, intraday interactive information available to all managers, traders, loans officers, and other authorized personnel—and the top of the organizational pyramid—is that the cost of converting established accounting systems can be prohibitive. It is necessary to convert procedures, not only change computer programs and this, many bankers say, can be quite expensive.

The answer to this comment is that the results achieved through the sophistication of internal accounting information systems currently used by top-tier companies suggests that costs are not a real obstacle. If changing accounting standards is expensive, the benefits to be obtained cover the expense and leave a profit. Alternatively, not changing accounting standards to an intraday practice may be prohibitively expensive, because of the huge risk that is incurred.

We have to rethink the purpose of financial accounting. The form of any reporting framework should be designed to provide a background for assessment. The presentation of information must be individualized while the basic data might serve various constituencies. Five levels of reference are pertinent in this connection:

1. *The management of the enterprise.* It used to be that all that senior management needed to know was deposits and loans (even maturities were not that important); investments in securities (without any great detail); accounts receivable and accounts payable; assets and liabilities in their classical form. All these items are still important, but they are not enough. Modern management requires a great deal more of information to be in charge. For risk control, for instance, it needs ad hoc real-time response regarding the distribution of exposures, their details, magnitude, and payoffs. All items have to be recognized, even if profits and losses are not yet realized.

   What is more, the nature of this information as well as the required frequency of reporting can be significantly improved at affordable cost through interactive computational finance and database mining operations. Top management reports should fully reflect changes due to market forces and counterparty weaknesses. Within a dynamic, globalized market environment, volatility, liquidity, and the company's own strategy are in full evolution. Furthermore, besides the company's own management, there are other constituencies that are interested not only in current assets and liabilities, but also care to know about long-term assets and liabilities, as well as capital at risk and the likelihood of downside.

2. *Stockholders have a prime interest in the valuation of the institution and its financial health.* Modern accounting aims to present much more than the classical mirror of A&L. Measuring potential earnings and evaluating inherent worth is a prerequisite to stock pricing by the market; hence, it is very important for shareholders. Alert shareholders also appreciate that the market's potential and the company's own action (or inaction) introduce stochastic elements into valuation.

   Besides earnings, financial analysts examine the public company from other angles. For instance, its discounted cash flow which has an intrinsic value; its product line and the market appeal of these products; its products in the laboratory and their timing—the so-called pipeline; the level of information technology that it uses; and, most importantly, the quality of its management.

   There are items in this list that don't show up in the classical balance sheet, yet their valuation is crucial in terms of how the company is going from here to there. Also, whether it is in the right course for survival in an environment more competitive than ever.

3. *Bankers extending loans and doing derivatives trades have other questions to ask.* Classically, liquidation value has been quite important to bankers, provided they have the right to ask shareholders to take the backseat. But not everything is answered through liquidation value, which essentially means a fire sale.

   While in classical accounting, the value of each asset and each liability is a well-defined concept, and net worth is found through value additivity, leverage changes all that. Temporarily, but only temporarily, gearing pushes up the value; but the way to bet is that as time goes by and gearing increases, it destroys value. These, too, are facts not found in the classical notion of a balance sheet.

Bankers who are the lenders as well as shareholders, bondholders, and underwriters are concerned about a potential default and would like to have the proof that the debtor is solid. But they are also interested in getting a measure of *event risk*. Is this company going to be subject to a leveraged buyout (LBO) which can turn its debt from AA to BB?

4. *For practical purposes, regulators are obliged to look at both sides of the fence.* Central bankers and other regulators evidently have an embedded interest in the financial health of the institutions which they supervise. Securities and Exchange Commissions are out to protect stockholders equity. Both central bankers and securities regulators aim to avoid systemic risk.

   Yet all parties, authorities, and supervised institutions know that in a deregulated and globalized market the presence of uncertainty is essential to business and has to be taken into account. This statement is equally true regarding uncertainty about future value of assets and liabilities; the risk and return connected to capital at risk; and the aftermath of gearing because of derivative financial instruments.

5. *Tax authorities responsible for corporate taxes usually serve themselves with the current balance sheet and income statement structure.* This, too, is changing.

   Because of globalization of business, local tax authorities start levying a tax which, while it still addresses local income, it applies a percentage based on a guestimated global income of the business. There are, furthermore, issues connected to bilateral and international treaties for the avoidance of double taxation which increasingly impact local tax authorities.

One reason this or that type of violation of transborder treaties starts becoming a rule, is that the current accounting system fails in measuring global business in a way protecting the interests of all parties (see Chapters 2 and 3). It is also weak in measuring future exposure as it tries to present a certified form of global income. There are many crevasses in international treaties because these were not made to account for deregulation and globalization. Even in terms of taxation, current accounting structures don't quite hold the position they are supposed to serve.

For all five major classes of parties interested in financial accounting information, there must be transparency and consistency in reporting. Algorithms and heuristics that permit to present critical information in a comprehensible and comprehensive manner are necessary. This is the focal point of new methods and systems designed for financial accounting and for reporting purposes—where the principles of COSO can provide a significant help.

NOTES

1. *Middle Office* (June 1998).
2. London (March 17–19, 1997).
3. D.N. Chorafas, *Chaos Theory in the Financial Markets* (Chicago: Probus, 1994).
4. *Business Week* (December 22, 1997).
5. D.N. Chorafas, *Advanced Financial Analysis* (London: Euromoney, 1994).

CHAPTER 14

Market Value Accounting

References were frequently made during the discussion of financial accounting standards and reporting practices (Chapters 9 and 10) and of international accounting standards and generally accepted accounting principles (Chapters 2 and 3) to the *accruals* method and *fair value*. In this chapter, the two terms are explained and their aftermath compared. Their effect on financial reporting is also discussed.

Keep in perspective the notions underlying the balance sheet: *Assets* and *liabilities*—or, more precisely, *their values*—should balance. The problem is valuation, and it comes from the fact that insiders and outsiders to the firm often see things differently:

- Sometimes insiders take big risks and expect these will result in big profits for themselves and for shareholders. This tends to emphasize assets over liabilities. Also insiders are more interested in future value of the assets they manage.
- Outsiders, like public accountants, investors, and regulators are more conservative in their valuation and for good reason. But conservative does not mean backward looking.

As we will see in this chapter, the problem with accruals is that the resulting book value has little to do with current reality and at times it may also be misleading. If fair value estimates are factual and documented, then they provide a better basis for appreciation of assets and liabilities.

Present value estimates make more meaningful the result of comparisons and tests. One of the criteria used in the analysis of balance sheets is the equity/assets ratio. This is more fundamental than capital/assets because capital may be bought, traded, or manipulated. Also, in some accounting regimes it is hard to define what exactly capital is.

Disclosure based on historical costs sees to it that when players in the derivatives markets cut a deal, it is hard to know how much exposure they take on.

It is not that simple to define capital in an unambiguous way. Leverage, creates major risks and leads to misinterpretations. The Long-Term Capital Management hedge fund had a leverage of 50 to 1. Many investors are basically going blind when they put their money in companies that deal in risky financial instruments or in unpredictable emerging country markets. The same is true when they buy stock in companies that aggressively use their treasury operations for profits. Both cases raise the risk that financial downturns could send investors scrambling to sell in a market void of buyers.

Internationally, accounting standards authorities are working to develop rules that would require a realistic appreciation of value in assets and liabilities, as well as a comprehensive disclosure of risks stemming from significant movements in financial markets by every company exposed to those shifts, whether financial institution, manufacturing, merchandizing, or other type of firm.

Many of the challenges faced by lenders, investors, and regulators boil down to the fact that the current accounting rules relating to bookkeeping and disclosure have been overtaken by market developments. It is not therefore surprising that fair value estimates, and reporting practices based on them, have attracted major attention on a global scale.

PLUSES AND MINUSES WITH THE ACCRUALS METHOD

Historical costs are the oldest approach in keeping the books. Depreciation and amortization are some of the updates. But what should be done if the market value changes upwards or downwards and the book value represent a small fraction of the assets or, alternatively, it is cloud 9 when related to market reality?

Both the law of the land and tradition provide one of the answers to this query. Traditionally, companies value their assets and liabilities at their historic costs and ignore fluctuations in their value. That makes accounting simple but wrong.

The accruals method cannot answer in an effective manner the queries in the preceding paragraph. Historical solutions have a rationale, but they do not always respond to changing market requirements.

This does not mean that historical prices are of no interest whatsoever. The advantage of historical prices and associated accounting records is that they reflect transactions as they have happened. But how actual is this information? To have it updated for some applications, we need to add accrued interest premiums and impairments:

- Accrued interest is generally added to the original carrying cost of receivables and payments.
- Accrued expense is an expense that has accumulated with passage of time and has not been paid.

The word *accrue,* as used in accounting, means to accumulate. Before the profit and loss statement is prepared and the books closed, the accountant must consider whether there are accrued income and accrued expenses—and take note of them. The principle is simple, when the accrual basis is used:

- Income is recorded for the fiscal period in which it is earned, whether it is received during that period or not.
- Expenses incurred in earning the income are recorded as expense, whether or not payment has been made for them during that period.

Depreciation is also calculated based on historical costs. The life of the asset is estimated and depreciation is applied according to a rule. For instance, with straight-line depreciation, an equal part of the depreciable value of the asset is charged off for each accounting period during the asset's life. But the algorithm may be accelerated by depreciation or something else that is legally admissible for financial reporting reasons.

In connection with premiums, historical costs may need to be amortized over the term a financial asset is used. If they have occurred, impairments should be subtracted from the historical price of a financial asset.

Until fairly recently, the method of accruals has been considered to be the proper way of calculating the periodic income of most business enterprises. This statement remains valid in the majority of countries and in many industries—though a change toward a different methodology, initiated in the United States and the United Kingdom is currently under way.

Older financial instruments can still use the accruals method to advantage. An example is loans. Because the interest is earned, some banks complain that fair value accounting will result in showing a loss with loans at the very moment that they are booked. Correctly, however, FASB statements don't permit cherry picking—while the securitization of loans by means of credit derivatives leaves the accruals method in the dust.[1]

A similar argument is valid in connection with interest rates and foreign exchange. With interest rate products, some banks favor the accruals method for calculating financial results, including discounted future margins on the balanced part of fixed-interest assets and liabilities. With currency exchange instruments this includes the sum of accrued foreign currency interest, but currency risk remains.

The same is true about interest rate risk. Interest rate exposure in loan positions can be closed in the banking book through an internal interest rate swap, exchanging fixed with flexible interest rates. The result from internal hedges in the interest rate business is offset by another transaction exchanging interest earned and interest paid.

This sort of transaction, however, does not fit well with the classical way of handling accruals. They constitute a modified method, made to respond to current trading and investment practices. Another alternative in accounting is the cash basis. With the cash basis, income is recorded only when cash is received; and expense is recognized only when cash is paid out. Frequently, the cash basis is modified to include the following:

- Accounts payable.
- Accounts receivable.
- Depreciation.

Professionals, nonprofit organizations and small businesses often use this method of accounting. Also, when a taxpayer's entire income is from such wages or salaries, dividends, and interest, the cash basis is simpler and is generally satisfactory.

If depreciation is recognized, it is computed periodically in the same way as if the company was on the accrual basis. But a firm that has a merchandize inventory cannot ordinarily operate effectively on the cash basis. For tax purposes, income may be calculated on either accruals or cash basis except where inventories are involved. In that case, an accruals basis is mandatory. Beginning and ending inventories must be taken into consideration in computing cost of goods sold.

When the accrual basis is used, income is included in the period in which it is earned, but expenses are deducted in the period in which they are incurred.

Accruals and cash basis are different, though the latter might be seen as a modification of the former. Comparing the cash method to accruals, when the cash basis is used, income is recognized in the period in which it is received and expenses are taken in the period in which they are paid: The receipt of income may be either actual or constructive. Constructive receipt means that the income was available though not yet collected. Interest credited to the taxpayer's savings account is an example.

A MILESTONE IN ACCOUNTING: THE NOTION OF FAIR VALUE

Fair value is a concept that has been briefly considered in preceding chapters. The simplest definition is that of an estimated value for a commodity in comparison to other similar commodities—other things being equal. But, as we will see, other things are not equal and there is need for a significant amount of accuracy.

Some people equate fair value to current value. This equation is not a happy one. Even under depressed market conditions there is usually a current value—but this statement can be open to abuse. In SFAS 107 and other places where the Financial Accounting Standards Board uses the term *fair value,* the price desired is not to be computed on the basis of a possible collapse in the market or any other worst-case scenario.

The term fair value, as used by FASB, denotes the amount at which an asset could be bought or sold between willing parties in a current transaction under conditions other than fire sale. We use this definition of fair value consistently because it is more descriptive than its alternatives and can lead to more accurate results.

The fair value definition by SFAS 107, the measurement that it suggests and associated documentation, are anchored in the realities of the marketplace. As such, the fair value definition is fundamental to economics and finance. Theoretically, fair value estimates are readily available in published form. Practically, this may be true for machinery, equipment, and sometimes real estate—though all these prices are subject to negotiation. Fair value can be available for financial instruments traded in the exchanges, such as stocks and futures, but listed prices are not available for over-the-counter instruments, where fair value is always negotiated.

For other assets, like currencies, information providers assure up-to-date market information on bid and ask. Bid is the nearest thing to fair value because if accepted it represents the price established between a willing buyer and a willing seller in other than liquidation or forced sale conditions. The desired price is the amount at which the instrument could be exchanged in a current transaction. In principle, when all assets and liabilities are written in fair value, hedging does not pose a problem.

This concept leads some people into saying that fair value implies a steady state, which for any practical purpose does not exist in modern financial markets. If the market has collapsed at the time the valuation must be made, SFAS 107 requires an entity to make its best estimate of fair value unless that is impracticable.

This leaves open a door of subjective interpretation of prevailing conditions. For instance, faced with thin markets, some financial institutions estimate a value based on similar instruments that are trading, while others have concluded that valuation is impracticable. This problem is of concern regarding how contents of a portfolio are priced.

An example of a good valuation technique using present value is that of expected future cash flows through discount rates commensurate with the risks being taken. The alternative left when this method is not applicable and current market price does not exist is marking to model.

The use of discounted cash flows and modeling should incorporate explicit assumptions regarding volatility and liquidity, including risk associated to interest rates, currency exchange, prepayment, and default. When all precautions are taken regarding fair value, as Statement of Financial Accounting Standards 133 aptly suggests, fair value is:

- The only relevant measure for derivatives.
- The most relevant measure for financial instruments.

Fair value estimates are always subject to periodic verification and update, whenever assets and liabilities are exchanged in transactions between willing parties. In a globalized market, there are as well other issues connected to fair value as, for instance, the impact of exchange rates, which is particularly important to multinationals.

Fair value of cash is subject to currency risk. The fair value of cash equivalents used as a basis for replacement value approximates the case of cash due in a short period of time to maturity. Typically, most companies take a timespan of less than 3 months while others accept up to 6 months in connection to cash equivalent estimates.

Fair values of short-, medium-, and long-term assets and liabilities must be based on quoted market prices or pricing models using current market rates. Examples are long-term investments, long-term debt, short-term instruments, swaps, currency forward contracts, currency options, and options hedging marketable commodities—whether these are real goods or financial instruments.

WHY MARKET VALUE ACCOUNTING IS NECESSARY

The trend toward fair value accounting started after the crisis of the savings and loans of the late 1980s (see also Chapter 15). The declining assets in the books of many S&L, because of interest rate mismatch, junk bonds, leveraging, and other reasons, would have been visible for many years if market values rather than historical costs constituted the assets and liabilities in the balance sheet.

Had greater transparency been the case, both the management of the thrifts and the examiners would have recognized declines in regulatory capital. Therefore, a timely action would have prevented the accumulation of losses, avoiding the meltdown and significantly reducing the cost of the salvage operation that had to take place.

In the United States, the Securities and Exchange Commission (SEC), Financial Accounting Standards Board (FASB), General Accounting Office (GAO), and a big chunk of the academic community have been in the forefront of the debate for fair value accounting because this method increases the transparency of assets and liabilities in the books by:

- Capturing declining asset values.
- Reflecting gains and losses with derivatives.
- Being sensitive to interest rate volatility.
- Offering an immediate appreciation of market risks.
- Improving the comparability of financial data.

Fair value accounting means current market valuation and it may be very helpful in internal control, the assessment of credit quality, and provides a clearer view of what exists in terms of assets and liabilities. In a dynamic market with significant volatility, historical cost accounting is misrepresenting the values in the books.

Because of the rapid expansion in derivative financial instruments, the 1990s have seen a flare-up in a long-running debate over basic principles in accounting. The whole issue of risk control hinges on which way assets and liabilities are priced. Reformers clamored for a truer picture of companies' profits, losses and resulting worth.

Derivative financial instruments and their bilateral transactions mushroomed, but hidden exposure made accounting changes necessary. Prior to this, banks mainly bought securities issued by federal and local governments and their agencies. There was little risk that these issuers would default. But now banks are taking gambles on exchange rates and interest rates.

Though Group of Ten governments do not default, the value of their bonds drops when interest rates rise. Under accrual type accounting rules, banks do not need to recognize this in their balance sheets.

Ironically, governments themselves practice a sort of creative accounting by tempering their own rules. Gold reserves are an example. With accruals, they must be carried at cost. But even the currently depressed gold bullion prices are higher than the ones at which most governments bought gold.

When a few years ago an ounce of gold cost about $400, the French and Italian governments made a nice profit (and plugged budget holes) by marking to market their inventoried bullion. But when the price of gold collapsed to $275 per ounce, neither of the two governments bothered to revalue its inventories. Switching between accounting systems is not allowed with private and public companies, but governments seem to have elastic rules for compliance.

Other entities don't like to be left behind. Encouraged by rules that demand a large amount of bank capital for loans and little for derivative instruments or government obligations, banks are replacing market risk with credit risk through derivatives—while as the case of Barings demonstrated, some of their branches keep double books, to take profits on successful gambles but ignore losses on bad ones.

Both lax regulations and spotty supervisions end in catastrophes. This was the case when the U.S. Congress authorized the thrift industry to use a new accounting standard that allowed savings and loans to amortize the losses on their loans over the life of the loans. If that was not a big enough loophole, the amortized losses could be offset against any taxes that a thrift had paid over the previous 10 years. In other words, the Internal Revenue Service returned an old tax for every dollar in losses reported by the thrifts.

No wonder so many S&Ls were bought by wheeler-dealers or outright bank robbers. A speculator could put up $3 million to open an S&L. He could offer very high rates to attract $100 or $150 million in government insured deposits. He could then lend this money earning a fat fee that could be used to cover his original investment, and still leave him ahead of the curve.

Because creative accounting practices are often (though not always) associated with market value estimates, many experts do not subscribe to market value accounting. Proponents of historical cost accounting argue that banks hold traditional assets for the long-term and that depositors expect predictable and steady asset values. By increasing volatility in assets and liabilities valuations, this school of thought suggests fair value accounting would weaken public confidence to the banking sector.

This argument forgets the strengths of fair value accounting, which outweigh the drawbacks the preceding paragraph stated. It is however a fact that, in connection with derivatives, market values are known with certainty only at the time the purchase is made or a sale is effected. Reliable estimates for most derivatives contracts negotiated over the counter are not available at other times.

To remedy this situation, we use models. Provided that we use marking-to-market and marking-to-model comprehensively, and that our method is dependable, we can reach results that are comparable among institutions. Model risk exists, but so far it has not been a top issue. The larger exposure lies in the side of the assumptions being made and whether or not these assumptions are correct. Rating agencies like Standard & Poors are now examining the fitness of a rated institution's eigenmodels.

FAIR VALUE, CASH EQUIVALENTS, LOANS, AND SECURITIES

The carrying amount of cash is essentially at fair value. Also cash equivalent instruments approximates fair value due to their short-term maturities and their liquidity. An example of cash equivalents is marketable securities that are highly liquid and have maturities of three months or less at the date of purchase. Short-term investments with maturities of less than six months also tend to be rather liquid.

The fair value of current and noncurrent marketable securities, long-term debt, as well as foreign interest rate and currency swap agreements, used to hedge third-party debt issues, is estimated based on quotes obtained from brokers concerning these or similar instruments. Sometimes this poses a problem of conflict of interest because the broker asked for quotes is the same entity who will market the instrument. It is therefore to its advantage to overestimate or underestimate some factors. In pricing marketable securities, for instance, the usual case is to underestimate future volatility, leading to a *volatility smile;* the broker says that he expects future volatility to be benign. This permits to underprice the instrument making it more attractive, but can lead to huge losses for the bank as it happened with NatWest Markets in the first quarter of 1977.[2]

The fair value of immediate annuities and annuities without life contingencies with fixed terms is estimated using discounted cash flow calculations based on interest rates currently offered for contracts with similar terms and durations. Fair values for fixed income securities are based on quoted market prices where available. Nonquoted securities are valued on the basis of discounted cash flows using current interest rates for similar securities:

- Equity securities are valued based principally on quoted market prices.
- Mortgage loans are valued based on discounted contractual cash flows.

Discount rates are taken using current rates at which similar loans would be made to borrowers with similar characteristics, using similar properties as collateral. It is not easy to find at the same time information on all these "similar" conditions. Therefore, some estimates are in reality guestimates.

Loans that exceed 100 percent loan-to-value are valued at the estimated fair value of the underlying collateral. The fair value of long-term debt is often estimated on the basis of quoted market prices for these or similar issues, or on the current rates offered for debt of the same remaining maturities. Short-term debt is valued at carrying value due to its pending maturity. The fair value of long-term debt and trust preferred securities is based on quoted market prices.

The difference between fair value and the carrying value represents the theoretical net premium the company would have to pay to retire all debt at a given target date. This is an issue requiring fairly sound assumptions.

The fair value of foreign interest rate and currency contracts, used for hedging purposes and long-term investments, is estimated based on quoted market prices. Usually, the fair value for interest rate, cross currency swap agreements and forward exchange contracts:

- Is calculated based on market conditions at year-end.
- Is supplemented with quotes from brokers.

These quotes represent amounts the bank would receive (pay) to terminate/replace such contracts. But it can be subject to a volatility smile as we have already seen. In certain cases, brokers quotes can be biased, particularly if those making them are part of the action.

There is also the case of foreign subsidiaries. Both for the parent company and its subsidiaries abroad, fair value is based on quoted market prices, or dealer quotes where those are available and taken to be reliable. Other factors may be considered where appropriate such as:

- Market prices for related or similar financial instruments.
- Pricing models that consider coupon, yield, credit quality, prepayment terms, volatility, and other economic factors.

The assets and liabilities of the company's foreign subsidiaries have to be translated at current currency exchange rates at the financial statement date. In case of virtual financial statements for internal accounting purposes only, this is done daily or at much shorter time intervals, depending on the frequency of such statements required by strategic and/or operating decisions.

PRESENT VALUE, REPLACEMENT VALUE, AND NET PRESENT VALUE

Whether obtained within the country of origin or from abroad, expected future cash flows are often discounted to their present value (PV). Present value is a computed value rather than market value characterizing fair value. Therefore, fair value and present value should not be confused.

Critical to the calculation of present value is the interest rate used for discounting, because it determines the economic meaning of the discounted cash flow.[3] The computation of present value is subject to a bifurcation:

- If expected future cash flows were discounted at a market rate appropriate for the risk involved, then the result is essentially market value.
- If future cash flows are discounted at the rate stated in the contract, or not discounted, the result is the stated transaction value.

If expected future cash flows are discounted at an interest rate, which equates future cash flows to the amount received or paid in exchange, the outcome is that particular measure. If a rate is used that ignores risks inherent in the instrument, then the outcome is not accounting for exposure.

The pros of expected future cash flows underline that these are the source of the value of receivables and payables, whether conditional or unconditional. Contrarians say that the problem is estimation may be difficult for conditional instruments and even for unconditional instruments for which credit risk is large.

Many banks use a computed value to express current exposure, with replacement value and add-on value the two principal components. Replacement value represents cost at the present time for the replacement of *this* transaction in the event of default. Because replacement value is essentially a risk factor, regulators tend to permit netting arrangements:

- Gross replacement value or GRV (also known as gross replacement cost) is replacement value without netting.[4]
- Net replacement value (NPV) is computed after netting, where and when netting is legally permitted.

I am no fan of netting because its rules are murky and it often ends as a loophole. The theory that transactions are hedged because they have two legs and what the one loses, the other gains does not stand. The case of Metallgesellschaft's bear-bankruptcy, and so many other examples, documents that pluses and minuses can be absolutely unequal.

More sophisticated than the computation of present value is that of *add-ons*, or additional charge for already recognized expenses connected to replacement value. Also, for possible future change in the replacement because of volatility in currencies, interest rates, and other factors. This leads to the concept of present value accounting of assets and liabilities along the framework shown in Exhibit 14.1.

Replacement value based on present value and add-ons should take into account risk premiums to be delivered for default risks and deferred earnings. How often should this accounting exercise be done?

- For traders, the result should be shown at least daily and even better intraday—with accuracy being more important than precision.
- For the trading lines, the result must be precise and available daily, weekly, and monthly, with profit and loss calculated just as frequently.

Let's recall what was written about the relative merits of accruals and fair value. Many banks apply the lower of cost, including funding costs, or market value. Particularly continental European banks do so with equities. However, unless prevailing accounting rules state otherwise, the difference between purchase price of equities, including funding costs, and higher market value becomes effective only upon sale of these equities.

Slow-moving accounting rules which (in many cases correctly) put greater emphasis on precision than on accuracy are not the best way for internal management accounting. Regulatory reporting requires precision that is attainable when the report is due quarterly or annually. But management accounting must be intraday capitalizing on current regulation that points toward a distinction in financial reporting between two types of assets and liabilities:

- Those that are recognized and realized, hence reported in the balance sheet and profit and loss statement (income statement).
- Those that are recognized but not realized because they are of longer maturities, reported in the balance sheet and in a separate statement.

Exhibit 14.1   A Framework for Present Value Accounting of Assets and Liabilities

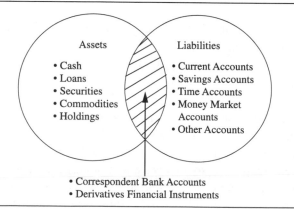

There are many applications with which the replacement value method can be effectively used. For instance, the result from counterparty risk can be calculated by means of GPV. For this purpose, the gross result before operating costs is determined by means of the algorithm:

Gross result = PV of the receivable contracted premium
+ Counterparty risk cash account
− PV of the required premium based on current assessment

Counterparty risk premiums due are credited to the counterparty risk cash account, while lacking payments are assigned to the parties responsible for products to the debit of counterparty risk cash account. Some banks deliver the outcome of this computation monthly to counterparty risk results; a better approach is to do it daily, and even better to have it available intraday.

Both for the interest business and for the non-interest business, in the case of transactions over several years the delivery of the counterparty risk premium can be made on an annual, quarterly or more frequent basis—as well as at termination of the transaction. Many banks see to it that for trading line products the risk premium is paid up front.

POSITIVE/NEGATIVE REPLACEMENT VALUE AND EXPECTED NET PRESENT VALUE

Counterparty risk is an important factor in any transaction, especially so in over-the-counter derivatives trading. With exchange-traded products, counterparty risk is negligible because changes in the value of positions are being offset by means of daily adjustments to required margins. With OTC and other deals of a bilateral nature, a valuable indicator of current exposure to counterparty risk is derived from gross and net replacement values of contracts outstanding:

- Positive replacement value (PRV) is the marked-to-market value of all receivables under derivatives contracts with third parties outstanding—without allowing for master netting or collateral arrangements.
- Negative replacement value (NRV) is the sum of all our liabilities to customers under contracts outstanding, also without netting.

As these examples document, the use of new definitions of financial value, and their associated metrics, helps to mitigate a bank's counterparty risk, improving on classical means for projecting credit risk such as the credit quality of counterparties. In essence, negative replacement value is the difference between positive and negative replacement values towards any one counterparty with which a master netting agreement has been concluded.

During the last few years, new regulations require that positive and negative replacement values of all derivatives are reported. For example, under Swiss law this is done under the heading "Other Assets" and "Other Liabilities" which essentially amounts in accounting in the balance sheet for off-balance sheet gains and losses. Prior to this change in reporting structure, only the replacement values of options were reported gross. In the case of other products, positive and negative replacement values were set off against one another.

Another issue is the role played by the notion (and the algorithms) of expected net present value (ENPV) in connection to loans. Its computation is performed within the framework of a grid whose nodes are indexed by:

- Time to maturity (or duration).
- Interest short rate which is applicable.
- Borrower risk rating by an independent agency.

A recursive algorithmic procedure can be employed to propagate backward ENPV, starting at loan maturity and ending at loan origination. This computation is done in reverse time and it can be helpful in testing certain hypotheses.

The product of such recursion is the ENPV of a loan at prescribed valuation time. A relatively new loan can be rolled back to its origination. A similar procedure may be used for revaluation and repricing of a seasoned loan. In an algorithmic sense, the suggested method parallels that used to value equity derivatives, where the elementary risks priced by the equities market are the underlying securities.

On the assumption that the equities market is arbitrage free, such elementary risks determine the risk neutral measure for equity pricing. With this, we may calculate the derivatives price as appropriate discounted expected value under the risk-neutral measure, leading to the Black-Scholes pricing formula for puts and calls on equity securities.[5]

While several banks are using this approach, it constitutes a simplification. Significant differences arise in applying arbitrage pricing to loans better approach is a Brownian model visualized as the limit of random walks, a property that is critical to this type of arbitrage pricing of equity risks.[6] This property is not present with credit risk using migration of ratings as for every nondefault-rating grade the borrower's rating can migrate at each node through a transition matrix.

Finally, there are some shortcomings with the net present value solution. Traditional approaches to the calculation of net present value rest on choice of a single risk-adjusted factor, such as discounted rate of return, to compute the probability distribution of a payoff function. Such methods do not properly capture the value of a trader's or investor's ability to modify a financial product as uncertainty is resolved or, alternatively, increases. Uncertainty unfolds and risk grows or shrinks; so does the risk-adjusted discount rate—and this means that no single discount rate may be appropriate for all cases or the same case at all times.

An evident answer is to use a process of adapting a financial operation or trade to futures contingencies. This, however, introduces asymmetries in future project value and it results in an overall increase in value, relative to the static type of net present value analysis. Methods can put up tolerances to this increase to keep it at realistic levels are still in their infancy, but eventually they will evolve.

THE LIMITS ON CHANGE IN NET PORTFOLIO VALUE

The Office of Thrift Supervision (OTS) has diligently computed guidelines for limits on change in net portfolio value, defined as the net present value of an institution's existing assets, liabilities, and off-balance sheet contracts. This measure is also referred to as the market value of portfolio equity (MVPE).

As a metric, net portfolio value takes account of embedded options and other off-balance sheet instruments. It is based on all future cash flows anticipated from a bank's existing assets, liabilities and derivatives contracts.

In its functions, as a regulator, OTS wants to see that each savings and loans establishes and documents quarterly compliance with limits in interest rate risk approved by the board. These limits should specify the minimum net portfolio value ratio (NPVR) the board of an S&L is willing to allow under current interest rates for a range of six interest rate scenarios.

Many institutions also set risk limits expressed in terms of the interest rate sensitivity of projected earnings. Such tolerances constitute a useful supplement to NPVR. Although banks are not required by OTS to compute limits and conduct analysis in terms of earnings sensitivity, the supervisors consider that a good management practice for a financial institution is to:

- Estimate the interest rate sensitivity of its earnings.
- Incorporate this analysis into its business plan, and for budgeting process.

To keep the system flexible, the bank is given by the supervisors total discretion over the type of earnings sensitivity analysis as well as all details of how that analysis is performed. OTS also encourages institutions to develop earnings simulations utilizing base case and adverse interest rate scenarios, and compare results to actual earnings on a quarterly basis, or more frequently.

The board of directors of a thrift is assisted by a quarterly OTS publication, "Thrift Industry Interest Rate Risk Measures." This is valuable in assessing the prudence of an institution's NPVR limits, as well as in evaluating current level of risk relative to the rest of the industry because it contains statistical data about key interest rate risk measures for the industry.

The board and senior management should appreciate that interest rate risk (IRR) limits reflect the bank's risk tolerance. It is therefore a sound policy to periodically re-evaluate the appropriateness of the institution's interest rate risk limits, particularly following a significant change in market interest rates.

While all changes should receive careful consideration, major changes lead to an IRR revision. Recurrent changes to interest rate risk limits for the purpose of accommodating instances in which the limits have been, or are about to be, breached may be indicative of inadequate risk management practices and procedures. OTS is watchful of such events and takes action before they become a torrent.

Good management practice suggests that if the institution's level of risk at some point does violate the board's limits, that fact should be duly recorded along with a documented explanation for that occurrence—including its background reasons. Then, it should be immediately brought to the attention of the CEO and the board for corrective action. Chief executives and directors should heed the advice of an Athenian senator in Shakespeare's *Timon of Athens:* "Nothing emboldens sin so much as mercy."

NOTES

1. D.N. Chorafas, *Credit Derivatives and the Management of Risk* (New York: New York Institute of Finance, 2000).
2. D.N. Chorafas, "Credit Risk Management," *The Lessons of VAR Failures and Imprudent Exposure,* vol. 2 (London: Euromoney, 2000).
3. D.N.Chorafas, *Financial Models and Simulation* (London: Macmillan, 1995).
4. D.N. Chorafas, "Credit Risk Management," *Analyzing, Rating, and Pricing the Probability of Default,* vol. 1 (London: Euromoney, 2000).
5. D.N. Chorafas, *Advanced Financial Analysis* (London: Euromoney, 1994).
6. D.N. Chorafas, "How to Understand and Use Mathematics for Derivatives," *Advanced Modeling Methods,* vol. 2 (London: Euromoney, 1995).

Definitions of Internal Controls and the Consensus of a Research Project

THE COMMITTEE OF SPONSORING ORGANIZATIONS OF THE TREADWAY COMMISSION (COSO)

Internal control is a process affected by the board, management and other personnel designed to provide reasonable assurance regarding the achievement of the following objectives:

- Effectiveness and efficiency of operations (i.e., basic business objectives: *performance and profitability* goals, safeguarding of *resources*).
- Reliability of *financial reporting.*
- Compliance with applicable *laws and regulations.*

THE AMERICAN INSTITUTE OF CERTIFIED PUBLIC ACCOUNTANTS' (AICPA) COMMITTEE ON WORKING PROCEDURES

Internal control comprises the plan of organization and all of the coordinate methods and measures adopted within the business to safeguard its assets, check the accuracy and reliability of its accounting data, promote operational efficiency, and encourage adherence to subscribed managerial policies.

This definition dates back to 1949 and is broad, recognizing that the system of internal control extends beyond those matters which relate directly to the functions of the accounting and financial departments to include budgetary control, standard costs, periodic operating reports, statistical analyses and dissemination thereof, a training program designed to aid personnel in meeting their responsibilities, and an internal audit staff to provide additional assurance to management as to the adequacy of its outlined procedures and the extent to which they are being effectively carried out.

A later definition by the AICPA divided internal control into two components:

1. Administrative control, which includes, but is not limited to, the plan of organization and the procedures and records that are concerned with the decision processes leading to the management's authorization of transactions. Such authorization had been defined as a management function directly associated with the responsibility for achieving the objectives of the organization, and as a starting point for establishing accounting control of transactions.

2. Accounting control, comprising the plan of organization and the procedures and records concerned with the safeguarding of assets and the reliability of financial statements, designed to provide reasonable assurance that:

    —Transactions are executed in accordance with management's general or specific authorization.

    —Transactions are recorded as necessary to permit preparation of financial statements in conformity with generally accepted accounting principles or any other criteria applicable to such statements and to maintain accountability for assets.

    —Access to assets is permitted only in accordance with management's authorization.

    —Recorded accountability for assets is compared with existing assets at reasonable intervals, with appropriate action taken with respect to any differences.

THE INSTITUTE OF INTERNAL AUDITORS (IIA)

Internal control is actions taken by management to plan, organize, and direct the performance of sufficient actions so as to provide reasonable assurance that he following objectives will be achieved:

*   The accomplishment of established objectives and goals for *operations and programs.*
*   The economical and efficient use of *resources.*
*   The safeguarding of *assets.*
*   Reliability and *integrity of information.*
*   Compliance with *policies, plans, procedures, laws, and regulations.*

THE BASLE COMMITTEE ON BANKING SUPERVISION

Internal control is a *process* effected by the board of directors, senior management, and all levels of personnel. It is *not solely a procedure or policy* that is performed at a certain point in time, but rather it is *continually operating* at all levels within the bank.

Historically, the internal control process has been a mechanism for reducing instances of *fraud, misappropriation,* and *errors,* but it has recently become *more extensive,* addressing *all risks* faced by banking organizations. Internal control consists of five interrelated elements:

1. *Management oversight* and the *control culture.*
2. *Risk assessment.*
3. *Control activities.*
4. *Information* and *communication.*
5. *Monitoring activities.*

The effective functioning of these elements is essential to achieving a bank's *operational, information,* and *compliance objectives.*

THE EUROPEAN MONETARY INSTITUTE (EMI), PREDECESSOR TO THE EUROPEAN CENTRAL BANK (ECB)

An internal control system (ICS) can be regarded as the process (including all the controls, financial or otherwise) effected by a credit institution's board of directors, senior management, and other personnel to provide reasonable assurance that the following objectives are achieved:

- Accomplishment of established *goals and objectives.*
- Economical and efficient use of *resources.*
- Adequate control of the *various risks* incurred and the *safeguarding of assets.*
- Reliability and integrity of *financial and management information.*
- Compliance with *laws and regulations* as well as *policies, plans, internal rules and procedures.*

(EMI underlines that regardless of how well designed it may be and how well it may function, an ICS can only provide reasonable assurance that the above-mentioned objectives are attained.)

CHORAFAS' COMPREHENSIVE DEFINITION OF INTERNAL CONTROLS

Internal control is a process established by the board of directors and by top management to provide themselves with a dynamic, proactive system on the way the institution functions. As such, it is affected by and is affecting all levels of personnel, because it brings transparency.

Internal control enables the senior executives to manage by tracking exposure from: credit risk, market risk, operational risk, reputational risk, legal risk, and other risks relating to transactions, to assets and to liabilities—as well as to fraud and to security. The aim is to:

- Safeguard the business assets.
- Assist in compliance and accounting reconciliation.

- Promote personal accountability.
- Lead to corrective action.

For its development, implementation, and proper functioning, an internal control system requires: Laws and regulations; rigorous supervision; corporate policies and objectives; organization and structure; reliable information and advanced technology.

Open communication channels are vital. To enhance internal control, institutions should use a wide range of tools and techniques, supported by real-time computers, sophisticated software, mining of the transactional databases, quality control charts, simulation models and interactive visualization of financial and other reports.

Because all systems can malfunction and they decay with time, internal control must be regularly audited. The proper functioning of internal control is part of the accountability of top management.

Index